Acadian
Odyssey

By
**OSCAR
WILLIAM
WINZERLING**

LOUISIANA STATE UNIVERSITY PRESS
Baton Rouge

To The Memory

Of

My Beloved Mother

Josephine Marie Winzerling

(1863 - 1939)

Who Taught Me To Love Research

Foreword

THE ACADIAN odyssey has inspired poets as well as historians to immortalize a displaced people who, for the sake of fidelity to conscience, wandered in valiant comradeship from the heart of Nova Scotia to Europe, South America, and the American colonies seeking the freedom to live in peace on land they could call their own.

With the fall of Fort Beauséjour on the Bay of Fundy, June 16, 1755, the world-wide deportations began, and the peregrinations of the victims continued for many decades. On the centenary of the exodus, celebrations were held September 18, 1855, in Nova Scotia, New Brunswick, Cape Breton, and Prince Edward Island by descendants of the exiles, who number thousands in the Maritime Provinces, French Canada, and Louisiana.

Quite opportune is the publication of the present volume at the close of the second centenary of the Acadian exile. Doctor Winzerling has contributed the fruit of years of study and research in America and Europe to the writing of this work, almost all of which is based on original documents that he discovered in the archives of Spain, France, and England. In presenting the account of a few of the countless thousands who sought freedom in this land of opportunity, he has immeasurably enriched the historical background of the colonization of America.

John G. Murray
Archbishop of Saint Paul

Introduction

THIS BOOK is an attempt to present one chapter in the vast history of the Acadians of Nova Scotia. It is the particular story of several groups of Acadian exiles who were sent to France after 1755. Resettled in the mother country, they resisted absorption, and, after twenty-eight years of neglect and deception by the French government, more than 1,500 of them realized, with the aid of Spain, their hope of returning to America. Few of the Acadian exiles who sought refuge in Louisiana demonstrated more fully their enduring attachment to America than did the members of those groups who originally were sent to France. This work follows these Acadian groups not only in their devious wanderings after the year 1763 but also in their bitter struggle for justice and survival. Their history, although heretofore neglected, is significant in American colonization.

In the year 1755 the English had expelled the Acadians from Nova Scotia. They then numbered about 18,000 in the various villages on the peninsula and the neighboring islands.[1] Months after their expulsion more than 3,000 of them eventually assembled in the port cities of France.[2] Of these one group of 866, the remnant of 1,500, had been banished from Nova Scotia to Virginia. The Virginians had refused them admission and sent them to England. After years of harrowing experiences as prisoners of war in England's seaport concentration camps, they finally arrived in France.[3] Another group of 2,000 were sent directly to France by Governor Lawrence of Nova Scotia.[4] And a small group of several hundred from the American colonies filtered into France after 1763 as a result of French intervention.[5]

After twenty-eight years of neglect in France these Acadians became thoroughly disillusioned by royal promises and in their hopes of retrieving their losses. The removal in seven expeditions of the greater part of these exiles from France to Louisiana by

Spain was one of the great mass colonization projects on the continent of North America. The chief promoter of their removal in 1785 was a Louisiana naturalist, Peyroux de la Coudrenière. But the responsibility for the success of the seven expeditions Spain placed on the shoulders of her ambassador in Paris, the Count de Aranda. The entire project with its devious backstage political activities forms a fascinating chapter in the history of the United States.

With exception of the first chapter, the author has based his narrative almost entirely upon original sources gathered during a year of intense research in a number of important European national and private archives and libraries, ranging from the Archivo General de Indias of Seville to the British Museum in London.

Many days were spent in field work too. The author visited every city of importance where the Acadians had lived—Poitiers, Châtellerault, Limousin, and the isolated Poitou hills where La Colonie Acadienne du Poitou had been established in 1772. He met many descendants of the Acadians still living on the Grand' Ligne; dug in the ground, examined the soil and its "bruyère blanche" and ubiquitous "la brande"; and verified for himself what the manuscripts described.[6] He spent a day on Belle-Ile-en-Mer, and wondered how man or beast could still live there. He gazed for hours on Choiseul's beautiful estate of Chanteloup commanding the valley of the Loire north of Amboise and pondered what ill-fated hand had prevented the poor Acadians from possessing those fertile meadowlands. He loitered for hours in the port towns of St. Malo, Morlaix, La Rochelle, Mindin, Paimboeuf, and in particular Nantes, where the Acadians had endured so much misery and suffering in the Old World, and which was the port of their final removal from France to Louisiana.

Individual French citizens whom the author met looked at him with mingled astonishment and curiosity. They apparently wondered why anyone should spend so much time and money to learn more about their all-but-forgotten Acadians. Yet they showed distinct satisfaction and pride in the enthusiasm and sympathy of the "American stranger." But no one displayed such willingness to co-operate and furnish whatever help and information the author needed as did the descendants of the Acadians themselves. With great pride an old Acadian escorted the author to Rue Dosdane près la tour Pirmil in Nantes. "There," he said, "Oliver Terrio had his shoeshop." And after pointing out what he considered the approximate location of the shop, he added with a sigh, "What a mistake my great grandfather made in not accepting Terrio's advice to go to Louisiana. See, Sir, how poor I am today."

The author owes a great debt of gratitude to his archbishop, the Most Reverend John Gregory Murray, Archbishop of St. Paul (Minnesota), who provided the opportunity for research in foreign archives. He owes special thanks to James Dixon and Hannah Kellogg, of San Francisco (California), who helped in many ways, and to Jane Brennan and Marie Brophy of Minneapolis, who assisted with the index. He acknowledges his indebtedness for help in reference work to Father Leonard Leander, Assumption, Minnesota, and especially to Joan Doyle of Washington, D.C., who despite her busy literary labors gave so generously of her time in revising the entire manuscript. He is most grateful to Lucia Kinnaird of Berkeley, California, for proof-reading, and in particular to Dr. Lawrence Kinnaird of the University of California (Berkeley), who inspired the subject. For whatever errors may be found in this work, the author alone assumes all responsibility.

O. W. W.

Taylors Falls, Minnesota
June 20, 1955

Table of Contents

Acadian Odyssey

CHAPTER ONE

Exile without End

How similar to the odyssey of Ulysses is the tragic story of the expulsion in 1755 of the Acadian nation from Nova Scotia.[1] As there are thousands who will read and reread the fascinating episodes in the Odyssey so also there will be many who will never tire of reading of the Acadian wanderings, of their bitter hardships, of their poignant sufferings, and of their heroic achievements; for their odyssey is a great drama which touches the human heart. In spite of their industry, their loyalty, and their patriotism, a relentless fate drove the Acadians even in exile to destruction. Their very virtues contributed to their collapse as a people.[2]

Uncertainty beclouds the origin of the name Acadia, or as the French pronounce it, "Acadie," which denotes the vast area of land, lying to the northeast of Maine, which English-speaking people today call Nova Scotia. In 1524 Jean Verrazano described to the French government a land "which is called Arcadie because of the beauty of its trees," [3] and almost a quarter of a century later in 1548 Gastaldi, in his account of the actual extent of Nouvelle Écosse, spoke of it as Lacardia. Zaltieri made use of the same name in the year 1556,[4] and Ruscelli labeled the region Lacardie on his map of 1561. André Thivet, in 1575, and Champlain in "Les Sauvages," his official report for the year 1603, described the region as Arcadia. Worthy of mention is the appearance in 1604 of the term la Cadie in the commission to De Monts: "The Royal grant to De Monts for the colonization of the lands of la Cadie, Canada, and other places in New France." [5]

Many modern historians have surmised that the name Acadia is nothing more than a corruption of the classical name of Arcadia.

But some American authorities hold that Acadia is derived from any of several Micmac words, such as "algaty," sometimes spelled "algatig," meaning a camp or settlement; from "quoddy," denoting fertile fields, and especially from "akade," signifying a place where fish, birds, fur-bearing animals, and forests of valuable trees abound. Whatever is the obscure origin of the name Acadia the sense of a fertile land, or a bucolic country seems to have been implied.[6]

The first successful colonization of Acadia was made in the year 1604 by Pierre du Gast de Monts with 150 colonists.[7] This band of colonists was made up of "convicts, laborers, some Huguenot ministers and Catholic priests, and some nobles such as Samuel Champlain and Jean de Poutrincourt." Armed with viceregal powers and a trading monopoly for ten years, De Monts made the first permanent settlement on an inlet on the southwest shore of Nova Scotia washed by the Bay of Fundy. Champlain christened the infant colony Port Royal. A few days later De Monts located a second settlement opposite Port Royal on the west bank of the bay and called it St. Croix.[8]

The small settlements flourished until the end of October, 1613, when Captain Samuel Argall of Virginia sailed up the coast on a hunt for Frenchmen. He shelled and set fire to both settlements, sending the colonists in flight to the woods, where for fourteen years they eked out a living like nomads, or dwelt in the homes of savages.[9]

France, consequently, was forced during the next twenty years to abandon all efforts to colonize Acadia. But during this interval great events followed on the heels of one another: the Pilgrims (*i.e.,* the Separatists), 102 in number, landed at Plymouth Rock in the year 1620. Then Sir William Alexander, a Scottish courtier at the court of James I, tried to settle the Scots in Acadia.[10]

Next, the Massachusetts Bay Company established nine hundred Puritans, first at Salem, later at Boston. These finally were expanded into seven villages between Boston and Dorchester.[11] When the treaty of St. Germain-en-Laye in 1632 restored Acadia once more to France, Armand Cardinal Richelieu welcomed the opportunity of furthering his schemes of colonization in North America, schemes which were temporarily checked by the vicious attacks of Sir David Kirke.[12] He immediately appointed as "lieutenant general of the king and governor of Acadia" his cousin, Isaac de Razilly, an enthusiastic promoter of French colonization in North America. Razilly successfully recruited some three hundred "picked men," all "engaged bachelors" from the villages of Brittany and Touraine.[13] Among these colonists was Charles d'Menou d'Aulnay. The settlers were of a sturdy, industrious, and religious element of Brittany and Touraine. In a few years they increased to such a number that they formed a people—the first successful colonizers of Canada.[14] But on the death of Razilly, civil war broke out between the colony's two leaders, D'Aulnay and Charles La Tour. This cruel strife not only halted all progress in the colony but it also threatened the very existence of the settlements. It brought upon the colony many evils, and the once beautiful and peaceful Acadia almost perished.[15]

The descendants of these colonists were not a learned people. Only a few of their number were even able to read or write. Simple, industrious, and kindhearted they lived unto themselves but with an open heart of justice and charity to everyone.[16] They were a gentle race. If a widow were found helpless through old age or infirmity, her neighbors would volunteer to cultivate her gardens and fields, cut firewood for her, and gather the harvest. An orphan was welcomed in any home and was treated like a natural child, while the poor and aged were given special care by the community. If anyone lost a sheep, a hog, or a heifer, or suffered any damage in his potato or wheat crop through vandalism or theft from Indians or French, he would work all the harder to overcome the loss, instead of wasting time, money, and the sweetness of his disposition for an uncertain remuneration in the courts of the elders.[17] They made their own shoes, clothes, tools, and cooking utensils. During the good seasons of the year, they cultivated their fields, trapped, and fished as a group. During the bitter winter months, groups of families would gather around the hearth, drink hard cider or maple syrup, tell stories, sing their old folk songs, dance, and relate their ancient history.[18] True, they lived a life "of unambitious peace" with all the world around them and wore out their lives in strenuous efforts to reclaim the soft marshlands and fresh-water fields—a work at which they were unequalled experts.[19] Socially, they clung tenaciously to the simple manners, customs, and old French tongue of their forefathers. It is not true that the Acadians spoke a "patois Acadien,"[20] though their language in time was naturally influenced by isolation from France and by English environment.[21] As an Acadian seldom married outside his home town, everyone in that town was in some way related to everyone else. They lived like ancient patriarchs in a state of innocence and equality comparable to that of the first centuries.[22]

One of the outstanding traits of the Acadians was their profoundly religious character. An English traveler wrote that in his dealing with them he rarely met with either malice or vengeance and that he did not know of drunkenness and swearing among them. A memoir in the Archives des Affaires Étrangères in Paris notes that crime, theft, debauchery, and illegitimacy were unknown in their communities for as long a period as forty years; that "paternal authority" policed their villages and towns.[23] Even to this day, their descendants in the French towns of La Puye, Archigny, and Pleumartin are noted for their strict respect in the observance of Sunday and their sincerely religious character. To them the Church was the very heart of their lives; in it they were baptized, were married, and hoped to be buried; and in it they found all that was of joy and interest to them. With childlike delight they would anticipate and prepare for the celebration of some feast day of St. Ann or of the Virgin Mary or of her Divine Son. These were events that called not only for personal piety and devotion but also for the gayest regalia of national costumes and communal generosity in its observance.[24] They prayed much and loved God ardently; they lived and let live in "comfortable poverty." Even in their hour of bitterest suffering and trial, they did not envy the wealth, power, or happiness of other peoples. As "a people" they opposed any act of carnage or war. They trapped for a living but objected to hunting for a living.[25] Good or bad they accepted their lot in life without murmur as the will of God. Their philosophy of life could be summed up in the verse written by one of their exiles:

> Eternal Judge, to whom revenge belongs,
> Forbear to visit for our num'rous wrongs;
> Let us in patience bow beneath the rod,
> And say with Christ—"Thy Will be done." [26]

Such a Christian philosophy was possible only in a people who were deeply moral and strengthened by a clear conscience.

The territory known as Acadia passed through four treaties and many vicissitudes before the English finally succeeded in wresting it from the French. The first blow, the unprovoked attack of Captain Argall of Virginia, fell in the year 1613. The second came in the year 1654, when the English of Massachusetts, taking advantage of the state of war between England and France, sent Robert Sedgwick with a strong fleet to demand the surrender of Port Royal in the name of Oliver Cromwell. The incompetent La Tour, taken by surprise, surrendered.[27] The success of the New Englanders, however, was short-lived, for the Treaty of Breda in the year 1667 restored Acadia to the French.[28] There were then a little more than four hundred people in the whole of Acadia, very few of whom were to be found north of the Bay of Fundy.[29] When Colbert came to power, however, he recognized the economic resources of the colony, and in the year 1670, to strengthen French control, appointed a governor for Acadia.[30]

The third attack occurred in the year 1690, under the leadership of Sir William Phips. At the head of a New England fleet that carried over a thousand men he not only stormed and destroyed Port Royal but also carried away his prisoners of war to Boston. But by the Treaty of Ryswick of 1697, the English were again forced to restore Acadia to the French crown.[31]

Four years after that treaty the population of Acadia stood at 1,450 souls—466 inhabitants at Port Royal; 498 at Minas; 189 at Beaubassin; 15 at Chipody; 75 at La Hève and vicinity; 6 at Megaïs; 40 at Miramichi, Chedebouctou, Népisigny; 15 at Passamacadie; 40 at Pobomcoup and Cap Sable; 25 at Pentagoët; 50 at River St. John; and 31 in various places in the interior.[32]

The final attack, and the one which resulted in a permanent conquest, came in the year 1710. Queen Anne, "the quarrelsome and petty queen of England," ordered Colonel Francis Nicholson, her outstanding colonial officer in America, to recover Nova Scotia for the English crown. Equipped with an army of 1,500 New England soldiers and aided by a powerful unit of the British fleet, Colonel Nicholson began the siege of Port Royal on September 24, and on October 16 seized the fort in the name of Her Britannic Majesty.[33] Thus, after four savage attacks, each one made with typical English persistency, the English possession of Acadia was finally ratified in the Treaty of Utrecht in April, 1713. At the time of the signing of this treaty the population of Acadia had risen to approximately 2,500 souls.[34]

In spite of her fourfold defeat in Nova Scotia, France still dreamed of a colonial empire stretching from Newfoundland to New Orleans. On the one hand she planned to restrict the English colonies to a narrow strip of land on the Atlantic seacoast. She built a line of forts from Bay Verte along the St. Lawrence, the Great Lakes, and across the Ohio country to New Orleans. She had already thirty forts in the disputed area with one at Crown Point and another at Sorel River.[35] On the other hand, she protracted as long as possible the negotiations over "the ancient boundaries" of Acadia,[36] until she felt that she was somewhat prepared not only to fulfill her plans but even to contest by force of arms, if necessary, the ultimate hegemony.[37] This dream of colonial mastery in the western hemisphere presaged ill for the Acadians, who were caught between English-hating Indians and bold and insolent French. Already, on May 23, 1754, Governor William Shirley of Massachusetts had reported to Sir Thomas Robinson that the settlers of Chignecto were working through the French garrison at Beauséjour with the Indians of Acadia and the St. John River to destroy all the eastern settlements[38] and by this means to encroach on His Majesty's territory of Nova Scotia and capture the province of Maine.[39] He showed the home government that his reports were substantially correct. He had caught among the Indians a few hotheaded Acadian youths, who, contrary to the stern advice of their elders, openly sympathized with England's enemies among French and Indians. Governor Shirley thereupon fancied the entire Acadian people were stealthily plotting to overthrow English rule in her adjoining colonies. He therefore painted the Acadians to the authorities in London as threatening "to twist the Lion's tail." [40]

Moreover, from the records there is no doubt that the English colonial authorities unfairly accused the Acadians of perpetrating or instigating all Indian atrocities committed in Massachusetts.[41] While it was true that a body of five hundred Indians and French, divided into several parties, fell upon the eastern settlements of New England,[42] the colonial English were not thereby justified in placing the blame on all Acadians for those attacks.

Later the English discovered that the savages of the Nova Scotia peninsula had guns, powder, and provisions. Again they blamed the Acadians, and thus a series of fancied acts of Acadian hostility were built up. In 1690 the English used these unproved charges to justify Sir William Phips' attack on the peaceful towns of Acadia, and as an excuse for the annexation by the colony of Massachusetts of eight hundred miles of territory northeast of its boundary and the placing of it under the governorship of Phips.[43] The roots of these accusations, however, reach much further back into the ancient Anglo-French rivalry, then fast reaching a climax.

The home governments of England and France had long sensed an impending struggle for colonial and maritime supremacy. The English were nearing their complete possession of the Atlantic coast between Maine and Florida, while the French were tightening their hold at the mouths of the two great rivers —the St. Lawrence and the Mississippi. By pushing into the valleys of the Ohio and Mississippi and those of their tributaries, the French hoped to bring the vast regions sandwiched between these two points of penetration under their control.[44] To strengthen the claims of the French, the Marquis de la Galissonière, governor of New France, dispatched Céleron de Bienville in the year 1749 to plant lead plates at important sites in the Ohio Valley, which the English were now preparing to occupy through the agency of the Ohio Land Company's grant of two hundred thousand acres of land just below the forks of the Ohio River.[45] The English completely outmaneuvered the French by planting more colonists along the narrow strip of the Atlantic seaboard than their rival did in the great basins of the St. Lawrence and the Mississippi; and they developed at the same time a reciprocally profitable trade with their colonies, a factor which bound them closer to the mother country.[46] Had Louis XIV poured into the Ohio Valley the manpower of one of his vainglorious wars, the history of this area might have been quite different. In the midst of these high-powered international politics, the honest but uneducated Acadians were caught as pawns on the chessboard of international rivalry. The English governor of Nova Scotia, Lawrence, laid at their door every imaginable charge—violation of the "old limits," "obduracy," "instigation of the Indians," "belligerent neutrality," and others, to all of which Governor Shirley of Massachusetts on December 14, 1754, heartily agreed and promised full and vigorous co-operation in Lawrence's scheme to drive the French out of Canada.[47]

Education is essential to the freedom and security of any people. The rustically simple, contented, and politically carefree life of the Acadians of the eighteenth century would have been ideal had the rest of society been as simply constructed as was theirs. But through their neglect of education the Acadians made themselves and their country easy victims of hardened, conscienceless statesmen. Their ignorance of political conditions enabled politicians to achieve success in any hostile scheme. Were the Acadians an educated people, they would have known their political duties and rights and would have known also how to fight those who were eyeing the resources of their country and their happy land. As it happened, however, when the vultures pounced upon them, they were not able to produce any competent leadership.[48]

When George Washington turned his stockade at Great Meadows into Fort Necessity, and when on July 3, 1754, he was attacked, defeated, and forced to abandon his fort, the French and Indian War, antedating the fatal struggle on the Continent by two years, had begun. Hopefully, the French boasted of their plans to drive the English out of the Ohio Valley, but for the Acadians they had little thought.

The character of Governor Charles Lawrence had much to do with the ultimate expulsion of the Acadians. Unlike his predecessors, Lawrence was as suspicious as he was treacherous and ambitious.[49] He was a governor who could see only the letter of the law; (the Acadians must take the oath of allegiance to England without reservation, or leave the country. The Acadians, on the other hand, insisted that the Treaty of Utrecht guaranteed them freedom from bearing arms, freedom of religion, and the free possession of their property.[50] In name as well as in attitude they regarded themselves as "neutrals" and refused to bear arms either in their own defense or in defense of their mother country. For this reason and also because they unanimously refused to take the oath of allegiance, England could not, on her part, consider them full British subjects.[51])

The Acadian position was the awkward one of having a foot in both camps. To live under English protection and in an English-owned colony while at the same time declaring loyalty to the French king was an attitude that could hardly win approval from the English government. Could the conditions have been reversed, one wonders if the French government would have tolerated the seemingly unpatriotic "status quo." [52] Even to the day of expulsion and for many years after it, the Acadians preserved a tenacious attachment to the person of the King of France.[53] There is no doubt that as a people the Acadians disliked being under British rule; but there is equally no doubt that as a subject people they were obedient.[54] When war came in 1754 most of them threw away whatever weapons and ammunition they possessed, declaring that they did not wish to hang.[55] On the surrender of Fort Beauséjour in June, 1755, however, the English caught two hundred of their able-bodied men fully armed. Provided with such evidence, Lawrence concluded that all Acadians were rebellious, untrustworthy, and in league with the French and no proof of loyalty offered by the overwhelming majority of the nation could change his view. He thereupon issued two drastic orders on June 4, 1755: first, every Acadian must surrender whatever weapons he might possess; and secondly, everyone must take the oath of allegiance without reservation. Lawrence had decided upon firm action.[56]

A council was held on Thursday, July 3, 1755, at the governor's house in Halifax. The inhabitants of Minas sent a handful of delegates to represent their people. The delegates presented to the governor and his council a tactlessly worded memorandum in which they requested that they be allowed to use their guns and canoes.[57] They stated that loyalty was a matter of conscience and that their people could never take any other oath but that tendered in September, 1727, by Governor Richard Philipps.[58] The new unqualified oath had a clause that demanded the bearing of arms,[59] and when Lawrence asked the delegates to take the unqualified oath individually, they refused that request also. As a result, the governor clapped them into prison.[60] At first he and his council thought of letting the Acadians migrate wherever they wished. But as their population on the peninsula of Acadia alone numbered at least 13,000 he feared that they might go to French Canada and that their able-bodied men would strengthen the French colonial army.[61] Lawrence was undecided what he should do. He was worried by rumors of an impending French naval attack, and suspicious that the tactlessly worded memorandum was founded on a secret knowledge of the presence or expectation of a French fleet in the Bay of Fundy. How else could one account for this boldness in the face of a common ruin? "I have ordered my deputies to be elected and sent hither immediately," he wrote on July 18, 1755, to the Board of Trade, "and am determined to bring the inhabitants to a compliance, or rid the province of such perfidious subjects." [62] The Board of Trade answered, "You are not to attempt their removal without His Majesty's positive order," [63] but later the home government upheld Lawrence's action of expulsion on the grounds that the province of Nova Scotia and the property thereof "did *always* of right belong to the crown of England, both by priority of discovery and ancient discovery." [64]

The Acadians thus became the victims of an ambiguity about "priority of discovery and ancient discovery" which England used as a handy wedge to push her claims on the North American continent.[65] It is true that at the time of discovery the French did not clearly define the exact territorial limits of Acadia. By the right of discovery of Jean Verrazano and Jacques Cartier,[66] they claimed all the vast domain in America "north of the sphere of Spanish influence."[67] Thus, roughly considered, Acadia would include all of the country northward and eastward from the river Penobscot. This would embrace New Brunswick, Nova Scotia, Prince Edward Island, and the northeastern corner of Maine.[68] This was England's contention in the treaty discussions of 1739; but France maintained that under Acadia "with its ancient boundary," she was yielding only the southeastern part of the peninsula of modern Nova Scotia, and that she had always applied the term to its 55,000 square kilometers, bounded by the Gulf of St. Lawrence, the Atlantic Ocean, and the Bay of Fundy.[69] In other words Acadia meant simply Annapolis and its immediate neighborhood. This would be admissible under the clumsy wording of the Treaty of Utrecht.[70] The Jesuit missionary, Charlevoix, stated in his report of August 23, 1749, that France ceded only the "old limits," that is, the southeastern half of the peninsula but that the English pretended that the term comprised *all* the territory of the peninsula of Nova Scotia with its "old limits," and the territory east of the Kennebec River.[71]

As the limits of Acadia were never definitely settled, they loomed in the year 1755 as one of the causes of the war between France and England. That the Acadians as a people were in league with the French because two hundred of their men were found in Fort Beauséjour upon its capture seems to have been more of a suspicion on the part of the English authorities than a proven fact.[72] Probably England's imperialism was the prime motive in the expulsion of the French Neutrals (as they were called) rather than her fear of their joining the French and thus constituting a potential enemy on her left flank.[73] The French scented England's motives, as early as April 6, 1691, when Robineau de Meneval, then governor of Acadia, mentioned to Pontchartrain that he should order a strengthening of the forts in Port Royal because the English of Boston were looking upon Acadia with great jealousy as a neighboring state under hated French control.[74]

There is no reason to doubt that the Acadians of 1755 were right-intentioned in their refusal to take the unqualified oath.[75] They honestly confessed their fear saying, "we do not yet know in what manner the English will use us." [76] As a people they were earnest and sincere in their loyalty to the English government. Their ignorance of English politics, however, made them suspicious of any English action; and their suspicions in turn made them obdurate. But they were by no means traitorous in their obduracy. They would have fared better had they shown a little diplomacy, but, influenced by their rustic culture and lack of education, they decided on a course of action which appeared to them as a nation honest but which spelled their ruin.

The English, on the other hand, were forced from a military point of view to be cautious. They had justifiable fears for the safety of their thirteen colonies from French imperialism.[77] Their ignorance of French naval movements fostered suspicions about Acadian boldness and obduracy, and their suspicions in turn begot a brutal and inhuman conclusion—expulsion.

Though expulsion was even then a recognized war measure, it may be asked, was Charles Lawrence, as head of the English government in Nova Scotia, justified in using such an extreme measure upon an inoffensive people because they refused to take his unqualified oath of allegiance? General Jeffrey Amherst expressed the opinion when he was in New York on August 30, 1762, that the "Acadians might have been kept in proper subjection while the troops remained in Nova Scotia," though he feared the possibility of trouble upon the removal of the troops.[78] When the Acadians had rejected to take a previous oath in the year 1714, Governor Samuel Vetch had recommended expulsion. At that time such a movement could have been accomplished without extreme hardship, for the Acadian population was a mere handful of 2,500 souls.[79] But in 1755 removal was complicated by the bitter political and religious rivalry that then existed between England and France, and by the huge increase in the Acadian population. The census of Canada estimated the Acadian population in 1755 to be between 10,000 and 11,000 inhabitants with an additional 4,000 or 5,000 living on Prince Edward Island, Cape Breton Island, and in other outlying districts.[80]

Another alternative to wholesale expulsion would have been a demand for hostages. It was a common practice in those days. But it was feared that the authorities in Quebec might find it convenient to sacrifice the hostages to secure the success of the French arms.[81] France, tardily remembering her Acadians in their hour of trial, proposed an alternative to mass expulsion. She petitioned the English government to grant the Acadians permission to leave the peninsula with all their effects, thus giving the English all of Acadia. But the British ministry refused the request.[82] When the threat of expulsion became an unavoidable fact the imprisoned Acadian delegates, reluctantly yet sincerely, offered to take the oath unconditionally. But Lawrence doubted their good intentions. "There was no reason to hope their proposed Compliance proceeded from an honest mind," he reported later, "and could be esteemed only the Effect of Compulsion and Force, and is contrary to a clause in an Act of Parliament, I.

Geo. 2.c 13, whereby persons who once refused to take the oaths cannot afterwards be permitted to Take them, but are considered as Popish Recusants; Therefore they would not now be indulged with such permission, and they were thereupon ordered into Confinement."[83] Lawrence with his council had decided upon wholesale expulsion. That was the surest way to destroy the Acadians as a military danger.

The method of dispersing the Acadians has scarcely an equal in history. "We did," said Edmund Burke, "in my opinion, most inhumanely, and upon pretences that, in the eye of an honest man, are not worth a farthing, root out this poor, innocent, deserving people, whom our utter inability to govern, or to reconcile, gave us no sort of right to extirpate."[84] How right was his judgment. The transports were few, inadequate, and unseaworthy. Hence a frightful crowding that bred disease during the long journey to exile resulted.[85] There were many pitiful separations in families, and even shipload destruction in midocean.[86] A well-known case of family separation due to the small number of transports was that of Réné LeBlanc, notary-public of Grand Pré. Le Blanc, his wife, and their two youngest children were put on one transport and landed in New York, but their eighteen other children and 150 grandchildren were embarked on different transports and dispersed among the different colonies.[87] Hutchinson, the historian of the Massachusetts Bay colony, tells how husbands, absent at their work when their families were captured, were separated from their wives and children.[88] The New York *Mercury* for November 30, 1762, told of deliberate separation of husbands from their wives and fathers from their children. Other colonial newspapers contained advertisements of members of families seeking their companions, of sons anxious to reach and relieve their parents, of mothers longing for their children.[89]

The plans of relocation (if such they could be called) depended much on the good will of the governors of the thirteen colonies.[90] The food supply for a long journey was insufficient, of bad quality, and unhealthy. Consequently, smallpox and other diseases broke out aboard the transports and death decimated the ranks of the exiles.

When the Acadians were placed under arrest, about 2,000 of them escaped into the surrounding forests.[91] For many years they wandered from town to town like hunted animals, half-clad and half-starved, but ever in search of some near relative. Many of them returned to their homes in Acadia only to find the old homestead in ruins. After the treaty of 1763 a part of them wended their way to the coastal towns of Buctouche and Richibucto in New Brunswick and especially to the villages along Chaleur Bay or to the river settlements on the Peticodiac and Miramichi, and to the town of Memramcouk.[92] Another part of them filtered into the French Canadian towns of L'Acadie, St. Gregoire, Nicolet, Becaucour, St. Jacques, L'Achigan, St. Philippe, Laprairie, Fort Frederick on the Kennebecassis River, and St. Anne. At Fredericton (formerly St. Anne) the English government forced the refugees once more to yield their cultivated lands to his majesty's soldiers of the American Revolutionary War.[93] They finally found homes in the Madawaska Valley and on the shores of Chaleur Bay.[94] Today the descendants of these escaped Acadians number over 230,000 souls.[95]

Many are the estimates of the victims deported in the year 1755 to the English colonies. The Acadian prisoners in England thought the number close to ten thousand.[96] They are probably right, for L'Abbé Casgrain, an accurate and reliable historian, estimates 8,200 as the correct figure.[97] Since the deportations of the Acadians continued until the peace of Paris in 1763, the total number must have been doubled. But the colonies were not prepared to receive such great numbers. The influx of large groups of exiles naturally placed a heavy strain on their economic resources. For that reason New Hampshire rejected outright Boston's appeal to receive some of the exiles.

Nevertheless, from Massachusetts to Georgia, Governor Lawrence kept unloading the Acadians along the American coast. Between 1755 and 1763 he had shipped 2,000 or more to Boston, where the Bostonians treated them like slaves,[98] 700 from Grand Pré and Port Royal to Connecticut,[99] and at least 250, "poor, naked and destitute," to New York.[100] Sir Harry Moore rid New York of the major part of her Acadian exiles by persuading them to emigrate to Santo Domingo, where the starved outcasts, "crawling under the bushes, to screen themselves from the torrid sun," perished miserably.[101] Lawrence had exiled 754 to Philadelphia. There the ships and their human cargo were kept in the harbor for three months, while smallpox killed 237 of them.[102] Of the 2,000 Lawrence had removed to Maryland, hundreds escaped to Louisiana, Canada, and the West Indies.[103] To North Carolina he sent 500, and to South Carolina, 1,500 Acadians. But the Carolinians cleverly enticed them to leave in some old boats for Acadia. Only 900 arrived at the River St. John.[104] Lawrence next banished 400 to Georgia from which the poor creatures immediately fled, preferring death anywhere in the tropics to slavery with the blacks in the rice fields and on the sugar cane plantations.[105] Penniless, destitute, and homeless, either unwanted or despised wherever they appeared, the Acadians in most cases were shunned, cheated, and heartlessly allowed to die without even the care and affection given to pet animals. Connecticut alone was prepared to receive the exiles sent to her and treated them as a group humanely.[106] There is no doubt that every Acadian would have preferred exile in France to banishment to any other place. But that decision was not in Lawrence's power.

Lawrence sent two groups of 650 to a watery grave in the icy mid-Atlantic aboard the unseaworthy ships *Violet* and *Duke William*. "On December 10th," observes Doughty, "the *Duke*

William came upon the *Violet* in a sinking condition; and not-withstanding all efforts at rescue, the *Violet* went down with nearly 400 souls." While assisting the *Violet* the Captain of the *Duke William* learned that his own vessel was doomed, despite the empty casks in the ship's hold. He had scarcely launched the overloaded longboat, when an explosion occurred which sent the *Duke William* and 300 of her Acadian passengers to the bottom of the ocean. The lifeboat finally reached the seaport of Penzance with only 27 survivors.[107] "I do not know," observes George Bancroft, "if the annals of the human race keep the record of sorrows so wantonly inflicted, so bitter and so lasting as fell upon the French inhabitants of Acadia."[108]

Did any of the exiled Acadians ever attempt to return to Acadia? Many groups did try in the face of every obstacle to reach again their native land. Typical of the fortune of those groups was that of 60 families who had assembled at Boston in 1763. Despite the presence of pregnant women in their number, they nevertheless determined to march back on foot to their old homes and farms at Beauséjour, Beaubassin, Grand Pré, and Port Royal in Acadia. Of money they had none, nor did they have any other resources except a spirit of determination, work in the palms of their hands, and an undying love for their native land. After a trek of 300 leagues over mountains and through forests, they arrived in Acadia only to find everything changed: English names, English inhabitants, English villages. "Above all wher-ever they appeared, everyone looked askance at them, as if they were ghosts from a different age," wrote Rameau. "Their very presence frightened the children, and alarmed the men and women of the villages."[109] Undoubtedly, they did seem like specters that had come from the grave. Broken in body by hard-ships, starvation, and fatigue, and crushed in spirit by human animosity and the very sight of their homes and farms either destroyed or possessed by strangers, these homeless people literally dragged themselves from hamlet to hamlet in search of some corner that they could call their own in a land that in all justice still belonged to them. Then the English authorities interfered. At this, some of the exiles fled to Prince Edward Island; others, not so fortunate in escaping, were forced to do the humiliating work of repairing the dikes of the new masters of their lands, for the new masters never achieved the success of the Acadians in developing the fertility of the fields of beloved L'Acadie. Another group of 130 were arrested, sent to Halifax, and again expelled,[110] only to realize that:

> Waste are those pleasant farms, and the farmers forever departed.
> Scattered like dust and leaves, when the mighty blasts of October
> Seize them, and whirl them aloft, and sprinkle them far over the ocean. . . .
> When on the falling tide the freighted vessels departed,
> Bearing a nation, with all its household goods, into exile,
> Exile without an end, and without example in story.
> Far asunder, on separated coasts the Acadians landed. . . .
> Friendless, homeless, hopeless, they wandered from city to city. . . .
> Asked of the earth but a grave, and no longer a friend nor a fireside.[111]

Among the deportations between 1755 and 1763 related in the preceding pages were three groups, around whose odyssey this narrative centers. The first group comprised 1,500 Acadians whom Governor Lawrence had dispatched to Virginia. But the Virginians, resenting the governor's imposition on their hospitality, would have nothing to do with them and forthwith ordered the ships to sail for England. On their arrival, the English government interned this group of Acadian exiles as prisoners of war in Liverpool, Southampton, Falmouth, and Bristol.[112] The second group, numbering about 2,000, Lawrence tried to dump on

French seaports after sensing a vigorous opposition in the American colonies to their reception. Of these, Dr. Brown noted: "Many of the transports having them on board were ordered to France, about 1,300 perished by shipwreck on the voyage, those who arrived, France would not receive, they were landed at Southampton and other ports where, taking smallpox, they were carried off in great numbers." [113] And the third group numbered about 500 exiles scattered on the North American continent. Encouraged by a special invitation from the Duke of Nivernois, the French ambassador in London, these escaped by devious ways to France from the various American colonies after the Treaty of Paris in 1763.

CHAPTER TWO

The Acadian Exiles in England [1]

FOR SEVEN YEARS on land and sea England and France struggled. All the major powers of the world were involved in their Seven Years' War from 1756 to 1763. This was truly the first "World War." England was fighting for supremacy on the North American continent, France to save her vast colonial empire which English imperialism of Pitt's genius was trying to wrest from her.[2]

When peace finally came on February 10, 1763, in favor of England, the climax of the Acadian expulsion was long since past. But still the wretched exiles cropped up like driftwood along the littoral of the Atlantic Ocean and the Caribbean Sea. In France they arrived by thousands.[3] To the American colonies,[4] to Santo Domingo and the Leeward Islands they came by shiploads.[5] By detachments they fled to the Falkland Islands.[6] And by dozens they lingered on the beaches of far-off Nicaragua and British Honduras, where, known as "Frenchwers," the forlorn outcasts, in dire necessity, lived on the scavenger catfish and finally succumbed to the malarial mosquito.[7] This work aims to follow only the wanderings of those Acadians who assembled in the maritime ports of France and from there "were removed to Louisiana at the expense of the Spanish King." [8]

We have seen that a group of 1,500 Acadians had been deported from Acadia to Virginia, and there disembarked. But as the Virginians regarded them as prisoners of war, they ordered the transports reloaded and sent immediately back to England. During that long return voyage many died of grief and the hardships of such primitive traveling.[9] On their arrival in England many more died from starvation and grief.[10] The English secretary of state ordered them distributed in the various maritime ports of the kingdom, with the largest group in Liverpool.[11] Decimated in their voyage from Acadia to Virginia, and from Virginia to England,[12] their numbers were further reduced during their captivity of seven years in England so that only 866 of the original 1,500 survived.[13] At the end of seven years of exile, Liverpool had 224; Southampton, 219; Falmouth, 159; and Bristol, 184. Eighty others were forced aboard a corsair.

Some months after their arrival, the English government assigned them a certain number of houses in a segregated quarter of each city with exception of Falmouth, where they were scattered throughout the city. In Liverpool, the government placed them under a commissioner named Langton. It granted to everyone over seven years of age six cents daily, three cents a day to children and infants,[14] and one dollar and twenty cents a year for lodgment.[15]

On September 2, 1762, the court of France sent as its minister plenipotentiary to the court of England Louis Jules Barbon Mancini Mazarini, Duke of Nivernois, Grandee of Spain, Knight of the King, Peer of France, to negotiate an end to the Seven Years' War.[16] The Acadian exiles who were kept as prisoners of war in a segregated quarter in Liverpool were the first to hear of his arrival.[17] They decided to inform the ambassador of their presence and plight. They made use of a certain Normand Duplessis, a French-born pilot of Le Havre, who had been ransomed from the hands of his English captors by M. de la Touche of Martinique. Duplessis could write. He promised the Acadians that he would not only draw up a narrative of their sufferings but that he would also present it to the Duke of Nivernois. But at the last minute he failed them, having been won over by the English commissioner to become a British subject.[18]

The Acadians in Liverpool nevertheless went ahead with their plans to contact the Duke of Nivernois. That was no easy task, however, because the English commissioner, Langton, censored all letters they wrote or received. But they had with them a daring young Irishman, Turney by name, who had married an Acadian girl. The wife had lost her subsidy of six cents a day through her marriage to a foreigner, and the husband was excluded from membership in the Acadian nation. He volunteered to take their letter to the Duke of Nivernois. All that he asked as a recompense for his services was the privilege of following the Acadians wherever it should please the king of France to establish them. After assuring him membership in their nation, the family heads collected twenty dollars to defray his expenses. The plucky, enloved Irishman got the letter through to the Duke of Nivernois.[19]

The letter presented a brief summary of what the Acadians in Liverpool had suffered because of their loyalty to France and to their religion.[20] In it they related the offer that the English government had circularized among them, a return to Acadia in full possession of their homes and farms, if they would take the oath of allegiance which they had constantly refused since 1742. The English government had given them from eighteen months to two years to make a decision. It also disclosed how their chiefs had drafted a petition to the minister of marine, how the English commissioner Langton refused them permission to mail it, and how they unanimously answered all his offers and demands that they renounce France: "We wish to live under the rule of His Most Christian Majesty for whom we are ready to shed our blood." Nothing that the English could promise or threaten could change their attitude. The letter ended with a petition that as French unfortunates they begged the ambassador's protection.[21]

The Duke of Nivernois was deeply touched by the knowledge of their sufferings, persecution, and unswerving loyalty to France.

He was convinced that the king had a duty to rescue these subjects who had given and were still giving such generous proof of patriotism.[22] Accordingly, late in October of 1762, he addressed a memoir to Étienne François, Duke of Choiseul, foreign minister of France, on their behalf. He observed that such faithful subjects could be used with profit in the French colonies.[23] Then on December 11, 1762, he opened negotiations with Lord George Grenville,[24] English prime minister, to secure the liberation of the 300 Acadians "who had been prisoners in England." [25] But before he had reached a settlement with Lord Grenville, he dispatched a messenger, "quickly and secretly," without the knowledge of the English prime minister, to the Acadian prison camp in Liverpool. This messenger was his own personal secretary, M. de la Rochette. He instructed him to make a sly visit to the Acadian prisoners of war in Liverpool, encourage them to the best of his ability, and ascertain all details about them since their expulsion from Acadia.[26]

In reply to the letter that the Acadians had written, the duke instructed La Rochette to transmit to them the following message: that he had informed the king of their inviolable loyalty to his person and also of the sufferings to which this loyalty had brought them; that his majesty was profoundly affected and wished them to return to France; that the king had promised to award them after the conclusion of the peace as good and faithful subjects with the legal ownership of farm lands in the most beautiful provinces of France, and with enough financial help to rebuild what they had lost;[27] and that in France he would treat them more advantageously than they would dare to hope.[28] That was the first part of the ambassador's answer.

The second part of the duke's instructions assured the Acadians of his full protection. But since he did not judge the time ripe to publicize his protection, he wished the Acadians to observe great caution in word and discretion in conduct.

And the third part of Nivernois' message wished the Acadians to supply his secretary with all details, not only about themselves but also about their confrères in other English ports.[29] On December 26, 1762, La Rochette departed on his secret mission to Liverpool.

But before he had left, Count d'Egremont, French secretary of state, had issued orders to Governor Vaudreuil of Canada to sound out General Jeffrey Amherst on the terms of an armistice. On the capitulation of Montreal, on December 8, 1760, Vaudreuil had presented fifty-five articles of peace to Amherst.

On the margin of the 39th article which stipulated that all the French must remain in Canada and not be deported either to England or to the English colonies, Amherst wrote, "Agreed, except as regards the Acadians." Again as a marginal note to the 54th article, which would guarantee a safe return to officers, militiamen, and Acadian prisoners in New England to their respective countries, the general scribbled, "Accepted; but with reservation to the Acadians."[30]

Louis XV, consequently, on January 20, 1763, refused to sign the armistice unless Amherst granted the Acadians a choice of returning either to Canada or to France. Amherst was adamant on the first alternative, but on the second he yielded.[31] That, in brief, was how some 2,542 Acadians assembled between the years 1758 and 1763 in the French maritime ports of Boulogne, St. Malo, Rochefort,[32] Morlaix, Lorient, Belle-Ile-en-Mer, Le Havre, Cherbourg, La Rochelle, and Bordeaux.[33] The authorities in Halifax had previously sent some of those exiles to France, as they did not know where else to dump them. The French authorities registered them in four classes of the most common names.[34]

Meanwhile, La Rochette had arrived on December 31, 1762, in Liverpool. He went immediately, but as secretly as possible, to the Acadian prison quarters. When he had them all assembled, he opened the meeting with a preface calling for great caution and moderation. Then he disclosed to them how the Duke of Nivernois had been deeply moved by the contents of their letter, and promised to be their protector in England. He assured them that the king of France also was shocked in learning of their great sufferings because of their loyalty to his person. But when he told them that Louis XV wanted them to return to France, that he would assist them financially until they became self-supporting, that he would grant them lands equal to those that they had lost in Acadia, and that he would allow them to settle in any part of the kingdom that they might choose, the outburst of their joy knew no bounds. They spontaneously broke out in shouts of "Long live the King." Such confusion arose in the meeting that some English people in the neighborhood were scandalized by the seemingly disorderly conduct of these French prisoners of war. La Rochette could do nothing to moderate their demonstrations of joy.[35]

Then tears of joy welled up in the eyes of all as they gradually grasped the meaning of the royal message. The end of the long years of captivity and painful heartaches of separation, exile, death, and misery in all its multitudinous forms had finally come. "All men, women and children were weeping for joy and muttering in their cries, God bless our good King. Many seemed beside themselves; they clapped their hands, raised them to Heaven, struck them against the walls, and sobbed like children"[36]

It is hard to describe the deep emotions of joy, gratitude, and devotion which shook this honest, simple, and cruelly abused people after they had realized the significance of their coming liberation. At last France had recognized their patriotism. They spent the whole night blessing the king and his ambassador, the Duke of Nivernois, and in consoling each other on the peaceful life that they would have in France. Before making any inquiries on the events that followed their expulsion from Acadia, La Rochette waited awhile until they had recovered from the first outbursts of their emotions. After they had regained their composure, he pieced together the following story.

Langton, the Acadian commissioner, was indeed a patriotic Englishman. He had tried hard to win the exiles over as British subjects. He had even resorted to the use of many ruses. When he saw that idleness of captivity was destroying them, that death, disease, and grief had reduced their number from 336 to 224, he promised them work after the peace was signed, if only they would declare themselves British subjects. As the Acadians mistrusted his word, he had tried another ruse—"a good-will policy." Early in December, 1762, he called a meeting of his charges and told them that after so many years of neglect there was no doubt that France had abandoned them. Therefore, His Britannic Majesty wished that they would now consider themselves as his subjects. If they would do this, the king would not only send them back to Acadia but he would also restore their farms, homes, and livestock. But still, their unanimous answer to him was, "We are French, and the king of France must decide our fate." [37]

After their rejection of these overtures, the commissioner treated them as rebels. He tried to break their morale by threats of imprisonment and even by a reduction of their pay. When he failed at this intimidation, he had recourse to a strategem which he was sure could not fail because of their attachment to the Catholic faith.

He deceived their chaplain, a Scottish priest, with false hopes and promises. He convinced him that His Britannic Majesty would appoint him parochial dean of the Catholic villages of Acadia, if he won the Acadians over to take the oath of allegiance as British subjects.[38] The deluded chaplain, consequently, began to preach such suave sermons to the Acadians that he enticed fifty-four of them, almost all old men, to volunteer to return to Acadia. The rest of them, however, thought the sermons of the chaplain "were scandalous." But it must be told to the credit of the fifty-four deserters that every one of them refused to sign any written statement presented by the commissioner.

But the bad example of these fifty-four elders had a far-reaching effect on the morale of the others. It thoroughly disheartened the remaining 170 persons representing thirty-eight families. They, too, would have volunteered later to return to Acadia. That they did not do so at the time they owe to the intervention of the French pilot of Le Havre, Normand Duplessis. He had argued so vigorously against such disgraceful action that they accepted his counsel. He promised them that he would present a petition on their behalf to the Duke of Nivernois when suddenly Duplessis himself fell for the wiles of the commissioner and the honeyed sermons of the chaplain.[39]

The commissioner then played his trump card. When he had sensed the purpose of La Rochette's visit, "he saw with chagrin the loss to English interests that the departure of the Acadians would cause." Consequently, he began to indoctrinate the Acadians of Liverpool with fear and discouragement. He broadcast subtle reasons why La Rochette and his assistants would not show any credentials of their mission: they had come to deceive the unsuspecting Acadians. They were spies who were working to lure the simple exiles to go to the French tropical colonies, where the heat would soon kill them off. And, even if by some chance the Acadians should survive the tropical heat, France would not give them the daily subsidy which England had given them for the past eight years.[40]

At their wits end, the Acadians of Liverpool elected two of their group to interview the Duke of Nivernois. They invested their representatives with the power of delegates to accept or refuse any of the conditions that the duke might propose. During the dead of night and at the risk of punishment, the two delegates sneaked out of camp to the French embassy in London.

During the interview with Nivernois, the delegates asked assurance on only one point: would France really claim them as her subjects? If so, they would all patiently suffer the cessation of their pay.[41] Given assurance, they divulged to the duke where he would find 600 more exiles scattered in the ports of Southampton, Falmouth, and Bristol.[42]

On learning of the cities where the English kept the other contingents of Acadians in England, the duke sent additional orders to La Rochette. He should also pay these other groups a secret visit. And he should use the same instructions given him on December 26, 1762, for Liverpool.[43]

La Rochette arrived at Southampton on January 18, 1763. As his visit was secret and not official, here as in Liverpool, he could not display any credentials by which the Acadians of Southampton could assure themselves of his authority. Southampton, situated close to London, was the summer rendezvous of the English nobility. Naturally, the Acadians of Southampton had been subjected to more dangerous ruses than were their confrères in the other English ports. For instance, General Mordant and the Duke of York had visited them and attempted to persuade them to renounce France. These poor exiles were then accustomed to the trickeries of English commissioners—trickeries which they thought were sufficient cause to distrust anyone. But trickery from the nobility was something new. And when La Rochette came to them as a secret messenger of the French ambassador, the Acadians of Southampton, fearing a repetition of English wiles refused to accept him or to believe his assurances, or even to listen to him. With their number reduced from 340, when they had left Virginia, to 219 souls, they felt that they had suffered enough from delusions.[44]

La Rochette left them without accomplishing anything, except picking up some data on their history. Before leaving, however, he told them that he was convinced that they were stanchly loyal to His Most Christian Majesty of France, and that it was this deep love for their king that made them so distrustful of him and his mission. As soon as he had left, the Acadians obtained permission from their commissioner to send two delegates to interview the Duke of Nivernois on the promises of La Rochette.[45]

From Southampton, La Rochette proceeded to Falmouth, where he arrived on January 25, 1763. He discovered in Falmouth 159 Acadians who were in a most wretched state of existence. Since the end of November, 1763, the commissioner had stopped their pay. It had been the same for them as for their colleagues in Liverpool: six cents a day for those over seven years of age, three cents for those under that age,[46] and one dollar and twenty cents a year for lodgment.[47] Normally, they should have had sixty dollars in their coffers. Instead, they were destitute. Those who had not a trade lived on loans, while widows and orphans made a living by begging.

The Acadians of Falmouth, moreover, did not live in a segregated quarter of the city. Instead, they were lodged in different houses of its citizens. Because of that system, many of their young people were apprenticed in the homes of English workers "with whom they contracted some very un-Frenchlike attachments." This grieved the parents deeply.

Few of these Acadians showed any good will towards La Rochette. They distrusted him and his assurances, and did not observe caution in conversation with the same accuracy as their fellow prisoners did in other ports.[48] Somewhat disappointed at the reception in Falmouth, La Rochette wended his way on January 31, 1763, to Bristol. Here he found the same distrust which he had experienced in Falmouth. But when he heard the story of their sufferings, his resentment at their aloofness yielded to sympathy.

Only 184 now survived of the 340 who had been shipped to

England from Virginia.[49] They told him that they had landed at Bristol 300 strong. "But the city was not prepared to receive them, and made them spend three days and three nights on the wharves, exposed to all the inclemencies of a winter weather. Finally, the English authorities locked them up in some old buildings where smallpox took many of those who had not succumbed to exhaustion and despair."[50] They had been deceived so many times, they told La Rochette, that they could not trust him, his mission, or his promises. And, moreover, in case he did not know, they had talked before he came with two Acadian delegates who were on their way from Southampton to consult the Duke of Nivernois.[51]

Just as in Southampton and Falmouth so also in Bristol, La Rochette left the Acadians thinking him a spy. But he himself was convinced that the Acadians of Bristol, like their associates in the other camps, were just as stanch in their loyalty to the king of France.[52]

With the exception of Liverpool, La Rochette had little success with the Acadians in the ports of Southampton, Falmouth, and Bristol. But he did accomplish what the duke had sent him to do. He imparted to the Acadians assurance of protection from the French court, gathered much data on their expulsion, their mode of existence after their expulsion from Acadia, and their present attitude toward returning to France. On his return to London, La Rochette presented the duke with the memoir just narrated, and concluded with the observation: "The Acadians of England fear a return to France."

La Rochette gave Nivernois four reasons for this general fear. The first was false reports of starvation. The Acadian exiles in England had heard that France allowed their relatives who had gone directly from Acadia to her maritime ports to starve for months without giving them help. Consequently they had a deep-rooted suspicion that they would meet the same fate.

The second reason was the anti-French influence of their English and Scottish chaplains. These priests were constantly describing France as a country abandoned by God. They were daily urging their spiritual charges to renounce France and return to Acadia as British subjects. But not every Acadian in England believed the chaplains. A good part of them openly showed distrust for and dissatisfaction with the spiritual administrations of those politically minded chaplains.

The third reason was deceptive English propaganda at home and abroad. The Acadians had misunderstood this propaganda and were foolishly imagining that they would ultimately be able to return to Acadia and enjoy the free exercise of their religion under protection of the French king. Those Acadians especially who were in the ports of Boulogne, St. Malo, and Rochefort persisted in that dream. They even wrote about it to their relatives and friends in England.

The fourth reason was a vague yet general hope of returning to Acadia as a group. The Acadians in England were convinced that the king of France would abandon the 10,000 of their dispersed brethren in the English colonies on the North American continent. Had not a few families of the dispersed Acadians in Boston escaped to Bristol? Those refugees reported that their people captive in Boston were dying of hunger, that the colonial English were still expelling Acadians every day, and that they had forced a large number of Acadians to labor on the new lands of the Chevalier de Ternay in New England. Since 700 Acadians still remained at Chebouctou or its vicinity,[53] they were resolved that should the king of France be unable to rescue all dispersed Acadians, or claim them as his subjects, or ransom them as prisoners of war, every one of them would try to return to Acadia. They felt that the greater part of their exiled nation could always make a return to Acadia, if they secretly informed every exile of the promises and tolerable treatment that they had received while prisoners of war in England.[54] What kept them from volunteering for the Antilles was the fear of family separations.

In regard to statistics, the present Acadian population and the port cities of their residence, La Rochette could get only an estimate. The Acadians in England informed him that he would find in France about 2,000 scattered in the various ports of Boulogne, St. Malo, and Rochefort, and in the English colonies of New England, Maryland, Pennsylvania, and South Carolina another 10,000.

Nivernois listened with deep attention and sympathy to La Rochette's account of Acadian suffering and loyalty to France. Now more than ever before, the French ambassador became convinced of the great agricultural and economic value of those exiles to France or her colonies.[55] He closed the interview with the determination that all Acadians everywhere must be rescued for France.

CHAPTER THREE

Nivernois Rescues the Acadians in England

O N MARCH 14, 1763, the Duke of Nivernois wrote to
the cousin of Choiseul, César Gabriel de Choiseul, Duke de
Praslin, to whom the foreign minister had committed the duties
of minister of marine:

> We would act wisely, were we to decide quickly on the
> plans we shall use to re-establish the Acadians. It will be im-
> portant that we settle these plans completely before the
> Acadians return to France. I ask you, Monsieur le duc, to
> send me your decisions on these matters as soon as possible
> so that I may be able to calm their fears, and answer their
> repeated questions on the treatment and destination that we
> shall give them. There is a rumor rife among them that we
> shall send them to Cayenne, and that disturbs them very
> much, because they fear the climate of our tropical colonies.[1]

The Acadians of England dreaded any change that threatened
to plunge them into greater misery. The story that France had
allowed their people to starve for many months in her maritime
ports made them very skeptical of French promises.[2] Realizing
their fear of losing the financial pittance from the English or of
being sent to Cayenne, the Duke of Nivernois offered to Praslin
a plan for their rehabilitation in France.[3] He pointed out that
prompt approval of that plan would enable him to publicize it to
the captive Acadians in England. He was confident that his plan
when known would not only calm their fears in regard to treatment and refuge that the French government would give them
in France, but it would also wean them from their growing
attachment to the English scheme of returning to Acadia.[4] He

36

was confident of more than that. He felt that if the French government treated the Acadians of England well it would attract all the others who were scattered throughout the English colonies to come to France. "What a great advantage that would be for France—to gain such stanch subjects! Their loyalty is only equalled by their suffering for their country," he wrote to Praslin.[5] Nivernois then disclosed to him a master plan to attract all Acadians to France. In it he itemized the expenses carefully. He concluded that the total expense the French government would incur in resettling the Acadians by advancing them one hundred and twenty furnished cabins, a daily subsidy of two cents to every one during the first year, liquidation of their debts in England, the grant of farm animals, poultry, grains for two years, garden tools, and transportation from England would run to about $24,220. Nivernois left the cost of hiring an agent to supervise the work open. He did not think it within his authority to determine such an honorarium. That depended on the generosity of the French court.[6]

Looking into the future, he pointed out again to Praslin the great social profit to the French crown in an honest and sincere rehabilitation of these Acadians. "The King," he computed, "will have to spend $24,220 to acquire 120 families. But these families in the course of 20 years will make a return of 240 families of faithful and industrious subjects." Then he entered into an explanation of how the state would make valuable financial gains. Deducting $4,000 (cost of transporting the Acadians) from $24,220 expended, would leave $20,220 that the state had used to settle the Acadians. Interest on that investment divided among 120 families would net the state more than 10 per cent for the second year in work, consumption of food, and farm supplies. In other words, the state would realize $2,000 interest the second year or $800 more than the interest on the total advanced capital of $20,220.[7]

The duke's plan not only obligated the French government to shoulder the debts that the Acadians of England had contracted during their seven years of captivity, but their current support as well. As soon as Lord Grenville realized that England would lose the Acadians he ordered the commissioners in Liverpool, Southampton, Falmouth, and Bristol to stop paying them the pittance of six cents.[8] The commissioners had already been threatening this cessation of pay to whip the Acadians into taking the oath of allegiance.[9] Now the English government fulfilled its threat. As the poor exiles had not received a subsidy for some time, they naturally contracted debts even in purchasing the barest necessities of life. One of their urgent necessities was medicine to allay the widespread sickness caused by the circumstances of their wretched condition. Their debts now amounted to twenty-six or twenty-eight thousand dollars, Nivernois informed Praslin. He further indicated that the English government would not permit the Acadians to leave unless they paid their debts. Some of them had earned a little money by their labors and had pledged themselves to pay part of their debts; but, even if they should succeed in raising a thousand or twelve hundred dollars, they would still owe a thousand or sixteen hundred dollars more.[10]

As regards settling those Acadians who were already in France or who would return from the English colonies, Nivernois strongly urged Praslin to locate them in Brittany rather than in Guyenne. "In Brittany," he argued, "the Acadians would find comfort not only in the climate but also in the closeness of their brethren on the island of Bouin, which is only twenty-four miles from Nantes." [11] To supervise the removal of the Acadians Nivernois recommended La Rochette as best qualified, since he knew all the rules and regulations pertaining to the emigration laws.[12] Hoping for a favorable reply and acceptance of his plan of Acadian settlement, the duke directed La Rochette on March 18, 1763, to write a circular letter to all Acadians in England's ports. The duke hoped that the Acadians would smuggle the letter on to their fellow exiles in the American colonies. La Rochette sent the following letter, addressed to the care of Anthony Kasthing of England, Coffee House, St. Martin's Lane.

Liverpool, England
March 18, 1763

My dear Countrymen:

We have an order of His Excellency, the Duke of Nivernois, Ambassador Extraordinary of His Most Christian Majesty. He has been in London now for some time, and has asked me to notify you that a definitive treaty has been signed. He will take immediate steps to remove you to France. As he can act in your behalf only after he knows exactly how many of you there are or how many of you would like to place yourselves under the protection of the King of France, he wants you to submit a census of your people as soon as possible. This registration must contain the personal signature of every man, woman and child; and in case anyone cannot write, he must affix his mark alongside of his name.

I have the pleasure to inform you that your treatment in France will be still more advantageous than you expect, and that you will be under the immediate protection of the king and his minister, his excellency, the Duke of Nivernois.

Communicate this letter to your brethren. Tell them of their coming liberation. And assure them that I am vouching for the duke's protection.

Your very humble and obedient servant,
(signed) La Rochette[13]

Reference has been made already to Nivernois' motives and enthusiasm. His plea that France should give the Acadians of England the best treatment possible was not free from selfish aims. As lord of the island of Bouin he was anxious to have the Acadians settle that island. He frankly confessed to Praslin that his majesty would flatter him if he should condescend to choose that island as home for the small number of Acadians who were in England. The duke at least appreciated the fact that these unfortunates were a great source of political and financial wealth, and that they were attached to king and France. Praslin forwarded Nivernois' master plan and petition to his superior and cousin, the Duke of Choiseul.

The Duke of Choiseul on April 11, 1763, wrote from Versailles to Nivernois. He agreed with Nivernois that France must shoulder the Acadian debt in England if she hoped to attract them. He, therefore, authorized Nivernois to liquidate their debt immediately, and ordered the treasury of the colonies to refund that sum to the French embassy in London. He furthermore notified the subdelegates in every maritime town of France to welcome all Acadians that might arrive in their respective ports and to grant each adult six cents a day.[14] That was as far as he accepted Nivernois' plan of rehabilitation, for Choiseul had his own grandiose plans and schemes. He dreamed of rebuilding a new French empire in Guiana of South America. Consequently, he shelved the ambassador's stereotyped plan of colonization.[15]

In the same letter he informed Nivernois that he had ordered Hocquart of Brest to reinforce two frigates in that harbor with two transports and to dispatch all four ships without delay to England: one transport to Liverpool, another to Falmouth, and the other two to Southampton. Hocquart would advise the captains of the ships to contact La Rochette upon their arrival in the English ports. "Then, you will instruct the captains to disembark the Acadians at St. Malo and Morlaix," he wrote Nivernois. "In France, Messieurs Isarn and Quetier respectively, will register them. I have informed both of them to expect the arrival of the Acadians. And, moreover, I have instructed Monsieur Guillot to send the four ships back to the English ports as soon as they have finished the transportation."[16]

A week later, on April 18, Nivernois once more sent La Rochette to visit the Acadian camps in the ports of Liverpool, Southampton, Falmouth, and Bristol. By that visit he wished to ascertain the exact number of families, the name, age, and sex of each person. He ordered La Rochette to give this information to each ship and also to send a copy of it to him in London. Moreover, he charged La Rochette to secure a signed statement from the English commissioner of each camp. Nivernois was anxious to know how long each commissioner had withheld the pittance of subsidy from his charges.[17]

When La Rochette visited the four camps again, he was stunned by the discovery of the number of deaths in Liverpool and Bristol. In the space of three months the Acadians of Bristol had lost twenty-four members, Liverpool seven, and Falmouth and Southampton each one. This heavy mortality reduced their number from 866 to 833 souls.[18]

The Duke of Nivernois was indeed most meticulous. He prepared for La Rochette a detailed outline for the removal of the Acadians in the English ports. First La Rochette should move the Acadians of Bristol to Southampton. He should arrange their departure in four divisions, one each day for four consecutive days, and not more than forty persons in a division. In this way he would find it much easier to secure nightly lodgment. Moreover, a small group would spare him possible embarrassment from the publicity of any large number of French traveling.[19] Next he should hire at least five wagons (and at the customary price) to transport all men, women, children, and baggage. Then he should grant visas to each Acadian, but in so doing be sure to respect the form and custom of England. Next, he must send a detailed report with all the names of the evacuees plus another of expenses incurred either to him or to the minister of the king, so that either of them could render an account to His Majesty on the progress of Acadian exiles from England.[20]

And last, Nivernois himself forwarded to Choiseul the tentative account of his procedure in Acadian transportation:[21]

From Bristol

Expense of 5 or 6 wagons	$ 10.00
Supposed debts of Acadians	6.00
Pay to the Acadians of Bristol during 8 days at 8 cents a day for 160 persons	102.40
	$ 118.40

From Southampton

Actual debts	$ 3.00
Cost of provisions for the journey of 218 Acadians of Southampton to unite with the 160 from Bristol, making a total of 378 persons at 8 cents a day for 9 days	272.16
	$ 275.16

From Falmouth

Debts of 158 Acadians, caused by the suppression of their pay	$ 30.00
Food for 158 persons during the journey of 9 days at 8 cents per head	113.76
	$ 143.76

From Liverpool

Debts of 217 Acadians	$ 6.00
Provisions for 217 persons during a journey of 20 days at 8 cents a day	347.20
	$ 353.20

In spite of Nivernois' carefully detailed plan and La Rochette's capable execution of it, the removal of the Acadians from England was not accomplished without problems. No doubt the troubles were beyond the control of either. England in June, 1763, was full of French prisoners of war—officers, soldiers, and sailors, not to mention the 833 Acadians—all of whom wanted to return to France. Nivernois made several attempts to get the Acadians safely out of England. He was aware of their weakened condition and their aversion to overcrowding. But France's foreign minister, Choiseul, sent only four transports to accommodate the great numbers clamoring to return to France at the earliest date possible and overcrowding was the inevitable result.[22]

On May 16, the 218 Acadians of Southampton sailed for Morlaix aboard the corvette *l'Ambition*. On May 26, the 160 from Bristol (then camping in Southampton) also departed for Morlaix on the frigate *Dorothée*. On the same day, the 158 Acadians of Falmouth left on the transport *Fauvette* but for St. Malo. And on June 8, commissioner Langton finally permitted the remaining 217 Acadians of Liverpool to break camp for St. Malo, but only upon payment of all their debts. These embarked on the transport *l'Esturgeon*.[23] In all 378 were sent to Morlaix and 375 to St. Malo. They all arrived, safe but exhausted, in their respective ports of Morlaix and St. Malo. The ministry immediately provided them with some temporary quarters in the barracks of each city but made no provisions for sanitation. The Acadians, worn out by the long road journey of many days, were oppressed to the breaking point by the intense heat and discomfort of the unhealthily overloaded transports.[24] They had hardly arrived when the scourge of their lives, smallpox, attacked them again, and again their number was decimated.[25]

CHAPTER FOUR

Nivernois Rallies the Acadians
in the American Colonies

THE LETTER from La Rochette of March 18, 1763, soon found its way to Acadian exiles on the North American continent. The captives responded immediately to the invitation and request of the Duke of Nivernois. They did not know, however, that Claude François Louis Regnier, Count of Guerchy, had replaced the duke as ambassador at the English court. Would their response have been the same had they known of the change?

Be that as it may, on November 22, 1763, Choiseul informed Guerchy that La Rochette had forwarded to him the census and letters that the Acadians in English colonies had addressed to the Duke of Nivernois. "Sieur de la Rochette," he began, "whom Monsieur le duc de Nivernois had entrusted with the task of assembling all Acadians dispersed in England and of removing them to France, has just sent me a general census of the Acadians dispersed in Georgia, Carolina, Maryland, New York, New England, and Nova Scotia. With the census he has included copies also of some letters which these people, thinking that Monsieur le duc de Nivernois was still in England, have addressed to him." [1]

From data sent by the exiles in the English colonies La Rochette had arranged the chart shown on the following page.

Choiseul had no intention at first of assembling the Acadian captives of the English colonies in France. But he did sincerely strive to secure their return to Acadia. Yet at the same time he

EXILES IN ENGLISH COLONIES[2]

Individuals	New England		New York	Nouvelle Écosse		Maryland†	Penn-sylvania	South Carolina	Georgia	General Total
	Admin. of Boston	Admin. of Conn.		Admin. of Halifax*	Rivière St. Jean					
Men	160	108	38	136	19	117	64	57	33	732
Women	167	109	40	123	17	139	68	65	37	765
Boys and Girls	716	449	171	435	51	554	251	158	115	2,900
TOTAL	1,043	666	249	694	87	810	383	280	185	4,397

* These figures do not include families scattered along the coast.
† There were as many in the districts of Baltimore as in the towns of Annapolis, Newton, Snowhill, Oxford, High and Lower Marl-borough, Port Tobacco, and Princetown.

was also making plans for their repatriation in one of the French tropical colonies should he fail to achieve his first aim.[3] He accordingly instructed his intendants and commissioners of the maritime ports to acquaint the poorest Acadian families immediately upon their arrival of the advantages of going to Guiana, or to one of the islands in the West Indies, such as St. Lucia, Guadeloupe, or Santo Domingo. Should they go to one of those colonies, His Majesty would not only continue the same subsidy that they had received in the past but would also grant them other privileges. Their departure from France Choiseul thought would ease the great strain on His Majesty's shrinking revenues.[4]

But the Duke of Nivernois and the English forced Choiseul's hand. In October of 1762, the duke had sent him a memoir. In it he stressed the Acadian claim on royal protection, and their possible usefulness after the peace in France or in French tropical colonies.[5] And the English, from 1758 to 1763, kept dumping the deportees of Acadia, Prince Edward Island, and Cape Breton into the French maritime ports,[6] until by the end of the year 1763 the Acadians, including those from England, who entered France after the fall of Louisbourg and the surrender of Canada, numbered between 3,000 and 4,000 persons.[7] Nivernois was correct in his advice to Choiseul. Assurance of good treatment would attract the Acadians in the Anglo-American colonies to retrieve their lost fortune and happiness in France.[8]

La Rochette's letter with the duke's kind invitation and promise of good treatment reached the 383 Acadians of Pennsylvania early in July, 1763. They were the first of all Acadians in America to send a signed petition to His Most Christian Majesty begging him to liberate them from Anglo-American slavery. "Since the English took away our lands," they pleaded, "we have always wished to return either to France or to one of her colonies so that we might enjoy the free exercise of our religion. We ask of our Sovereign no other kindness but only deliverance." [9]

The exiles in Maryland had heard of the appointment of the Duke of Nivernois as ambassador extraordinary as early as November, 1762. As soon as they learned of his kindness to their people in England and of his desire to liberate them, they addressed a letter to him dated December 2, 1762. In it they depicted a brief but touching picture of their wretched existence. In brief the English had indentured them on the farms of Maryland, "where the robust ones worked as laborers, and the old and sick eked out a living by begging." [10]

But their hopes of deliverance rose as they read the duke's message in La Rochette's letter. They hastily gave him all the information he wanted about their people. They told him especially how their numbers had dwindled from 2,000 to 810—a figure that included the children who had been born in Maryland[11]—and how and where their people were scattered among the towns of Maryland— 26 at Lower Marlborough, 33 at Princess Anne, 44 at Newton, 58 at Upper Marlborough, 68 at Georgetown, 68 at Snowhill, 77 at Baltimore, 78 at Annapolis, 157 at Port Tobacco, and 169 at Oxford. They concluded their letter with a humble petition: "Your poor servants ask only the privilege of being counted among His Most Christian Majesty's subjects." [12]

In Connecticut 666 Acadians survived. They probably fared the best of all, as the state legislature had made provisions for their rehabilitation. But these poor exiles nevertheless longed to be united with their own people. And as soon as the content of La Rochette's letter was noised abroad in August of 1763, they besought the Duke of Nivernois not only to take them under his protection but also to take them back to France.[13] They told him that he would find an isolated group of twenty families comprising 122 persons at Preston. They were cut off from the rest, and now almost forgotten by the majority of their own people. The names of these families were: Hébert, Bourgois, Carsot, Lor,

Caumeaux, Simon, Doucet, Grangèr, Martin, Michel, Braux, Babinot, Richard, Brun, Fauret, Prijean, Savoye, and Amiros. Of all the Acadian exiles in America, none had cause to rejoice more heartily at the good news of possible reunion than this lost colony.[14]

For the Acadians in South Carolina the news of La Rochette's letter was heartening. They were only a handful—280, including men, women, and children—many of them orphans. Once they were 2,000. Misery had so crushed their morale that the content of La Rochette's letter did not stir them to any show of enthusiasm.[15] Nevertheless, each one placed himself under the duke's protection and ardently besought him for an early return to France. As a group they begged him above all things to obtain from His Majesty an order for "the return of some of their children who had found work in the homes of certain English subjects."[16]

The most enthusiastic response came from the Acadians in Georgia. When La Rochette's letter reached them they all fell on their knees and gave thanks to God. True, they had waited long for a liberator, but He did not fail them. He had sent them the Duke of Nivernois.[17]

They wrote for the duke, on August 23, 1763, a brief history of their miserable life in Georgia. There remained only 187 of them, comprising 37 families. They were there through sheer necessity. They could not avail themselves of Governor Reynold's permission to leave Georgia, because they had no money or skilled workers who could build boats.[18] Every day they had to fight against the intrigues of the English who were trying to trick them into a renunciation of France.[19] But their greatest sorrow—and one that was shared by ecclesiastical authorities as well—was the absence of chaplains. During their eight years of residence in Georgia they had had no priest to minister to their spiritual needs. Consequently, they had not confessed themselves or received the sacrament of the Lord's Body for eight years. Nevertheless they met regularly in a special house to say their prayers in common, and to observe Sundays and all feast days as the Catholic, Apostolic, and Roman Church had taught them. They pleaded with the duke to use his influence in ordering the return of several of their children who had been kidnapped and indentured to plantations on the seacoast, and of others whom the English had sold. They regarded life without their religion and among the English as the greatest evil that could befall their children.[20]

The 249 Acadians in Boston were equally enthusiastic. As soon as they learned of the substance of La Rochette's letter, they signed the petition to return to France. But a cruel fate was in store for them. Just as they were ready to slip aboard a French vessel, the captain, a native of Nantes, refused to book them passage. Thus, only a few of them were fortunate enough to wheedle their way back to Bordeaux. On October 15, 1763, Choiseul severely censured that unpatriotic French captain.[21]

In New York some three hundred of the exiles were living under circumstances of great wretchedness. So great was their misery in that state that they merely pleaded for admittance to any French colony just so they might escape Anglo-American slavery. One hundred and fifty of them, accordingly, seized the first opportunity of escaping aboard a French merchant ship bound for Martinique. Choiseul would have liked to repatriate them to France, but he felt that the expense of chartering a special ship would add to the heavy strain on the wobbly treasury of France. He did all that he thought he could do with safety for them. He granted them subsidy for a whole year in Martinique.[22]

Such in brief were the reactions of the Acadians in the Anglo-American colonies to La Rochette's letter. After studying the chart and letters La Rochette "had just sent him," Choiseul sent a note to Guerchy. He informed the French ambassador in England that many of the Acadian exiles in the American colonies had expressed the desire of going to French tropical islands. Since the governors of the American colonies were not putting any obstacles in their path of escape, Louis XV had ordered Martinique and Santo Domingo to send ships to rescue the exiles, especially those stranded in Boston and New York.

> Nevertheless, I am asking you to sound out the English Minister on this subject. Find out for your own satisfaction if His Britannic Majesty would countenance the return of the Acadians; because if he should consent to it, we could take other efficient means to bring them home. You see how important it is for you to proceed tactfully with your questions on this matter in order that you do not get for your efforts a formal refusal, because if you should meet with the least opposition there, we would do better to continue the indirect means which we have already been using in sending ships from Martinique and Santo Domingo. I ask you to give me your opinion as well as an account of your discussions with the English Minister, so that I might take His Majesty's orders.[23]

However, as soon as the English court learned of Nivernois' scheme to attract the Acadians to France or to her tropical colonies, it registered a formal protest with the French ambassador. Consequently, on December 6, 1763, the Duke of Guerchy wrote to Choiseul his opinion. He advised him not to approach the governors of the English colonies, and even less the prime minister in London, for official permission to remove the Acadians, but just keep on sending some ships to Boston and New York. The Acadians marooned in those cities would find a way to get out.[24]

Governor Wilmot of Nova Scotia also learned of La Rochette's letter. On January 8, 1764, he wrote to Lord Halifax that he had conclusive proof that the Acadians of Nova Scotia had applied to the king of France to repatriate them. He asked Halifax if he did not consider removing the remainder of the exiles in Nova

Scotia to the recently conquered islands in the West Indies as advisable. Such a step would keep them as English subjects.[25]

Lord Halifax' answer of June 9, 1764, was not only clear but decisive.

> With regard to the Information you have received [he informed the governor] of the Acadians having applied to the Court of France to be removed out of His Majesty's Dominions, there is great Reason to believe that such Application (if it should be made) would not meet with any Encouragement, as His Most Christian Majesty's Ministers assured me, in Answer to my Remonstrances occasioned by some intelligence of the same sort received from Boston in September last, that His Court had no intention of Interfering with Respect to the Removal of the Acadians. . . . But you will never suffer them to be carried away by the open attempts or secret Practices of any Foreign Power.[26]

Seventeen months later, on November 8, 1765, his lordship reversed his attitude. When Stephen Landry in his own behalf and in that of all Acadian groups in Maryland and Pennsylvania had presented a petition to General Gage to settle again in either Acadia or Quebec, the Board of Trade at Whitehall rejected the request even though the exiles were willing to take the oath of allegiance.

> It would not be advisable or expedient [ran the wily excuse to General Gage] to permit Monsieur Landry and his associates either to return to Nova Scotia or to settle in Quebec, where the irreconcilable enmity that they have ever borne to your Majesty's Government, may probably operate more to the prejudice of Your Majesty's interests than it can do in any other situation, and where their attachment to the crown and subjects of France will lead them into a correspondence and connection of the most dangerous kind.[27]

But when Colonel Haldimand applied on December 2, 1765, to take the Acadians of St. John's Island to his estate in Canada he received immediate permission.[28] Why the discrimination against Stephen Landry and his associates?

There were still 1,249 "irreconcilable" Acadians representing 324 families dotting the seacoast of Nova Scotia.[29] They were chiefly located in:

1. Isles Madames......Neirichak......	33 families of	174 souls	
2. Petit Degras......................	9	"	37	"
3. Des Kousses......................	15	"	73	"
2 Isles Du Cap Breton			
1. St. Pierre-Lardoise..................	11	"	63	"
2. Labrador........................	7	"	32	"
3. Louisbourg.......................	4	"	22	"
4. Baye de Gabarus..................	6	"	38	"
1. Windsor..........................	72	"	82	"
2. Halifax and vicinity...............	24	"	118	"
3. Chegelkouk.......................	17	"	96	"
4. Cap de Sable.....................	12	"	50	"
5. Baye Ste. Marie...................	24	"	98	"
6. Rivère St. Jean...................	37	"	158	"
7. Fort Cumberland..................	16	"	70	"
8. Memramkouk.....................	23	"	87	"
9. Petkoodiak......................	14	"	51	" [30]
Total......................	324		1,249	

When this marooned remnant of Acadian natives learned of the Duke of Nivernois' intention in their regard they all rallied to his call. They begged and pleaded with him to obtain for them either an "improvement in their position . . . or a chance of settling in France or in the French colonies." [31] But the Board of Trade on June 9, 1764, sealed their fate.[32]

Halifax had denied Stephen Landry and his associates in Maryland and Pennsylvania permission to return to Acadia or even to distant parts of the Quebec province. As the reason for his decision he alleged fear lest their "irreconcilable enmity" towards the British crown and "their attachment to the Crown and subjects of France will lead them into a correspondence and connection of the most dangerous kind." [33] Had he forgotten the half century of loyalty in the face of provocation from Halifax that the Acadians gave the British crown?[34] How different is Dr. Andrew Brown's estimate of these Acadians whom Lord Halifax declared as steeped in "irreconcilable enmity." "The King has no subjects more loyal or better disposed to defend his rights." [35]

There is no doubt that Nivernois partly understood the Acadians when he too wrote Choiseul that good treatment would attract them to France. But only Martín Navarro, intendant of Louisiana, fully understood their character as a people, when he told José de Gálvez, "The Acadians are in need of good treatment and human kindness." [36]

CHAPTER FIVE

Acadians Appeal to Louis XV
at Compiègne, 1772

As THE Acadians arrived in France they settled in the maritime towns of Normandy, Brittany, Aunis, and Guyenne.[1] They lingered in these towns for ten years under charge of the first lord of the admiralty whose chief commissioner was Antoine Phillippe Lemoine of Rochefort.[2] His first act was to secure from the minister of finances an appropriation of $57,900[3] for support of the exiles until he could achieve their incorporation into the economy of the French nation, as willed by Louis XV. Until that time, he allotted to each one six cents a day.

There is no doubt that Lemoine was a man of good intentions. All that he visioned and wished to do he did, not only for the Acadians but also to honor his own sense of charity and humanity and to demonstrate as well his zeal in fulfilling the king's will and in promoting his sovereign's glory.[4] He realized that there were citizens in the maritime ports who were anxious for an opportunity to enrich themselves by exploiting any settlement of the Acadians or by victimizing the simple character of the exiles themselves. To save them from being victimized by unscrupulous merchants and land sharks, Lemoine fixed a limit to the entire expense which their support would cause the king. Then with keen foresight and ability he pondered for a long time on the best means of establishing them profitably to themselves and to France.[5] But he made one grave mistake: he pondered too long.

While Lemoine was mulling over his plans, early in February

1763 the Duke of Nivernois was doing his best to influence Choiseul to accept at least one of several plans he had for the Acadians. He called the duke's attention to several factors in the character and nature of the Acadians that militated against any settlement of them in French tropical possessions. As the Acadians were all laborers their life had been devoted to farming, fishing, or a laborious trade. Acadian farms demanded assiduous cultivation, and their cabins and dikes continuous repairing. What time those daily labors left them they would spend in making clothes, sails, twine, baskets, straw hats, sabots, rakes, and other needed implements.

Moreover, the Acadians by their nature were unfitted to the climate in French tropical possessions. They even had "a prejudice of repugnance" for tropical climates. In Acadia they had lived in a rough climate of 44° latitude above the equator. Being inured to cold they suffered little sickness. When the English, however, began to deport them to warmer climates, over 600 soon died from smallpox, a disease unknown to them in Acadia. Were they settled in the tropics, half of them would die.

In addition, the Acadians by their poverty were unfitted for any of the French tropical colonies. The insular plantations of sugar, coffee, indigo, and cotton demand a financially well-fixed class of colonists. And there was not an Acadian who was not poor. The colony of Cayenne, on the mainland of South America perhaps, was the only one where Acadians might live with some hope of success. They could perhaps invest their labors in plantations of cacao trees, but in those only, since their poverty would forbid them plantations of sugar, indigo, or any of the others that require some years of development before they could give a profitable livelihood. Consequently, Nivernois proposed three plans which he thought showed harmony between the interests of the state and those of the Acadians with equity.[6] Two of his three plans were:

First, the physiocrats of France have been discussing for a long time the utility in clearing the *landes* of Guyenne and of Gascogne.[7] There is no doubt that settling the Acadians on these *landes* would give the government great profits. The Acadians would transform these desert-areas into such thriving colonies that other settlements would benefit from them and their industry. The climate of Guyenne indeed differs very much from that of Acadia; but it is healthy, and I think that the Acadians could adjust themselves to it without danger. I think, in addition, that we should settle them on the seacoast where there are some harbors. They would soon build up a coasting trade which would give them new resources.[8]

Second, in the Province of Brittany. This province has shown a marked depopulation through the number of soldiers and sailors which it has furnished the government during the Seven Years' War. It has advantages, but they are undeveloped because of its dearth of population. For instance, its ground is fertile, and its coast waters abound in fish. The fishing of herring offers the possibility of a considerable commerce and profit to the government.

After the Seven Years' War the eastern section of Brittany offered huge regions of uncultivated lands. But those regions had a disadvantage in that their fishing was hardly sufficient to sustain the local farmers. But Nivernois thought that the Acadians would find compensations such as prompt settlement, subsidy from Brittany's agricultural society, and livestock breeding.

Nivernois' third plan was to establish the Acadians of England as a special colony on the island of Bouin just off the coast of the lower Poitou. Considering the size of the island, its scant population, and the possibilities of its fishing industry of sardines, an Acadian colony there undoubtedly would have brought new life to the island.[9]

Of all the islands off the coast of France [he informed Choiseul], the climate of the island of Bouin resembles most

that of Acadia. For that reason I consider this island most
suitable for these Acadians. Besides, when these unfortunate
prisoners learned that the Duke of Nivernois was the owner
and lord of the island of Bouin, they ardently desired to
settle there in preference to other places, because they look
upon him as their liberator and only friend.

The island of Bouin,[10] on the other hand, from time im-
memorial has enjoyed certain privileges. King after king had
repeatedly confirmed these privileges to its insular inhabitants. They have exempted the islanders from taxation, from
the duties of the corvée, of defense of the island, of maintenance of the dykes, and of the barges on which the sub-
sistence of the island depends. The Acadians would find
themselves more happy there than elsewhere, and consequently would be more useful. They would bring new life
to the island, and new possibilities to its fishing business.
True, the island could not support all the Acadians from
England. But I offer as a satisfactory solution the placing of
the remainder in Brittany, where they could settle with profit
to themselves and to the state.

I will not hide my feelings here that I would feel greatly
honored if His Majesty had the kindness to settle a small
part of the Acadians in England on the island of Bouin,
considering that these exiles are very attached to the King
and France, and represents great economic possibilities.

As regards the establishment of the Acadians who are already in France or who will return from the English colonies, I strongly urge His Majesty to settle them in Brittany
rather than in Guyenne, because there, they would enjoy the
comfort not only of the climate but also of the closeness of
their brethren on the island of Bouin, only eight leagues
(twenty-four miles) from Nantes.

The Duke of Nivernois ended his memoir to Choiseul by re-
minding him that the state would have to encourage the Acadians from reasons of politics as well as of equity. Colonies in
1763 were a great expense to a tottering France, but the expense
was only a loan that she would make to her subjects, who every

year would develop an interest that would not cease to grow. Ultimately, France would have the capital returned to her, but in a different form: the increase of her population and the expansion of her commerce and trade.[11]

None of Nivernois' plans for the Acadians materialized, even though Choiseul had written to him, "His Majesty willingly accedes to your plan and grants you leave to establish the Acadians on the island of Bouin. He will subsidize them in the same way as he is assisting those who are already in France." A week later he wrote again, "The King will be happy to know of the number of Acadians whom the Duke of Nivernois has destined for his island of Bouin before their arrival in France. His Majesty will distribute the rest in the ports of Brittany." [12] Despite these assurances, all Nivernois' efforts failed to captivate the imagination of French authorities. The government later, on March 27, 1767, bought the island from him for $140,000 and turned it into a fortress.[13] With the sale of the island of Bouin, Nivernois passed out of the picture of Acadian rehabilitation, and with him went the Acadians' best chance for a satisfactory settlement.

Lemoine, in the meantime, kept pondering over his own projects so long that the ministry of marine had a change of executives twice. When Lemoine was finally ready to execute some of the many projects that offered a satisfactory settlement of the Acadians in France, the new minister of marine made so many objections and alterations that none of the plans proposed appeared feasible. Yet the Acadians did not refuse any of the projects, however poorly organized, even though they knew that a great number of their confrères would die in every attempt.[14]

Nivernois' plans, however, had this effect: they encouraged Choiseul to execute his own pet project. Choiseul had plans of his own whereby he hoped to become viceroy of a new New France—a New Canada in Guiana, South America.[15] There he would create a new colony that would help the rich sugar colonies in the West Indies and over which he would have no clash with England.[16] He had saved those colonies from the insatiable greed of England by ceding in the Treaty of Paris (February 10, 1763) all the French possessions east of the Mississippi River.[17] As he later vengefully remarked, "I ceded it on purpose to destroy the English. They were fond of American dominion, and I resolved that they should have enough of it." [18] He even rid France of the "unprofitable servant" of Louisiana in the secret Treaty of Fontainebleau (November 3, 1762) in order that he might have more funds and more colonists to lavish on his cherished project of empire in Guiana, besides saving Spain's friendship. This tropical empire he could then populate and strengthen with loyal, industrious Frenchmen. And the Acadians fitted his idea of the right type of empire-builders.[19] But they dreaded the tropics and did not respond to his appeal. Consequently, he recruited only 138 of them, 26 being from Prince Edward Island and 50 from Cape Breton.[20] His whole attempt to build an empire in Guiana was a colossal failure, and of the 10,446 colonists—8,000 of them Germans—that he poured into this tropical inferno in the years 1763-64 at the cost to France of $5,790,000, scarcely 5,000 survived the first year.[21] Of the 138 deluded Acadians, many perished. The rest he was forced to repatriate to France.[22]

After the collapse of Guiana, Choiseul was swamped with projects from every land shark and swindler. Everyone fancied he possessed the solution to the problem of the Acadian settlement. Lemoine was correct in his suspicions that there were many who wished to exploit the Acadians.

In August of 1763, Louis Elizabeth de la Vergne, Count of Tressan, presented a plan for settling 120 Acadian families in the county of Bitche in Lorraine, a desolate area made more desolate in 1632 by ravages of Gustavus Adolphus. The Count of Tressan asked a ridiculous reward for his plan and services, $8,000 plus an annual income of $1,600.[23] Choiseul barely glanced at the money-making scheme.

Choiseul thereupon thought of settling 150 to 200 of the Acadian families on his own "de luxe" estate of Chanteloup commanding the valley of the Loire, north of Amboise.[24] On June 7, 1765, he wrote to l'abbé Louis Joseph le Loutre to come to Paris to discuss the plan.[25] This was a genuine offer of "good treatment" to the Acadians, and one that undoubtedly would have been a true solution had it been put into action. Unfortunately, the project did not materialize.

By 1765 discouragement and idlenesss were breaking the morale of the Acadians. Any opportunity now seemed good; and they grasped whatever was promising. Hence, between 1763 and 1766 many families volunteered for the Falkland Islands, where they had heard that the climate was excellent and the soil fertile. But diplomatic tension between England and Spain over possession of those islands forced the exiles to seek refuge once more in France. And by 1775, the majority had fled.[26]

Colonization of Belle-Ile-en-Mer in 1765 was one project that rose above the stage of discussion. Later it became a typical example of failure. Promoter of this project was l'abbé Le Loutre, friend, protector, and unflinching advocate of the Acadians. While the Acadians were still prisoners in England, he had conceived the plan of settling them on Belle-Ile-en-Mer, an island off the west coast of France. As early as July, 1763, the prospects of settlement on the island favorably impressed a delegation of three Acadians.[27] Le Loutre himself worked unsparingly to recruit families from among those who were prisoners in England. He enlisted fifty-five families from Morlaix and twenty-two from St. Malo—in all seventy-seven families.[28] Later Choiseul added to the Belle-Ile expedition an Acadian family from Boulogne, making a total of seventy-eight families.[29]

Le Loutre wrote from Paris on August 5, 1765, to the governor
of Belle-Ile, Baron Warren:

> My Acadians are ready to leave; they have been awaiting
> my arrival only. But I am detained here by a project which
> I can reveal to you alone, and I only beg you not to tell any-
> one else. The Duke de Choiseul wishes to buy 15,000 acres of
> land to establish a colony of our Acadians, and he has asked
> me to keep it as a private matter until he has closed the con-
> tract. But that plan would only delay the establishment of
> Belle-Ile. Yet we have enough Acadian families to fill both
> projects. My project asks of the Duke leave to depart in or-
> der to settle the seventy-seven families on Belle-Ile. Next
> Spring I will go to establish the rest of my Acadians on his
> lands. I ought to leave, therefore, next Thursday for Com-
> piègne, and on my return, I should have the honor to inform
> you of the arrangements on which we have agreed.[30]

L'abbé Le Loutre presented to Choiseul the consideration of
the following figures. To settle one Acadian family on Belle-Ile
would cost the state approximately $160, since the Acadians
would work as carpenters and laborers in the construction of
their own buildings.[31] The total cost of establishing seventy-eight
families on the island would not exceed $12,479.98. Le Loutre
explained to Choiseul that the king had granted him some help
in the erection of boathouses and purchase of materials and animals, and that he himself was not keeping anything as a remuneration for his personal services.[32] With great enthusiasm Le
Loutre broke ground for the first cabin in 1765. With willing
Acadian labor the province of Brittany built all the necessary
buildings, barns, and roads of about 20 measures of plowable
land, and granted proportionate meadows, pasture lands, wood-
lands, and wastelands in fief.[33] The state moreover allowed them
six cents daily for five years for all children born in England, and
the same for life for those born in Acadia.[34]

Le Loutre organized the seventy-eight families into four parishes: eleven families formed the parish of Palais, sixteen that of
Locmaria, twenty that of Sauzon, and thirty that of Bangor.[35]

The contract called for an exemption of taxes until the year
1769 and expulsion for failure to meet payment after that year. It
also granted them, on the one hand, the right to increase their
acreage of cultivation without any increase in their rent and to
plant, dig, and fence as they wished. But, on the other hand, it
obligated them to help in the maintenance of roads and bridges
of their villages and to pay a tithe in grain as fief-holders.[36]

On March 2, 1766, Le Loutre proudly wrote to Choiseul:

> Monsieur abbé Le Loutre, former Vicar General of the
> diocese of Quebec, testifies to the following: in the month of
> October 1755, the English had transplanted the Acadians,
> now settled on Belle-Ile, to Boston and other English colo-
> nies; that in the year 1756 they transferred these Acadians
> from those colonies to the sea ports of Old England; that in
> the year 1763, after the treaty of peace, the French king re-
> moved them in his own ships to France, and settled them in
> the various maritime towns; and that in the present month
> of October, 1765, Monsieur le duc de Choiseul, Ministre de
> la Marine has allowed them to migrate to this island.[37]

The good abbé did not enjoy his success very long. The
drought came—six years of it! Crops failed so miserably that the
Acadians could not even save enough seed for the following
year. Added to drought, an epizootic distemper destroyed their
livestock. Disaster upon disaster stared them in the face.[38] Then
in 1768 came the crushing blow. Someone erred in sending them
a bill for the first payment of taxes, the tithe. In a general meeting they were unanimous that the colony could not possibly meet
the taxation. They were bankrupt. They agreed to fight any payment of taxes this year because the contract of 1765 called for
payment in 1769, and moreover someone had overcharged
them.[39] They then presented to the province of Brittany a re-

spectful petition in which they pleaded for a reduction of taxes in consideration of their unavoidable misfortunes of four successive years. The answer was "Pay or Leave." [40]

Le Loutre was frantic. He worked unsparingly to save his colony from being expelled. But the Acadians were now also thoroughly disillusioned and discouraged. By the end of July, Le Loutre saw the handwriting on the wall.

> I have made hundreds of trips to Versailles [he wrote to Baron de Warren]. I have been to Compiègne and Fontaine-bleau. I have called on Monsieur le duc de Praslin several times. I have begged and pleaded to the point of importunity. Finally he answered me that hereafter I should see the assessor of taxes, since this matter was no longer his duty. I then presented in the name of my Acadians a very detailed memoir to the public assessor.[41]

In this memoir, l'abbé Le Loutre pointed out to the public assessor of taxation the urgent necessity of the government's subsidizing the Acadian colony of Belle-Ile:

> I received an answer [Le Loutre continued in his letter to Baron de Warren], but I got it through the influence of some important persons who were interested in my poor Acadians. I knew well that the public assessor wished to see the Acadian colony saved. But the cost frightens him. He has no money I am told. And on the other hand, it seems a shame to allow such good farmers to leave France.[42]

Belle-Ile-en-Mer consequently collapsed in 1772, and the twice-expelled exiles retired again to the maritime ports.

The colony of Belle-Ile might have continued for a while despite great hardships. But it could never have been a huge success for the island is too poor, barren, and wind-swept.[43] It is hard to understand how the delegation of three Acadians who inspected Betlle-Ile in July, 1763, could have been so favorably impressed with its potentialities. There is no doubt, however, that the adamant attitude of the noble landowners in demanding their "pound of flesh" was the chief cause of its collapse. Probably the Acadian leaders thought that life on Belle-Ile, poor, barren, windswept as it was, was far better than the life they had known in England's prison camps of 1763.

When the Count d'Hérouville saw the initial success and threatening collapse of Belle-Ile-en-Mer, he proposed to the minister of marine the settlement of 200 to 250 Acadian families on his vast estate in Flanders. His plan was similar to that of Le Loutre. But the government, seeing the approaching collapse of the Belle-Ile colony, hesitated to accept his offer.[44]

By now the Acadians in the maritime ports were ready to attempt any project that would give them a semblance of decent livelihood. So desperate were they becoming, and so thoroughly disillusioned in the sincerity of the efforts of the French ministry, that they were even willing to return to New Brunswick or Acadia under any British conditions.[45] Choiseul appreciated their plight. "This nation, which has sacrificed all for love of France and to whom royal help had been promised, is restless and worn out by their inactive life." [46] Le Loutre had warned the French ministry of the growing desperation among Acadians.[47] Fearing loss of the Acadians to the English, the French government itself now proposed to them a colony on her islands of St. Pierre and Miquelon.[48] Many Acadian exiles had fled to these islands during the turbulent years of the expulsions with the hope of recuperating their losses there. During May, October, and December of 1767 about 551 exiles embarked from St. Malo, Cherbourg, Rochefort, and La Rochelle for these God-forsaken sand bars.[49] To shorten a long sad story elsewhere well told by Émile Lauvrière, the majority returned crestfallen a few months later to swell the list of Acadian pensioners in France.[50]

Auguste René, Count de Chateaubriand, offered 2,500 measures of his barren lands to the Acadians of St. Malo. But so thoroughly disillusioned were all Acadians with aristocratic promises that not one of them volunteered even to consider the possibilities of his offer. They suspected beforehand what the offer held out to them.[51]

Antoine Philippe Lemoine had a close friend in the Marquis de Saint-Victour, governor of Tulle. He was lord of an extensive estate in Limousin near Limoges. In 1769 he offered the Acadians 150 acres of small farm lands—again the dregs of his handsome estate. His conditions were reasonable enough: clear the *landes,* give him a part of the produce for twenty years, and after that he would grant legal ownership.[52] The very sight of the poor soil and the wretched conditions of the few sharecroppers whom the visiting Acadians saw dwelling on those *landes* turned them away. Yet seven families, thinking that the tolerable life of a sharecropper was far preferable to that of inane idleness and beggary, accepted the offer of the Marquis de Saint-Victour. In the year 1772 Limousin petered out as did all the other projects before it. And the disillusioned families returned to the maritime ports to join their idle brethren.[53]

In 1771 the Acadians came under care of a new department: the ministry of finances. This department also had the misfortune of a change of heads, shortly after it had inaugurated plans for a new expedition to the island of Corsica. The director of finances invited some leading Acadians to inspect the potentialities of farming on the island, and the Acadians as usual accepted the invitation. Their investigation disclosed a rotten scheme to get them out of France: they would have had to face "poor treatment," high rents, sterile lands, and an unhealthy climate. Upon learning this the whole Acadian nation rejected the scheme, and thus ended the first Corsica project.[54]

Many were the other projects proposed, but "none succeeded because none was capable." [55] Causes of their failure are not hard to find: change of heads in the departments of marine and finances which crippled whatever plans or arrangements Lemoine would make;[56] Lemoine's own prolonged delays and indecisive actions;[57] negligence and want of sympathy on the part of the French high ministry;[58] hostility of the local citizenry who regarded the Acadians as unwelcomed intruders;[59] always the same award of the dregs of French soil;[60] the almost unbearable irritation of a heavy tax-ridden eighteenth century France to a people accustomed to the freedom of a "forest primeval," teeming in bird, animal, and fish life; and above all, discouragement—a waning faith in France and royal promises,[61] and a growing conviction that "the poor treatment" they had feared while prisoners in England and in the American colonies was fast becoming a reality again.[62] All that they could see for their future was the dole with a homeless, aimless, penniless life.

After the attempt to settle the Acadians in Corsica failed l'abbé Joseph Marie Terray, secretary of finances, found the Acadians very burdensome. Without work for nine years and living on dole and charity, the Acadians themselves felt that they were a burden, not only to Terray but to themselves as well.[63] Discontentment and disillusionment beset everyone. Tired of the vacillating and neglectful conduct of the French high ministry, their leaders determined on a last attempt to obtain a fulfillment of the promises made to them by Louis XV through the Duke of Nivernois. They decided on a direct appeal to the king himself in order to accept the Spanish offer of settlement at Sierra Morena in Andalusia, "with the secret hope that the king would not think it suitable to let them go." [64] They sent a delegation which represented 600 families of 2,500 members. This delegation met Louis XV at Compiègne in July of 1772. They humbly laid before him the circumstances of their wretched condition in France.[65] They begged him, in case he could not help them, to grant them the necessary passports to leave France in order to accept the offer of the Spaniards.[66] Europe of 1772 was alive to the wonderful success Charles III had achieved in settling thousands of Germans and Swiss in Sierra Morena. The Spaniards had assured the Acadians of excellent advantages.[67]

To the director of finances no news could have been more heartening than this Acadian request. Their departure would free him from an embarrassment of $173,700 a year.[68] But to Louis XV the Acadian petition was most humiliating. He listened kindly to the review of their nine years of misery and poverty and deception. Their loyalty to his person and their sufferings for France touched him deeply. He showed openly his displeasure at the negligence of his ministers, "who seemed to make so little of these unfortunate people," and who " had not yet fulfilled the promises he had made to the Acadians nor obeyed his orders of ten years ago." [69]

The Acadian petition was submitted to the council of state. Every member followed the advice of the secretary of the treasury to grant the Acadians full liberty to leave France, except the king. He refused to part with such faithful subjects and noble patriots; he overruled the decision of his ministers and decided to keep the Acadians in France, "attachées à la glèbe," that is, by incorporating them into the class of farmers. By keeping them as farmers he would make them useful and happy as he had promised them.[70]

He ordered Jean Berton, secretary of state, to be sure to find arable lands this time, and Terray, secretary of public finances, to furnish the funds necessary to establish the Acadians as useful farmers.[71] Thus he had solemnly promised ten years ago through the Duke of Nivernois.[72] And thus, as a result of the displeasure he had expressed in his ministers, came the Acadian colony of the Grand' Ligne at Poitou.[73]

CHAPTER SIX

The Acadian Colony of the Grand' Ligne

WHEN Louis XV had charged his secretary of state, Berton, to find arable lands for the Acadians, the latter found himself in an uncomfortable situation. He knew that there were no more free arable lands in France.[1] Yet he had to fulfill his royal master's orders and save his own reputation. He recalled that a certain Marquis de Pérusse des Cars had petitioned him for an exemption from taxation on his great estate of about 13,186 acres in Monthoiron,[2] and in addition to this, was asking for a loan of approximately $90,000.[3]

The Marquis de Pérusse des Cars had been a colonel of a French regiment in Normandy, but in 1755 turned a noble Physiocrat experimenter. In that year he bought a huge estate in the vicinity of Monthoiron, comprising sixteen parishes. At the end of the German wars, in October of 1762, he agreed to clear the immense *landes* of his estate, of which some 9,890 acres were wooded and uncultivated for want of the settlers driven away by civil wars and the revocation of the Edict of Nantes. To achieve this great undertaking he invited four German families to clear a part of his property. He contracted to pay for their transportation, to feed them for three years, and to grant $13.20 and other tax exemptions to every man as a yearly salary, $6.60 to every woman, $3.60 to every adult between fifteen and eighteen years of age, and $2.40 to every child under twelve years of age. Soon a hundred other families applied, and in the year 1763 another four. On February 14, 1766, he obtained Louis XV's permission to undertake whatever was necessary.[4] The marquis' contract with his settlers was liberal and his expenses high, but his profits were small. The project had cost him nearly $4,800—all the capital he possessed. Hard-pressed he presented to the king a report of his aims, the results he had achieved, and the success he yet expected. When the marquis concluded with a petition for an exemption from taxation and a loan of $90,000, Berton just shelved the petition.

Now, Berton found himself distressed. He remembered the Marquis de Pérusse des Cars petitions and saw in them—at least he thought so—a loophole through which he could escape from his own embarrassing situation and a criticism of neglect from his royal master.[5] In an interview with Lemoine, who became commissioner in 1766 for all Acadians in France, he disclosed his intention of establishing the Acadian families on the estate of the Marquis de Pérusse des Cars, and of leaving to the marquis the task of making them into good farmers. He pointed out to Lemoine that the council of state ever stressed the necessity of the Acadians' remaining farmers. Farming was their only and their surest hope of a comfortable life in France, of their usefulness to the state, and of the state's acquitting itself of a duty it owed to a people who had merited its help through their unflinching loyalty. Lemoine was overjoyed, and heartily supported Berton's idea. Berton commissioned him to work out a plan of Acadian settlement on the marquis' estate.[6]

Early in 1773, Lemoine presented to Berton a plan in which he had arranged with the greatest clarity all terms and conditions for a successful establishment of 1,500 Acadians on the estate of the Marquis de Pérusse des Cars. First, the commissioner made a careful census of all Acadians in France.[7] He tabulated the present Acadian population, number of families, and maritime ports of their residence.[8] Then he outlined the main features and terms of the contract between the state and the Marquis de Pérusse des Cars. It was a tentative contract of six points. The first point pro-

posed that the government could accomplish a final settlement of
626 Acadian families of 2,370 members at the initial cost of
$120,000.[9] From his labor classifications of the Acadians in 1773,
he showed Berton that all Acadians in France fell into three
groups: the first class comprised 1,347 laborers or persons fit for

LABOR CLASSIFICATION OF ACADIANS, 1773*

Classes	Number of Families in 1st Class	Number of Families in 2nd Class	Number of Families in 3rd Class	Total of Individuals in Each Class
1st Class *Laborers*				
Good laborers	172			
Laborers and sailors	25			
Laborers and carpenters	48			1,347
Laborers and blacksmiths	2			
Laborers and pit-sawers	17			
2nd Class *Trades related to Agriculture*				
Surgeons		1		
Sabot-makers		3		
Cart builders		3		
Blacksmiths		4		
Lumber jacks		11		
Lime burners		1		153 ⎤
3rd Class *"Gens de metiers" who could stay where they are*				
Ship carpenters			10	⎥ 1,023
Boat builders			1	⎥
Barbers			1	⎥
Tailors			4	⎥
Bakers			1	⎥
Joiners			3	870 ⎦
Upholsterers			1	
Jewelers			1	
Rope maker			2	
Fishers, sailors, caulkers			151	
	264	23	175	2,370

*Colonies C[11] D, VIII, f.303, A.N.

farming; the second class, 153 persons whose trades supplemented the needs of the great class of farmers; the third class, 870 mechanics whose trades were related to their abode of city life and for whom any change would only destroy them as useful citizens. On these assets, Lemoine pointed out to Berton, the state could build an efficient Acadian colony at Poitou.[10]

Of these there were 35 men and 45 women too old or sick to assist in clearing the fields. All the others were able-bodied men and women capable of building their own homes and of supporting themselves.

The second point of Lemoine's plan dealt with the division of land and houses. Lemoine suggested that the government should combine the first and second classes of Acadian laborers into one class on the estate of the Marquis de Pérusse des Cars, and keep the third class of 870 mechanics in the seaports. But it should grant to every Acadian of both divisions legal title of ownership to approximately two acres of land which the marquis would offer for cultivation. But in the case of the 1,500 farmers, the government should grant, over and above legal ownership of two acres, legal title to a house and a special subsidy also in order to give the class of farmers a security in farming.[11]

The 4,687 acres of land granted by the marquis, Lemoine proposed to divide into 5 equal sections of slightly over 937 acres. Each section would form a village. Each village would comprise 30 cabins, and each cabin would house 10 persons. Each village, therefore, would have 300 farms, and the 5 villages together would have 150 cabins with a population of 1,500 persons.

Of the 937 acres in each village, 593 acres would belong to the village farmers at approximately 20 acres to a cabin. The other 344 acres would be divided, in proportion of 2 acres to a person among the families of the second class of mechanics dispersed throughout France.[12]

In point three Lemoine outlined the execution of his plan. He

thought that by October 1, 1773, the marquis could have 30
cabins ready to lodge 300 Acadians. Those Acadians who could
not be lodged in the 30 cabins could locate themselves in the
barracks of Poitiers and Châtellerault, two towns quite distant
from the site of the settlement. The marquis could then direct his
Acadian farmers to clear one third of their farm lands. Lemoine
moreover calculated that by the summer of 1774, the marquis
should have all contracted houses finished and in condition to
accommodate the Acadians. And in autumn of the same year he
should put them to work again in clearing another third of their
land.

By 1775, Lemoine pictured all cabins and clearing of land
finished. By January of 1776, the Marquis Pérusse des Cars should
have the 1,500 Acadian cultivators fully settled and every farm
operating. Then, the 1,023 Acadian mechanics, if they wished,
could sell or lease the farms to which they had acquired legal
title, as those farms would then be under cultivation.[13]

Under the fourth point, Lemoine asked for full collaboration
from the ministry. He would have the government continue the
pay of six cents (sous) daily to each Acadian, without distinction,
up to January 1, 1774. After that date the Acadians remaining in
the maritime ports would not receive any more pay. Then the
state by guaranteeing the legal ownership of approximately two
acres of land to each Acadian from the first of January, 1774,
would have paid off its debt to the Acadian people. But the
Marquis de Pérusse des Cars would have the responsibility up to
January 1, 1776, of paying or supporting those Acadians occupied
in clearing the land, and those lodged at Poitiers or Châtellerault.
To the government, however, would fall the responsibility of
transporting the Acadians to Poitiers or Châtellerault, and to
expedite all transportations by corvées, especially in regard to
building materials.[14]

The government must grant the Marquis de Pérusse des Cars the

sum of $120,000 in eight equal payments, every three months.
And it should grant him the first payment immediately to purchase necessary building materials, animals, and harnesses. At the
request of the marquis, however, the government should change
those installments to $5,000 a month.[15]

In the fifth point, Lemoine sketched the entire outlay to the
state of the colony Poitou. He estimated the cost of each farm at
$560. This figure included one well-built cabin, two pairs of oxen,
two cows, two ploughs, one cart, small farm tools, and fodder for
the oxen and one cow only during the first year, but not the purchase of seed. Lemoine thought the Acadians could borrow the
oats needed for their first harvest. He hoped and figured, moreover, that their farms would produce five parts to one from the
first harvest, and that that ratio would net them enough not only
to repay their loan but also to purchase the necessary grain for
the second sowing.[16] Thus he concluded that 150 farms would
amount to $84,000; financial help of 6 cents daily to 1,500 Aca-
dians for the years 1774 and 1776, $65,700, or a total expense of
$149,700 to the state. He then deducted the appropriation of
$120,000 to the Marquis de Pérusse des Cars and arrived at a small
deficit of $29,700. This sketch looked impressive on paper.

Lemoine indeed planned the construction of La Colonie Acadienne du Poitou in a fashion that was not only detailed but
almost miserly. He threw the burden of the deficit of $29,600 on
the Marquis de Pérusse des Cars. He would have the marquis indemnify himself for that deficit from a questionable revenue of
$2,000 which the new seigneurial rent on each acre of land might
give him at thirty-five cents an acre (or arpent). He intimated,
moreover, that the marquis could meet a part of that deficit by
economizing in the purchase of needed materials. And certainly
he would find some saving in the corvées.[17]

Lemoine's sixth point was taxation, for which he had worked
out a simple system. The government must exempt the colony

from taxation for thirty years, and from the tax of "la dîme," that is, the tithe, for five years beginning from 1773. For the first year the Acadian colony would pay only one twenty-fifth in fruits. But he would have every family pay recognition of property rights to the marquis at one-sixteenth field rent in kind.[18]

Berton eagerly but cautiously studied Lemoine's outline of an Acadian colony at Poitou. He accepted every point of the plan, even though he thought that some features were somewhat expensive to the state. Lemoine on the other hand was confident of the colony's success, because he had the marquis' friendship. Consequently, he had no great difficulty in calming Berton's fears in regard to finanical outlays.[19]

After Lemoine had won Berton's approval on every point of the contract submitted, he sent some of the leading Acadian farmers to inspect the site and soil of their prospective farms. They looked site and soil over carefully. Their answer was unfavorable: "We have found only a barren area and sterile soil." They confessed to Lemoine that they were apprehensive of the entire project and could see only failure. They gave, moreover, as reasons for their apprehensions, "a general scarcity of water in the area, great difficulty to cultivate sterile ground, absence of good pasture for the cattle, want of firewood, and above all, the bad and incorrigible quality of the soil, which hid under a very thin bed of good earth, a kind of alkali substance that rotted the plants as their roots reached into the subsoil." [20]

Nevertheless, in spite of their apprehensions the Acadians did not refuse to accept the project. The land assigned to them was indeed a barren area, of which 2,637 acres were situated in the parishes of D'Archigny, Cenan, La Puye, and Saint-Pierre-de-Maillé. The colony itself was built on a plateau between the rivers La Gartempe on the east and La Vienne on the west. In his generosity Louis XV built then a highway from Monthoiron to La Puye with a connecting road from Pleumartin in the north

to La Bussière in the south. The Acadians called this highway
"La Grand' Ligne," or the King's Highway. And later the colony
was popularly called "The Acadians of the Grand' Ligne."

General Papuchon described that area very well:

> The region was never specially fertile. It was always
> known under the name of Des Gâtines, that is, the badlands.
> Elsewhere it is called Grande Gâtine or Gâtine Oriental, de-
> noting the area of the plateau between La Puye and Saint-
> Pierre-de-Maillé. The Acadian colony of Poitou was situated
> in la Petite Gâtine, which was once covered by an immense
> forest, known as Noah's Forest in the bad lands. The whole
> area was wasteland.
>
> The soil of La Gâtine is almost entirely composed of
> silicious sand, very hard, containing traces of limestone. This
> ground is almost impermeable to water. It follows that in
> this plateau region whose soil is impermeable to water that
> the small area of tillable ground is saturated during the
> greater part of the winter.[21]

Much of the depopulation and devastation of the Grande
Gâtine came as a result of the civil wars, the religious wars, the
revocation of the Edict of Nantes, and the heavy taxes of
Louis XIV. All these combined drove the farmers from the field
and drained the district of men and gold. Then after the Seven
Years' War came bands of ex-soldiers, who roamed over this area
and completed its devastation.

After the depopulation of the Grande Gâtine and the destruction of its forests, a second-growth vegetation characteristic of
sterile and sandy soil became established. Sage and scrub brush
mixed with furze covered the region, as far as the human eye
could see.[22]

Into that man-cursed and God-forsaken area, devoid of water,
wood, pasture, and fertility came the Acadians in October of
1773. What nature despised, Berton had asked the Acadians to
conquer. Four hundred and ninety-seven came and set to work

with great enthusiasm—men, women and children.[23] The remaining 1,003, including their confrères from Belle-Ile, had yet to come.[24] These the government thoughtlessly housed in a street on the south side of Châtellerault, still called "Rue Acadienne," instead of quartering them in the nearby villages of Cenan, D'Archigny, and La Puye. Residence in distant Châtellerault only bred suspicion and discontent. Despite all blunders the Acadians kept on working hard. Seeds germinated well, but as was inevitable, "in proportion as the roots dug into the ground the plants became yellow and died." There was no harvest in 1774. And again despite their utmost efforts, they had no harvest in 1775. The Acadians were stunned.[25]

Other setbacks arose over which the Acadians had no control. First, the houses were not finished in 1775. The marquis had to recruit Acadian labor and use the materials abounding in the area, such as stone, clay, and sagebrush to build cabins. Then the lands were not cleared as contracted. The contract called for the marquis to have one third of the land cleared by March, 1774, and by 1775 all lands cleared and cabins finished so that by January of 1776 the Acadians could claim legal title of ownership to their farms.[26] Next, the aristocratic proprietors imposed high rents despite protests of the state. As seed fell short, and prices of material rose high, the marquis reported that he could not finish a cabin for less than $700. On that basis the government saw with alarm that the cost of 150 cabins would be at least $211,272.50. And as decency of living quarters demanded more cabins so that 1,500 Acadians would not live like cattle herded in pens, the estimated number of 150 cabins rose to 215, or a total cost of $302,823.93, instead of the stipulated $120,000. The whole plan began to loom as a great illusion.[27] And the poor Acadians were just stupefied by all that was happening around them.

Added to these reverses, the Acadians felt keenly disappointed that no one wanted to buy or rent the farm lands of the mechanics. That was natural since the farm lands were in a bleak and remote country. Consequently a rumor sprang up that "the government will have to assume great expenses in order to treat the Acadians with the same respect as its other citizens so that no one can accuse it of injustice and wastefulness."

Lemoine saw the impossibility of keeping the expenses of the Acadian colony of the Grand' Ligne within the budget, and he began to fear the death of the colony. The entire cost had already exceeded by one sixth the total sum promised the marquis, although he had not yet done one sixth of that which he had contracted to do. All these unforseen expenses put the cost of the colony twelve times higher than he had calculated under point five of the contract drawn up for Berton.

Lemoine's report on the progress of the Acadian colony, the sterility of the soil, the rising discontent among the colonists, the lag in construction of the cabins, and the sharp rise in their cost, frightened Berton. He immediately restricted the number of cottages.[28] The Acadians already perplexed by the quick succession of reverses could only see ruin in store again for them, and turned in bitter criticism on the kindhearted Marquis de Pérusse des Cars and the idealistic Sarcey de Sutières, secretary of agriculture at Compiègne.[29]

Moreover, the discouragement, disillusion, and bitterness of the Acadians were intensified by agencies which had keen interest in the failure of the colony. That those agencies succeeded in hiding from the marquis their machinations to undermine the colony was evident. He made no mention of any evil plotting in his report of June, 1774.[30] Nevertheless an agent of some firm was active among the Acadians. He was known as "the Fleming." Whether he represented foreign interests or local interests of the depopulated and devastated provinces of Brittany and Normandy was not certain. This much, however, was certain—great fortunes came into the hands of the corsairs, shipbuilders, and merchants of the maritime ports, especially of St. Malo and Nantes, from the capture of 2,539 ships of the English marine in the naval wars of 1755-59. Equally well known were the facts that vacant areas of Normandy and Brittany needed good farmers, that business interests of the maritime ports needed reliable families in which to invest their new wealth, that many merchants of the French seaports had not forgotten that they were first in assisting the Acadians upon their arrival from Acadia and during their long wait of nine years preceding their appeal at Compiègne to Louis XV. That most business interests knew the sight of sterile ground at Poitou would fill the Acadians with discouragement, there was no doubt; that they sent "the Fleming" to incite the exiles to return to the maritime towns was strongly probable.

Whatever the story behind "the Fleming," he nevertheless did his work well. He posed first as an agriculturalist sent by the secretary of agriculture to study the soil of Poitou. After he had established his position he began a whispering campaign that the soil was no good, and that it could never produce anything in ten years of hard labor. Then he ridiculed the idea of the Acadians even attempting to plough the ground. Next he promised them secretly that on his return he would secure for them arable lands in Normandy.[31]

The effect of the whispering campaign upon the morale of the Acadians was destructive. Suspicion begot distrust, and distrust yielded to discouragement. They were convinced that they had been tricked and cheated. At a general meeting, the major part of the 1,500 Acadian farmers voted to return to the maritime ports. Their first exodus began toward the end of 1775, and the last, in the first part of 1776. Only 160 clung to the vain hope of ultimate success.[32] The government was stupefied at the sudden failure of the Acadian colony of the Grand' Ligne; but it watched its disintegration with a secret feeling of relief, since the colony had threatened to drain the treasury. It finally permitted 1,340 Acadians to retire to Nantes.[33]

From Nantes, the Acadians dispersed in two groups,—those who went to Rouen, Caen, La Rochelle, and Bordeaux, and those who settled in Nantes living on their pay until the time when they should get the lands promised to them.[34] After January 1, 1776, the government owed them $80,000, which in turn they owed to the merchants who had furnished them on credit the necessities of life. The Acadians were able to contract these legitimate debts in Nantes upon authority of their commissioner or his delegate, who issued I.O.U. billets to them.[35] A memoir had summarized their existence from 1775 to 1777 in the maritime towns as aimless and hopeless: "The Acadians of Belle-Ile and those of Poitou have lost their pay. They cannot till the soil, because it is no good."[36] The Acadian colony of the Grand' Ligne at Poitou was the straw that broke the camel's back. Its collapse threw the Acadians of France into a state of idleness, discouragement, and uncertainty of both dole and future. Their plight of 1776 led to a rift—a rift that threatened to destroy them as a people.

CHAPTER SEVEN

Disillusioned Acadians, 1777

WHEN Jean-Étienne-Bernard Clugny de Nuys be-
came general director of finances in 1777, the pitiful plight of the
Acadians, their constant petitions for payment and fulfillment
of Louis XV's promises to them, greatly disturbed him. Consequently, he made one last supreme effort to do what he thought
just to them in fulfillment of Louis XV's assurances. He decided
to settle them in Corsica again, but on a very fair and well-
planned contract. For in Corsica alone he saw some hope of
giving them arable land, since that island had some immense
uncultivated estates.[1]

To supervise all colonization in Corsica, Clugny appointed a
gentle, wise, honest, and understanding person, M. de Trelliar, former secretary of the cabinet of l'Enfant, Duke of Parma. He
ordered De Trelliar to visit the chief leaders among the Acadians
in Nantes in order to sell them the new project. De Trelliar's
pleasing personality and honest ways won the Acadians, and
2,366 of them accepted Clugny's project. But unfortunately
Clugny died a few days later. And his death suspended all work
on settling the Acadians in Corsica.[2]

Clugny was succeeded by Louis Gabriel Taboureau. The new
director studied his predecessor's Corsica project, liked it, and
began to work with ardor and interest for its accomplishment.
But his sudden retirement from office again suspended all
arrangements.[3]

Jacques Necker succeeded Taboureau as general director of
finances. At first he appeared opposed to any plan of settling

the Acadians again in Corsica. The expense he foresaw in such
a colony frightened him. Moreover, he knew very little about
the history of the Acadians that would warrant his full support
for such an expensive undertaking. He did not know what the
Acadians had cost the state nor what they might yet cost. Before
making a final decision, however, on the Corsica project, he
decided to inform himself fully on every phase of Acadian
history, beginning with Acadia itself. He ordered Joseph
François Coster, his secretary, to prepare a detailed account on
the following points: First, the history of the Acadians since the
Treaty of Utrecht, April, 1713; second, a census of all Acadians
in France; third, a report of their pay charged to the king's
name; fourth, a report of what was due them under that
account on November 1, 1777; fifth, a history of the Acadian
colony of Poitou; sixth, an estimate of the cost for a new Acadian
settlement in Corsica.[4] After a few days, Coster gave Necker a
minute and accurate report on all six points. Later he prepared
a memoir based on authentic records concerning the Acadians in
France and deposited it in the controller's office.

At a meeting held on November 10, 1777, attended by the
intendant of Brittany and De Trelliar, who had been promoted
to the office of director of colonies in Corsica, Coster presented
the work of his research on the Acadians. In his memoir he
offered such cogent arguments from justice, politics, economics,
and utility to the state in settling the Acadians in Corsica that
he completely won Necker over to the support of the second
Corsica plan.

But Coster by his scholarly report accomplished more than
that. When Necker learned of Acadian loyalty to France and of
Acadian sufferings for the Catholic faith, he was so deeply
touched that he resolved to better their lot. He announced to
the meeting that he would increase the Acadian land grants
from three to ten arpents, that is, from two to six and one half

acres approximately. He pointed out to his colleagues that this increase was just both to king and to Acadians. To the former it would give a greater rent at 4 per cent on his capital investment; to the latter, greater wealth and productivity. He also pointed out to the ministry that in the first Corsica concession the government had expected the rent on the two acres of land to pay 6 per cent of the interest on the cost of transportation and buildings. But in the second Corsica plan he would only manipulate a change in funds; for he would still give the king profits in taxes on commodities needed to establish the Acadian families.[5] Such was Necker's decision in the meeting of the ministry on November 10, 1777, at Fontainebleau.

While the ministry at Fontainebleau was pondering ways and means of fulfilling the promises of Louis XV to the Acadians, and of making them useful and happy citizens, a rift in national unity arose among the Acadians themselves. Two Frenchmen who had married Acadian girls incited some of the younger element with the hope that the American Revolution might bring about their return to Acadia. Then some of the elders of high repute who had relatives and friends happily established under the Spanish in Louisiana, openly declared themselves in favor of that colony rather than Corsica. This gave the young element the needed support and encouragement. They thereupon clamored for return of their compatriots who had already gone to Corsica and for abandonment of that project. That was a serious step. It involved national honor, for the Acadians had pledged themselves to De Trelliar to settle in Corsica. But the young element persisted in their demand and won the support of about eighty families. Flushed with success, that aggressive group determined to elect without a general assembly of the Acadian nation two delegates of their own to represent their constituents at Versailles. It further decided to establish itself as a rump assembly. In so doing it created for the first time in the odyssey of the Acadians in France a rift in national unity.[6]

The intelligent people among the Acadians, especially those who merited the confidence of the nation by their sagacity and understanding, were alarmed at the decisions that the rump assembly precipitated. In fact, they considered the actions of the rump assembly the fomenting of a schism. They warned all of the dangers involved against their future aspirations and national unity.

The national leaders of the Acadians, those delegates whom the nation in an earlier general assembly had elected as their representatives to treat with De Trelliar on the conditions of their settlement in Corsica, addressed a memoir to him. In it they begged him not to impute the rash actions of some impetuous and inexperienced youths to the whole nation; that they, "the best and largest part of the nation," not only protested against the conduct and decisions of the rump assembly but also disavowed any connection with it. They told him that in Nantes alone there were more than two hundred families which had no part in this rump assembly and which openly opposed its policies. They besought him to save their honor and protect the good opinion Necker had of their loyalty. Later they sent a similar memoir protesting their loyalty and condemning the conduct and actions of the rump delegates to Necker himself.[7]

Paying no attention to the memoirs and protests of "the best and largest part of the nation," the rump assembly of eighty families went into action and elected two delegates to represent it at Versailles. The first delegate was an Acadian, honest but inexperienced, a man who never had any part in the direction of the nation's affairs. The second was a friend, a Spaniard named Grinnau, whose wife was an Acadian. He was not only less experienced in Acadian affairs but also excitable and gullible.[8] The character of those delegates showed clearly the mentality and incapacity of the secessionists who elected them. Because the

Acadians then had in their midst men who were skillful, understanding, sagacious, and intelligent in their national matters, they would never have elected by a unanimous vote representatives mediocre in ability, academic in experience, and narrow in national vision.

Early in November, 1777, the larger part of the entire nation elected its true delegates. Those representatives had authority to treat with the government on only one point, namely, settlement of the pay due the nation. At that conference, when the ministry tried to present to them a plan of settling all the Acadians comfortably in Corsica, they shrewdly answered that they were not empowered to treat on that subject, that their mission had been restricted solely to the request for financial help, and that they could not give a definite answer in the name of the nation. Nevertheless, they admitted that they perceived advantages in the new Corsica plan. They promised the ministry to explain the plan to their people and to return. And they kept their word.[9]

The national schism continued to exist, and in their return conference the major part of the Acadian nation authorized its delegates to transact two matters only. The first was to give the ministry a correct picture of the present misery of the Acadian people, and to petition for the back payments due to them so that they could pay their lawful debts. To obtain this first point was the general vow of the entire nation. Now that there was a split, both parties still clung to the same objective. The second point was to explain to the ministry that the eighty families which had broken loose from the unity of the nation feared the climate, the unhealthy air, and the inhabitants of Corsica, and were begging to be freed from their promise to settle on that island. At the time of De Trelliar's visit, they had only given their consent to go to Corsica through fear of losing their pay.

The greater part of the nation had come to beg the ministry to save the Acadian people from the serious consequences which such a rift could cause.

Disregarding all pleas of the major part of the nation, the rump assembly went ahead with its own program. It sent the two delegates to Versailles to submit the wishes of its constituents: a picture of their misery, the need of their back pay, release from the obligation of going to Corsica, and freedom to go to Louisiana or Acadia. Necker was in a quandary. Finally he proposed to the two delegates a new plan whereby he would free the entire nation from its contract with the government to settle in Corsica.[10] So inexperienced were the two rump delegates that they not only accepted the new plan for their own party but also obligated themselves to make the major part of the Acadian people accept it.[11]

Necker's new plan was a clever one. By it he aimed to free the French treasury forever of an almost endless drain on its resources in supporting a people of no use to France. He planned four points of compromise, two in favor of the government and two in favor of the Acadians:

1. The Acadians should free the government from its obligation of back payments due to them. (This was the chief aim of both parties.)

2. The Acadians should not hold the government responsible for debts contracted by individuals of the nation under the authority and quasi-guarantee of the commissioners.[12]

3. The government would continue its support of the Acadians for two years more, but would reduce the support from six cents to three cents daily for each person.

4. During the course of those two years the government would grant every family head the free right to decide the place or province where he would like to settle in the kingdom. And it

would subsidize every family in proportion to the number of persons in that family over and above the payment of three cents daily for two years.[13]

The inexperience of the rump delegates did not enable them to foresee the evil consequences contained in the second article. They did not stop to think that the debts of the Acadian nation were the property of its French creditors, and consequently neither delegates nor the entire nation of Acadians could compromise that credit without the consent of the creditors. Since the Acadians were not the possessors of any property that could cover the payments of their debts, the consent of the rump delegates to the second article subjected the persons of the Acadian debtors (and practically all of them were debtors) to arrest for failure to pay. Secondly, the stupid willingness of the two rump delegates to accept the second article opened the door to protests from their creditors against the government for payment of commodities. The Acadians had bought those commodities of life on a guarantee given by the provincial intendants of ultimate payment.[14]

Necker saw that the rump delegates had no authority to give such a definite assurance of acceptance in the name of the entire nation. He saw clearly, too, that they could only represent their own constituents, the eighty families totalling 300 persons, at Nantes. And he did not like the fact that the rump delegates could not present any credentials of their mission. Besides, he foresaw that before he could act legally he would have to have the consent of every family to the propositions of his new plan. At first he thought of putting the propositions down in writing for the rump delegates to ratify for their followers. But in the last moment he changed his mind and dismissed the rump delegates with a promise that in a short time he himself would present the same four propositions of his new plan to the entire Acadian nation.[15]

The objections of the rump delegates brought Necker back to his first project of November 10, 1777, namely, settlement in Corsica. But his sense of justice made him abandon that solution, because he saw that the entire Acadian people could and should accept his new plan of four propositions. He himself regarded it as the best solution that he could offer for their happiness and usefulness in fulfillment of Louis XV's promises to them.[16]

As a result he ordered M. de la Bove, intendant of Brittany, to familiarize all the Acadians in his province with the new plan. La Bove, however, passed the orders on to his subdelegates, and the subdelegates presented the four propositions not as an offer but as an ultimatum. The ultimatum was crushing. That sudden harshness on the part of the French government caused much uneasiness and agitation among all Acadians. From that day in 1778 to 1783, strife, despair, and poverty continued to gnaw at Acadian national unity and aspirations.[17] The efforts of the rump minority to persuade the entire nation of 626 families of 2,542 souls to accept Necker's plan of four offers only widened the breach of disunity and charged it all the more with destructive animosities.[18] Brother fought brother, husband opposed wife, children threatened to desert parents, families were torn asunder. Few seemed to agree what to do. Some insisted on settling in Louisiana;[19] others in any of the American States; many, on returning to Poitou; and still others, to Corsica.[20] An Acadian leader, Oliver Terrio, described the effect of the ultimatum on the families: "So poor, with many children and no schools, eaten up with despair and the constant deception of false promises—I say poor, because our pay, which was six cents was reduced to three cents . . . Wait! That was the only answer we ever got from the authorities—in regard to the promises of our receiving lands as the reward of faithful attachment to France. Some were so sick from this constant deception, that they were unable to work for a living." [21]

Four months later, March 1778, Necker found the Acadian people not only idle, miserable, and bankrupt, but now terror-stricken, and torn asunder by internal strife that threatened their complete disintegration as a nation,[22] and as a body of people living on their pay until the time when they should get the arable lands which Louis XV in 1772 had promised them at Compiègne.[23] Necker knew that the heavily-burdened French state of 1778 was quivering with the distant rumblings of revolution. He also knew that the treasury could not much longer carry the Acadians on its payroll. He then saw a legal opportunity of easily dispersing the Acadian people. He obliged every family to yield to the force of circumstances and authority. Then for the first time since the expulsion in 1755 the Acadians fully awoke to the fact that France, which they loved so much and for which they had sacrificed all, was officially and cunningly planning the destruction of their cherished national unity. "When we arrived in France," they wrote, "His Majesty received us with touching kindness; and until he was able to give us some lands equal to those which we had lost in Acadia, he granted each one of us six cents daily. Moved by a just gratitude for these benefits, there was not one among us who did not wish to live and die under the French government." [24] To their bitter grief they discovered that to beloved France they had been and still were a useless burden.[25] The disillusion was paralyzing.

No one grieved over their uselessness more than they themselves did. Choiseul admitted that the Acadians were "a race sluggish by nature but very ingenious and good farmers, in general fitted for all things, because in their own country they were obliged to make all things." [26] All that these "ingenious and good farmers" had asked were good lands. "The lands of this kingdom," they wrote, "belong to the nobility who have offered us only the most sterile." [27] True the French government did pay millions of dollars in Acadian support,[28] but had the officials been honest both in fulfilling the promises and order of Louis XV, and in carrying out the different plans of settlement, the French treasury would have saved thousands of dollars. Because of that neglect of duty, want of sincerity, and possible selfishness of those in authority, the Acadians lingered for years idle in the seaports of France, suffering bitterly, and sinking every day deeper into poverty.[29] "But Monseigneur, see our present situation," they wrote to Charles Gravier de Vergennes, "after twenty-eight years, after the loss of our property, we find ourselves in poverty and misery. The landlords daily refuse to house us, and without his majesty's pay we cannot live. We are grieved that we are a burden."[30] That was the Acadian situation in 1783, when Peyroux de la Coudrenière with his wife appeared in Nantes.[31]

CHAPTER EIGHT

Peyroux de la Coudrenière

WITH THE ADVENT of peace in 1783 between Eng-
land and the thirteen American colonies, a leader and organizer
appeared among the Acadians of France in the person of Peyroux
de la Coudrenière.[1] Peyroux was once a druggist in Nantes.
Prior to his appearance in Nantes, he had spent seven years in
Louisiana, where he had amassed a fortune.[2] He was forty years
of age, married but without children.[3] He was the youngest of
three brothers, one of whom was married "and had a farm just
outside of New Orleans," and the third had died in Nantes in
March, 1784.[4] As Peyroux reported, on "my return to Nantes,
I found my family in mourning because of the death of my
brother." [5]

Peyroux was in Louisiana during the term of Luis de Unzaga
y Amezaga's governorship. It was there that he conceived the
plan of transporting the Acadians of France to Louisiana at the
expense of the king of Spain. The idea first occurred to him
during conversations with leading Acadians, who told him that
the desire of all Acadians in Louisiana was to have their unhappy
brethren in France join them. That general wish encouraged him
to offer his services to the Spanish ambassador in Paris, Don
Pedro Pablo Abarca de Bolea, Count de Aranda.[6]

When Peyroux called at the Spanish embassy he met Ignacio
Heredia, personal secretary of the Spanish ambassador. As soon
as Heredia heard Peyroux's plan he immediately arranged an
interview with Count de Aranda. The Spanish ambassador was
truly delighted to learn of Peyroux's plan of removing every

Acadian in France to Louisiana under the patronage of the king of Spain. He saw in Peyroux's plan of colonization an opportunity whereby Spain could use the Acadians in Louisiana as a bulwark against the English. "Removal at the expense of the king" would be money well invested. By promoting the plan at the Spanish court, would he not increase his own prestige in the eyes of his royal master? [7] Had not he himself, on October 17, 1777, succeeded in getting from the French government two Acadian families of twenty-two persons and sent them to Cabahannocer in Louisiana? [8] But Peyroux asked Aranda a price for his plan and services, namely, that Spain should recompense him with some public office and a position in Louisiana.[9] Aranda was agreeable to Peyroux's demands, and gave him tacit consent to begin work immediately. A few days later Heredia reported his impressions of Peyroux to the prime minister of Spain, Count de Floridablanca. "From the two conversations I have had with him, he impresses me as a mild man, wise and well balanced. His only ambition is the study of Natural History in the study of which he has told me, he has spent almost all the time of his residence in Louisiana and in Canada. He has published some essays on these two countries in *Dianode Physica,* a monthly publication here." [10]

Assured of tacit support from the Spanish embassy, and urged by the hope of public office and a position in Louisiana, Peyroux began his work by contacting some of the leading Acadians in Nantes. On July 12, 1783, he persuaded several of them to send a written petition to the Spanish ambassador in Paris. Among those whom he had persuaded was Oliver Terrio, a shoemaker of Nantes. Peyroux saw in this simple man a willing tool, and began to work on his pride by upbraiding him and all Acadians that they preferred to remain poor in France, live on charity, be idle, and take the miserable pittance of three cents a day instead of going to Louisiana, where many Acadian families were living happily and prosperously. Terrio explained to him that it was the dream of every Acadian family in France to migrate to Louisiana; that the ambition in everyone was growing stronger every day as letters with news of Acadian happiness and prosperity in Louisiana kept coming; that they had approached the French government several times on migrating to Louisiana, but that it rejected them and even criticized them as being ungrateful.[11] "As for myself," Terrio replied, "if I am suffering, it is not because of my own circumstances, as because of the plight of all Acadians."[12] From several conversations with Terrio and other leading Acadians, Peyroux pieced together the Acadian attitude toward France.

After the failure of the Poitou settlement in 1775 and the schism over the second Corsica project, Peyroux learned that the Acadian exiles in France had become a serious problem for the government.[13] The Acadians kept insisting on arable lands in fulfillment of Louis XV's promise in 1763 as a reward for their unswerving loyalty to France and to his person.[14] The French authorities, however, were becoming more and more irritated by that Acadian attitude. Guillot, commissioner at St. Malo, had remarked that the Acadians are making all officials dizzy. "Do the Acadians imagine that they will become noble landowners?" he asked. "The aim of the state is to incorporate them through their skill into the class of farmers. But they seem to resent being treated as peasants."[15]

By 1783 Peyroux gathered that the Acadian situation economically and morally had gone from bad to worse.[16] As the French government had practically bankrupted itself in aiding the American Revolution,[17] it had been forced to discontinue even the pittance of three cents to the greater number of Acadians from Poitou and Belle-Ile-en-Mer.[18] However, it was still giving them some help in provisions and clothes in I.O.U. paper notes, issued by the respective intendants of the provinces.[19]

Peyroux scented a bitter spirit of criticism against Necker. He had failed to establish the Acadians either in Brittany or in Corsica. But the director of finances became frightened when he learned that the cost to the wobbly treasury of the first project would be $600,000, and of the second $236,000. He refused to risk so much money for what he termed uncertain results from a people of no value to France. That attitude of the government the Acadians resented.[20]

Peyroux gathered further that ever since their assemblage in France in 1763, The Acadians had expressed themselves as disappointed in the treatment they had been receiving.[21] After the death of Louis XV, the Acadians felt that the government was hoping that in the course of years the general French population would absorb them. But that tendency the Acadians had been steadfastly resisting and, to counteract it, had formed themselves into a separate body of people begging the government for the back pay it owed them and the arable lands that Louis XV had promised.[22] They could not go to Louisiana in the year 1783 because of the American Revolutionary War and also because they had no leader. That they had made isolated attempts was certain from a letter of Count de Aranda to his secretary, Ignacio Heredia, "I am sending you a letter from José de Gálvez on some Acadians who are seeking to settle in Louisiana."[23]

Encouraged by all he had heard and discovered, and especially by the Acadian attitude of discontent with life in France, Peyroux sought next to win the active services of Oliver Terrio in the execution of his plan for removing the Acadians from France to Louisiana. He began by telling Terrio that he had a good friend in Ignacio Heredia. Then he convinced the cobbler that he had business connections with the Spanish ambassador's secretary. And lastly, he divulged to Terrio that he would like to have him as intermediary, since he knew all the Acadians. He also assured Terrio that working for Spain would bring a very lucrative reward from Charles III. And if Spain should fail to reward them, or if the undertaking itself should collapse through no fault of theirs, Peyroux assured Terrio with a most solemn promise that he would share with him "his last piece of bread."

Terrio could not resist the honeyed promises of Peyroux. He saw his position in life suddenly changed from that of a poor, humble shoemaker to that of being the right arm of Peyroux de la Coudrenière, friend and associate of Ignacio Heredia, secretary to Spain's powerful ambassador. He described his being catapulted into prominence as "elegance" while Peyroux's position was only that of "representation." Terrio was delighted to be a manager.[24]

The first point on which Peyroux and Terrio agreed was that the latter should reanimate the Acadians. Terrio's duty was to inspire them with a hope of migrating to Louisiana and of finally achieving the desire of their hearts: a new Acadia. Terrio did his utmost to enkindle enthusiasm among the Acadians and to get them to send a signed petition to Count de Aranda so that the Spanish ambassador could intercede with the king of Spain on their behalf. He was tireless in his correspondence with Acadians in St. Malo, Morlaix, Cherbourg, Rennes, and even in Flanders. "But, alas," Terrio wrote, "the first report of my work was not promising; only four signatures besides my own. But just as it was, Monsieur Peyroux sent it to Count de Aranda."[25] The four signatures were those of Simon Masrolle, Marin Gatreau, Pierre Jamlo, and Étienne Terrier.

The petition stated that after twenty years of exile, a great number of Acadians were still stranded in Brittany. It complained that the Acadians had no fixed means of livelihood except the pittance from the king of France. And it criticized France for offering them only sterile lands and the unhealthy area in Corsica.

We have asked after many years the king and his ministers to permit us to go to Louisiana [it pleaded] where there
are many of our friends and relatives. Now we beg you to
obtain from His Catholic Majesty permission to enter Louisiana, where we have yearned for such a long time to be
numbered among his faithful subjects. We are all farmers;
we know several kinds of crafts and trades; we will be able
also to attract to Louisiana a considerable number of our
people who are scattered among the Anglo-American states
and in Canada. Thus His Most Catholic Majesty will have
the satisfaction of having gathered under his government the
remnants of an unfortunate people who sacrificed everything
for their religion and for the love of their King.[26]

Count de Aranda answered that the petition was very equiv-
ocal and that he could not make himself responsible for its success, because it did not have enough signatures. Nevertheless, he
promised to send the petition to Madrid with a strong note of his
approval.[27] On August 8, 1783, Peyroux wrote from Paris to
Terrio that he might have to go to Madrid in order to push the
petition at the court, since the Spanish were notorious for their
"mañana spirit, and therefore, they might have to wait a month
before getting an answer." [28]

In the meantime Peyroux was busy writing his "Memoir on
the Usefulness of Establishing an Agricultural School in Each
Province and Colony of Spain." [29] The memoir reflects the aims
of the Physiocrats of the eighteenth century. In it Peyroux proposed to Charles III a system whereby Spain could strengthen
her grip on her colonies and get from them the greatest possible
economic profits. He pointed out to the king that Spain could
achieve these ends through agricultural schools attached to mon-
asteries and open to all children of both sexes over four years of
age, especially the homeless. These schools would give the children a thorough yet practical education in all things pertaining

to farming life, from the uprooting of weeds to the building and interior decoration of a farmhouse. "Some might say," Peyroux countered, "that this education embraces too much. They must not forget that the ancient inhabitants of Acadia, who today are scattered throughout Canada, Louisiana, France, and the United States, individually possessed all those talents. The human spirit is capable of a greater development than is commonly believed. The success of this development, therefore, is in making the best use of the first years of youth." [30]

Experience has shown that colonists from agricultural schools can establish and support themselves in climates and places where it would be impossible for unschooled colonists merely to survive. Peyroux observed that the Spanish authorities have been sending to the colonies untrained colonists, and that they perished miserably because of their want of agricultural education. With trained farmers in her colonies, Spain could dispense with the purchase of slaves, who not only corrupted the blood and morals of the colonists but also destroyed their purity of language, patriotism, and desire to work.[31] The demoralizing influence of the blacks on her colonists, he contended, had robbed Spain during the past century of great wealth which she should have reaped from her vast and fertile colonial possessions.[32] In the Acadians, Spain would have schooled colonists.

Heredia sent Peyroux's memoir, together with the petition, on August 21, 1783, to José de Gálvez in order that he might see and consider Peyroux's ideas on the improvement of Louisiana. Coinciding with the arrival of these messages at the court of Spain was the arrival of the captain-general of Louisiana, Don Bernardo de Gálvez, who, as his uncle wrote to Floridablanca on August 24, 1783, "just happened to arrive for a short time and wished to give the king his opinion in regard to the petition of the Acadians." But Charles III was at first reluctant to accept the Acadian petition and Peyroux's services. He dreaded failure—especially an expensive one such as the Acadian colonization in Louisiana would be to Spain's drained treasury. And he also feared Spain's ability to hold Louisiana against the onrushing Americans. Nevertheless, on October 22, 1783, after much reflection he issued a royal order accepting Peyroux's plan of removing the Acadians in France to Louisiana. But the royal order was not sent immediately to Aranda in Paris. Consequently early in January, 1784, Aranda left Paris for Madrid. He hoped to add his pressure on the king to accept Peyroux's plan of using the Acadians as colonists in Louisiana.[33]

On January 21, 1784, Peyroux wrote Terrio that he was in utter despair of any success for the Acadian plan of colonization. He thanked Terrio for his services. He was leaving Paris for Nantes. But just as he was leaving his residence, the Spanish consul of St. Malo, Manuel d'Asprès, caught him. Breathlessly he told Peyroux, "I am the recipient of great news. Our king has not only given his consent to admit the Acadians to Louisiana, but he has also assumed the expense of transporting and settling them on the banks of the Mississippi River."

Peyroux was beside himself with joy. Hurriedly he penned another letter to Terrio, "We will begin preparations in Nantes with speed, and do not fear of compromising yourself in being very active in this work. Tell the news to all your people in Nantes, and if you wish, break the news to those Acadians in St. Malo, and Morlaix, and write me at my address, St. Denys, No. 4, Paris." [34]

Heredia also was delighted when he learned that Charles III accepted the whole scheme of transporting the Acadians to Louisiana. He was now convinced of the integrity, character, and motives of Peyroux. Moreover, he saw in the agricultural ability of the Acadians a direct blessing for Louisiana.[35] But he also foresaw some problems. What would be the definite advantages to the king of Spain in assuming the entire expense of transporting the Acadians? Would the French court permit the Acadians to leave

France? What would be the obligations of the Spanish government to Peyroux? And would the Acadians accept the leadership of Peyroux?

While Peyroux was negotiating with the court of Spain for the transportation of the Acadians to Louisiana, the plight of the 140 Acadians in St. Malo had grown so desperate that they begged the French king to permit them to migrate to Boston. They offered as an excuse their desire to free the government of the burden of their support, and to regain their children who had been apprenticed to the English and were growing up in the Anglican faith.[36]

Back in Nantes, Terrio became very active as Peyroux had ordered him. He disseminated the news of Charles III's consent to remove the Acadians to Louisiana.[37] But he cautioned his fellow Acadians to observe the strictest secrecy as the king of France had not yet given his consent to their departure.[38] Peyroux himself then went to Brittany to coax the greatest number of Acadians possible to sign up for Louisiana.[39] Those to whom he spoke expressed a deep sense of gratitude to Spain in opening several of her harbors to them. They told him, moreover, that they thought that France would gladly accede to Spain's request in order to rid herself of the burden of supporting them. But this puzzled them—who would pay their debts?[40] Peyroux regarded the Acadians as a simple people who would accept his leadership without raising a question.[41] But by 1784 the Acadians had become an experienced people, skeptical of any agrarian scheme and reluctant to be victimized again. Instead of keeping the news of their departure a secret among themselves, they went in a body to the subdelegate of Nantes to learn if the ministry had given them permission to go to Louisiana and if Peyroux de la Coudrenière had any authority to transport them.[42] The same excitement and mistrust occurred in St. Malo, Morlaix, and other towns. All were in a state of impatience and difficult to control.

I see with pleasure this general ardor [Peyroux wrote to Heredia], but I am nevertheless angry that this news is so well known, because the landlords and the merchants are now refusing to give the Acadians credit, and that increases the misery of these people. Finally, there is no doubt that Monsieur subdelegate is going to write to the French court to inform it of all these matters; and since the Ministry has not yet been informed, something disagreeable could well happen to me from this affair.

From all these consideration, I beg you, Sir, not to delay any longer your request of the French court. The equinox is passed, and the beautiful season begins, and if this affair drags on much longer, the Acadians cannot be disembarked in New Orleans until autumn, and that is the season of many tempests on the Gulf of Mexico. Moreover, this people, arriving at the beginning of winter would not have time to prepare their fields for the following harvest, and it would be a year lost.[43]

The indiscreet conduct of the Acadians in going to their sub-delegates embarrassed the Spanish embassy. Nevertheless, it had the effect Peyroux desired of galvanizing Heredia into immediate action.[44] The Spanish chargé d'affaires decided to make a frank confession to Charles Gravier, Count de Vergennes, of the whole matter so that he might see that the Spanish embassy in Paris was acting with candor and good faith.[45] With this objective in mind he addressed a short note to Vergennes[46] on Tuesday, March 24, 1784, informing him of Spain's contacts with the Acadians and of the desire of Charles III to settle them in Louisiana, provided that His Most Christian Majesty would give them a free exit from France.[47] On March 31, 1784, Vergennes notified Marshal de Castries that the king of France had granted permission to the Acadians to leave the kingdom in deference to the request of Charles III of Spain.[48]

Acting on Heredia's hint that the Acadians would do well in supporting his request by sending a petition themselves to the

French court, Peyroux drew one up.[49] He got thirty-five family heads to sign it. On April 6, 1784, he mailed it to Vergennes.[50]

After giving a brief review of the history of the Acadian expulsion, of their loyalty to France, of their sufferings during twenty-eight years, and of their ardent desire to join their relatives in Louisiana, the petition concluded: "The Squire Heredia, chargé d'affaires for Spain has informed us of the proceedings of his court. We wish to support his request. We, therefore, beg your Excellency to obtain for us a free departure from France, so that we may join our relatives in Louisiana. We do not relish leaving our country, but we find a quieting comfort in the knowledge that the kind power that invites us is allied to our dear fatherland. We therefore beg that you be favorable to our petition." [51]

Vergennes passed this petition on to Charles Alexander de Calonne. On April 27 De Calonne returned a written answer that Louis XVI had not only approved the request of the Spanish court but even offered to facilitate the free emigration of the Acadians by paying all their debts. But he cautioned Vergennes not to allow the Acadian departure to result in an emigration of the French people. He expressed deep regret that the Acadian experiment had turned out a total loss to France after such heavy expenditures.[52] But on May 11, 1784, Vergennes sent a note with the king's approval to the Spanish embassy.[53]

While Heredia and Vergennes were interchanging notes on the transfer of the Acadians from France to Louisiana, Peyroux's secret activities were being watched by Balais, judge and intendant of Nantes. As early as August 1783, Vergennes had ordered La Bove, intendant of Brittany, to arrest all secret agents who were plotting a mass migration of Acadians from France.[54] Judge Balais as commissioner of the Acadians was proud and jealous of his authority. Unfortunately for Peyroux, the commissioner had not yet received any official communication of the harmonious agreement between the Spanish and French courts in regard to the Acadian migration. As soon as Judge Balais therefore learned the names of the two men who were "violently intriguing against his post," he ordered his "archers" to arrest them. "On the 21st day of May, 1784, Monsieur Peyroux was arrested and thrown into jail, but I escaped," Terrio wrote.[55] "I had taken refuge in the house of Monsieur Bourgoin, judge of the criminal court in Nantes. I stayed with him a whole week. While I was in hiding there, I wrote Monsieur Heredia that I was very discouraged that the progress of our whole work was so abruptly suspended by the imprisonment of Monsieur Peyroux." [56] When the two officers had arrested Peyroux, they found on his person three letters. Two were from Heredia, and the third was the copy of a letter Peyroux had written to him expressing joy on learning that the king of Spain had decided to settle the Acadians in Louisiana.[57]

As a consequence of the discovery of those letters the intendant of Brittany ordered the release of Peyroux. He stopped all further prosecution against him or his agents, for he saw that the Acadian emigration was under the consideration of the two courts and therefore out of his jurisdiction.[58]

Four days after Peyroux's release, José de Gálvez authorized Aranda to legalize Spain's agreement with Peyroux and achieve the removal of the Acadians from France to Louisiana with the least expense to the king.[59] With this Aranda wrote to Peyroux that he was much disturbed over his arrest, and that for his future security he was sending him a copy of Vergennes' note to Heredia. He authorized Peyroux to get the signatures of all Acadians who might wish to migrate to Louisiana. But he clearly cautioned him against the use of any force. The aim of both courts was to secure only those Acadians whose choice to go was of their own volition.[60] His Catholic Majesty wanted only free and faithful subjects.

With his work now officially established, Peyroux felt less and less the need of Terrio's services. On July 18, 1784, he ordered

Terrio to publicize the agreement of the two courts and his new status as Spain's official agent.[61] And on August 1, Peyroux announced that he was ready to receive the signatures of all Acadian volunteers.[62]

All these instructions Terrio accepted as a part of his duty, but when Peyroux requested the Acadians to nominate two family heads to help him identify true Acadian from pseudo-Acadians, Terrio felt humiliated. "I didn't read his letters without a feeling of anger and resentment," he commented, "for I could see that his confidence in me was waning as my usefulness was less needed. I will quote a part of his letter: 'As I [i.e., Peyroux] do not know the majority of the Acadians, I think that they should nominate two family heads to be present at the registration in order to eliminate those who are not Acadians and would pretend to be Acadians.' So I didn't know my Acadians! I who was in constant contact with them since 1783! Or was he trying to eliminate me, to rid himself of his manager?" [63]

Peyroux showed little concern that Terrio almost met death in the course of his duties as intermediary. When Terrio announced to the Acadians that Spain would welcome the French married to Acadian women, some of the French, fearful lest the government might suppress the pay of those who had to remain in France, opposed the plan of emigration. "It so happened that I was in an inn," Terrio explained, "when some of these trouble-makers began to threaten me, and the most furious of the three was armed with a stick, I believe. He trampled on me like a desperado, struck me many times, and would have killed me but for the interference of some friendly Acadians, who with great difficulty took his knife away. I was bleeding very much. The next day, when I complained to Monsieur d'Asprès, he answered, 'I am sorry; but what do you expect? One must have paciencia!' " [64]

Peyroux spent the summer of 1784 in canvassing Acadians in

the towns of Paimboeuf and Nantes. The report he sent Aranda on August 10 showed 224 family heads, 259 mothers and 741 children, of whom 392 were boys and 349 were girls. In a separate class were 23 adult orphan boys, 25 orphan girls "who have reached their majority; and 53 orphans who were minors." In all he canvassed 1,325 signatures.[65]

Of all the Acadians in Nantes, only those who were rich enough to live without government help refused to volunteer for Louisiana. Besides those, there were some poor families who could not sign up for Louisiana, because the family heads were at sea.[66] At Bordeaux, Rochefort, and Belle-Ile, Peyroux received incomplete reports from certain families, and so could not report on them as definite volunteers.[67] Of every family that volunteered, the family head, if he could write, affixed his personal signature, or if he could not write, a cross beside his name. Peyroux completed his work in those two towns without encountering any confusion. Even the subdelegate of Nantes, his enemy, was "a little more obliging" in giving some co-operation.[68]

When Aranda received Peyroux's census of volunteers for Paimboeuf and Nantes, he urged him to push his canvassing more vigorously in St. Malo, Morlaix, and all other towns where there were Acadians.[69] But Peyroux was to meet deep disappointment in the results of his canvassing volunteers in those towns. He wanted to see the Acadians at work on their farms in Louisiana, at least by the end of the summer of 1784.[70] But he met so many obstacles that he wrote to Aranda, "As far as I am concerned, Monseigneur, I have been humiliated and treated with contempt in my efforts to serve humanity." [71]

The first obstacle Peyroux met was Spain's dilatory attitude. He had sent a request for a prompt answer to eight questions, inquiries which, if immediately solved, would have expedited his work in St. Malo and Morlaix. When Peyroux was about finished canvassing Acadian volunteers in the maritime towns of France, he received an answer. He had applied on July 17; he got his answer on September 1, 1784. Spain was in no hurry.[72] The summer was gone.

Peyroux's first question to Charles III was, "When will His Majesty remove the Acadians from France to Louisiana?" Charles answered that he would remove the Acadians either at the end of 1784 or in the early part of 1785,[73] or just as soon as Aranda got the bids from the shipowners in Nantes.[74]

Peyroux's next question was a touchy one. "Will the Acadians receive any pay at all while awaiting the day of departure? " Charles III, with Spanish generosity, answered, "Spain will grant them the same pay which France had given them, and it will begin on the same day on which France ceases her payments to the Acadians." That delighted both Peyroux and every Acadian.

But a doubt still lurked in Peyroux's mind. "What if France takes offense after granting the Acadians permission to depart for Louisiana? Who will give the Acadians their gratuity, the king of Spain or the king of France? " Charles' answer was short. "His Christian Majesty [that is, France] saw no just reason for the continuation of the pay, since he must consider his royal treasury."

In his fourth query Peyroux pointed out that it was possible that the intendants of Brittany and Normandy might neglect to carry out the orders of the French king to grant the Acadians their pay until July. How would those poor people live until the day of departure? To which Charles III answered that if France did not object he would order Count de Gausa to give the Acadians credit on the day France ceased to, by ordering the royal treasury to draw on Paris.

Peyroux's fifth question was whether or not he should assemble all Acadians in the port of Nantes immediately after their registration as Spanish subjects? The answer was that he should bring them all together at Nantes where they would be under the care of the Spanish consul, Manuel d'Asprès.

The defrayal of expense in local transportation was Peyroux's sixth problem. Who would pay for Acadians far away from Nantes? Charles' answer was that each Acadian must meet his own local traveling expenses. Only in the case of the very poor would Spain give a reasonable help.

The substance of the seventh question was the admission of Catholic foreigners into Louisiana along with the Acadians. Three foreign families wished to be classified as Acadians in order to enjoy Acadian fishing and agricultural privileges in Louisiana. Would the king of Spain grant Peyroux the authority to promise them those advantages? "You may admit those foreigners," came the reply, "but only after each family has registered as a Spanish subject, presented its credentials giving origin, occupation, or trade." [75]

As Peyroux loved authority and display, he angled in his eighth question for Charles' permission to don a uniform as a Spanish official. "Peyroux in a uniform would inspire more confidence," he wrote. "Since the Acadians are a simple people, they judge a person more by his dress than by the authority invested in him." To this question Charles III agreed, that for the present he had no objection to Peyroux's assuming that distinction.[76]

The promoter encountered a second obstacle, however, in the absurd stories that certain persons were circulating at Nantes in order to dissuade the Acadians from volunteering for Louisiana. Those stories gave rise to many disturbing questions on the Acadian settlements in Louisiana and of the treatment the Acadians would receive from Spanish officials. Peyroux, in default of prompt official answer from Madrid to his eight questions, could only calm the excited Acadians with "paciencia," and "Trust the magnanimous character of Charles III." [77]

Peyroux's third obstacle to a speedy completion in registering Acadian volunteers was the poor transportation and traveling facilities in France of 1784. "I am angry," he wrote to Aranda, "that I cannot execute your excellency's orders with as great celerity as I desire, since stage-coaches have been abolished in Brittany. With the return of the old fashioned four-wheeled wagon, travel has become very slow and annoying." [78]

Gálvez followed up the answers of Charles III with an order that an official of the embassy with the aid of Peyroux should make a strict review of the entire group of volunteers on the day of embarkation. [79] On September 13, 1784, Peyroux sent to Aranda a long report, stating that he had completed the work of canvassing Acadian volunteers. But there was a note of disappointment in that official report. "Of the 3,000 Acadians supposed to be in France, there are only about 2,300," he told Aranda. "A great number of them had gone to Saint-Pierre and Miquelon, while others had secretly abandoned France." [80]

The letter went on telling of Peyroux's successes and failures. At Morlaix he had recruited 92 more volunteers for Louisiana, but discovered 34 others who were waiting to see what the Acadians of St. Malo would do. They had promised to follow them. Of the 500 Acadians at St. Malo, Peyroux had succeeded in getting only 81 to sign up for Louisiana. The others told him that they were expecting an answer on their private petition to the French court. They asked for a delay, for should the French court fail them, they preferred Louisiana to any other offer. Since the Acadians of Cherbourg and Havre de Grâce had expressed the wish to follow the majority in St. Malo, the greatest number of volunteers Peyroux could recruit was 1,508. There was a possibility of his mustering another 65 volunteers from Bordeaux, La Rochelle, Brest, and 35 from Belle-Ile. He wrote Aranda that those 1,508 volunteers were anxious to leave for Louisiana immediately, and that the delay petitioned by the families in St. Malo would only increase the hardship for the majority in finding nightly lodgment. He pointed out that many of the Acadian fishermen had to remain idle, fearing that they might be at sea on the day of departure.[81]

Peyroux came upon thirty families where there was an intermarriage of French and Acadian. He urged Aranda to grant these families permission to go with the rest to Louisiana. Refusal would only beget sorrow and possible divorces.[82] De Calonne suspected that many of those marriages were only business marriages. To many French, the Acadians represented potential wealth. They had legal right to six cents daily and to about two acres of land in France. The Spanish offer of settling the Acadians in Louisiana was very tempting to many idle Frenchmen.[83]

Peyroux informed Aranda that three French priests had appealed to him for permission to go to Louisiana as pastors of the Acadians. The first was a young vicar, named Guiard, zealous and well-liked at Nantes. Besides ministering to the Acadians, he would like to open missions among the savages. The second was a Capuchin of the province of Brittany. His name was Paul Marie. He had been born at Rennes, but now resided in the little convent of l'Hermitage at Nantes. He had the confidence of the Acadians, and was confessor for the majority of them, but he could not leave unless Count de Vergennes sent a petition on his behalf to the provincial of his convent. The third was a diocesan priest, the old Vicar-General of Acadia, Huet de la Valinière, who was unhappy in France and was daily begging to go to America.[84]

Peyroux also got several surgeons to volunteer to migrate with the Acadians to Louisiana. He told Aranda that at least one surgeon should go with every transport ship. He suggested that Spain should pay their transportation in return for their services during the voyage.[85]

Finally, Peyroux reported the petition of a noble Acadian of

St. Malo. His name was D'Antremont. His ancestors had been governors of Acadia. He was in poor circumstances and consequently could not obtain much education. He longed to leave France to escape the humiliation of military service, and asked of Spain some small position that would save his honor.[86]

On the same day, September 13, 1784, on which Count de Aranda had received Peyroux's official report, he dispatched to Madrid a note in which he stated, "Peyroux has finished his work of canvassing signatures in Nantes, Paimboeuf, Morlaix, and St. Malo. . . . He has 1,508 Acadians for Louisiana." [87]

CHAPTER NINE

Aranda Achieves Removal of the Acadians

THE ENTIRE RESPONSIBILITY for removing the Acadian exiles from France to Louisiana, Spain placed in the hands of her ambassador in Paris, Count de Aranda. José de Gálvez, minister of the Indies, urged him to discharge diligently the trust that the king placed in him by accomplishing as economically as possible and in good order the removal of the 1,508 Acadian exiles whom Peyroux had canvassed for Louisiana.[1] Gálvez made no secret of Spain's need of the Acadians "to populate the fertile province of Louisiana."[2] To aid Aranda in the successful achievement of that aim he placed unlimited funds at his disposal.[3] Aranda answered that he would "not disappoint his majesty in the confidence that he has placed in me. I will see that the removal is achieved with exactitude and with the greatest possible economy."[4]

Aranda began his work by seeking for diligent and trustworthy servants. He had one already in Peyroux de la Coudrenière, who had done secret work in securing some data from French ship companies. But he found his most reliable servant in the person of His Majesty's consul of St. Malo, Manuel d'Asprès, who not only drew up the contracts but also canvassed an additional group of volunteers, saved the entire colonization plan from failure, and supervised the removal of the exiles to Louisiana. "There is no better person," Aranda wrote to Floridablanca, "to supervise the removal of the Acadians with the aid of Peyroux than Don Manuel d'Asprès."[5]

Early in the secret negotiations Heredia had made the suggestion to Madrid that the Acadian colonists for Louisiana should present themselves in the ports of Spain for transportation in Spanish ships.[6] But the Acadians were opposed to that idea, and petitioned through Peyroux that Spain should charter ships in Nantes.[7] Peyroux anticipated the probable consent of Spain to their wish and, with tacit approval of Heredia, secretly began inquiries on bids from local ship companies in Nantes[8] on the removal of 3,000 Acadians from France to Louisiana.[9]

Peyroux indeed lost no time in gathering data on "the most economic transportation possible" for Spain. During the first week of March, 1784, long before France gave her consent to the Acadians to leave, he had contacted one Michel, one of the wealthiest shipowners in Nantes. Michel estimated that the cost of transporting one passenger from Nantes to New Orleans would be at least $60.00. That would include all incidentals such as hammocks during the voyage, transportation of passengers and baggage for thirty-nine miles down the Loire to the ports of Mindin or Paimboeuf, where his ships were at anchor. His bid also included well-balanced meals during the layover of twelve to fifteen days, until he could condition his ships for the long voyage to Louisiana. His lowest estimate was $54.80 per capita. He allowed a deduction of $1.20 if he did not have to supply the hammocks, and of $4.00 if he did not have to transfer passengers from Nantes to Mindin. Payments could be arranged later.

At the request of Peyroux, Michel sent that bid, drawn up in his own hand, to the Spanish embassy. He appended a statement that his estimate was not final but subject to modification should the Spanish government permit him to sell a cargo of foodstuffs such as flour, wines, and brandies at New Orleans, and permit him to take home a cargo of Louisiana wares and products.[10]

Peyroux wrote to Heredia that he considered Michel's bid exorbitant.[11] He thought that Spain could transport the Acadians more cheaply by chartering two or three ships herself. In fact,

he was confident that he himself could achieve the removal of
the Acadians for less than $40.00 a person, if Spain would only
trust him with the contract. He promised to use the best in
equipment and provisions. But Spain gave him no encouragement.[12] On March 31, 1784, France gave the Acadians her official
permission to migrate to Louisiana. Peyroux was now free to
seek bids openly.

Early in April, therefore, he approached other companies of
shipowners. He had heard that they were very anxious to secure
the contract for removing the Acadian exiles from France to
Louisiana, but he could not get them to give a definite bid.[13]
Then on April 27, 1784, Peyroux consulted one Dupuis, who had
been a royal commissary for twenty-three years. Dupuis estimated
that a daily menu consisting of bread, biscuits, cheese, codfish,
salt meats, light vinegar for aspersions, and fresh foods for the
sick should not cost more than 15 cents a day for each person,
and not over $13.50 for a journey of three months. Peyroux inti-
mated to Heredia that he also considered Dupuis' estimate very
high as it did not include water bottles, bedding, small baskets,
measures, tin pumps, balances, weights, lamps, and iron-hooped
water barrels. Water barrels of "thirty Wellers" in Nantes cost
only $3.00 apiece. One barrel per person should be sufficient.[14] He
further pointed out to Heredia that Spain could get cheaper
transportation by fitting out Spanish ships in Nantes than by
having the Acadians take off from ports in Spain.[15] Moreover,
"the utensils and provisions left over at the end of the voyage,"
he observed, "would reduce the cost of the transportation for His
Catholic Majesty. Thus, Sir, as I have just told you, it seems that
this estimate is the cheapest that we can get." [16] Dupuis' expert
advice at least gave Peyroux a general and honest idea of individual costs. That knowledge was of great help to Manuel d'Asprès
when he had to work out contracts with the ship companies.[17]
Next, on August 21, 1784, Peyroux interviewed the prominent

shipping firm Tourgouilhet and Rousseau of Nantes. They showed him two newly built ships, all ready to transport 800 Acadians. The first ship had been built in 1781, had a 115 foot keel with 4 feet and 8 inches between decks, and would be ready to sail on September 10. The other ship was smaller and somewhat older, its keel of 85 feet having been laid in 1778; but it was more spacious between decks with its 5 feet and 5 inches, and could make the Atlantic voyage at the end of September.

Thinking that Spain wished to remove 3,000 Acadian exiles at once to Louisiana, Tourgouilhet and Rousseau offered to assume the responsibility for hiring the other ships needed without additional cost. But they also offered an alternative. Should Madrid prefer only their two new ships, they would order these two to return immediately from New Orleans. They would then remove 800 passengers at a time, and so on successively until all Acadians had been transferred to Louisiana.[18]

Tourgouilhet and Rousseau submitted a twofold bid for the consideration of Aranda. In the first bid they offered to remove the Acadians from Mindin directly to New Orleans; in the second, from Nantes to the mouth of the Mississippi River only. They had four stipulations in their first offer. First, they asked a flat rate of $36.00 covering passage, meals, and equipment for each passenger without distinction of age. Second, every passenger must transfer himself and his baggage at his own expense from Nantes to the wharf at Mindin. If, however, His Catholic Majesty wanted the company to assume that responsibilty, they would have to ask an increase of $1.00 a person, making their flat rate $37.00. Third, they would assume the cost of provisions only at the moment when the ships would leave the harbor of Mindin. Fourth, after embarkation at Mindin, should contrary winds prevent the ships from sailing, Spain would be expected to pay them twelve cents daily for the support of each passenger as long as the ships were detained in the harbor of Mindin.

In their alternate bid Tourgouilhet and Rousseau also made a flat offer but without any conditions. If Spain preferred the shipping company to remove every Acadian passenger directly from Nantes to Louisiana, the flat rate would be $40.00. That price would include any layover at Mindin during the preparation of the ships and any risk of delay from contrary winds. Under either bid Tourgouilhet and Rousseau asked Spain to make payments in the customary three drafts on some bank in Paris, in proportion to the number of passengers, and beginning immediately after the ships departed.[19]

Aranda forwarded the bid without any comments to Madrid.[20] Floridablanca had informed him that the orders of José de Gálvez were that neither he nor any other person should decide any particulars of the terms.[21] Meanwhile, Peyroux wrote to Aranda in favor of Tourgouilhet and Rousseau's flat rate of $40.00 a person. He reminded Aranda that the price was very reasonable in comparison to what the king of France paid for transferring colonists to Cap François or to Martinique, places less remote than was Louisiana.[22]

On September 6, 1784, Aranda sent to Floridablanca another bid that Peyroux had secured, that of Giraud and Raimbat. And to the minister of the Indies, José de Gálvez, he dispatched a list of the Acadians who were ready to leave in September of 1784 for Louisiana.[23] But to the suggestion of any early departure, Aranda got no official answer from the minister of the Indies until February 4, 1785.[24]

On September 27, 1784, Aranda took Manuel d'Asprès into his special confidence. He revealed to D'Asprès the royal cedula of Charles III, entrusting him with the removal of 100 Acadian families from France to Louisiana. There would be other expeditions, and he needed expert help. He asked D'Asprès if he would accept the responsibility for organizing the details of the expeditions. If he would, he should proceed to Nantes without delay, assemble there as many of the families as possible, and determine the best time of departure. With the aid of Peyroux, he should make a list of the Acadians ready for immediate departure. But above all, he should reduce the terms of Tourgouilhet and Rousseau, and of Giraud and Raimbat. He assured D'Asprès of his deep appreciation for all services.[25]

Aranda had in D'Asprès a representative who was able to drive a hard bargain. D'Asprés wrote his superior on October 10, 1784, that he had visited all three companies. First, he discovered that Giraud and Raimbat had declared bankruptcy just after submitting their bid. And he further learned that even if they had not done so, they would not have been able to meet his demands because their ships of 300 tons were not constructed to accommodate 250 passengers.[26]

Tourgouilhet and Rousseau came immediately to see the Spanish consul as soon as they learned of his arrival in Nantes. Reminded of their promise to Aranda of a reduction, they offered a bid of $5.00 per head less. But they refused to assume the responsibility for transporting the Acadians beyond Balize at the mouth of the Mississippi River, as they feared that their ships could not navigate that channel. Each one of their ships could accommodate 300 passengers at $31.00 a person. They could leave on October 10. Tourgouilhet and Rousseau's terms of indemnity for delays were reasonable.[27]

On October 9, 1784, Antonio Marcorelles, another shipowner, gave D'Asprès a bid of $30.00 a person from infants a few days old to any age. His conditions were considerably more exacting than those of Tourgouilhet and Rousseau, indemnities for delays higher, time of departure later, and ships much smaller.[28] And he worried more over the depth of the channel than did any of the other companies. From him especially and from the other companies, D'Asprès gathered the impression that all the shipping companies feared the use of large ships, thinking the Mississippi channel was only nine to ten feet in depth. But all sailors claimed that the depth was from eleven to twelve feet.[29]

> Both companies are equal [D'Asprès observed in his report to the ambassador]. Neither one has more to offer than the other. Both have large and small ships. It seems to me that, reducing both to one price and to equal conditions as I hope to do, it would be better to deal with each one for the number of passengers that he is able to handle, and to give to other companies (which I know there are) the rest of the passengers on the same price and conditions. Placing the removal in the hands of different companies has the advantage of a speedy accomplishment with a minimum of fraud[30]

D'Asprès did not fancy any of the bids. He wrote Aranda to that effect on October 10, 1784, adding that he would have to iron out many wrinkles in them before he could present a satisfactory contract. For instance, a day of departure had to be fixed, as well as the obligations of the contracting parties if the ships were unable to sail on the appointed day, the fare of infants a few days old, the cleanliness of living quarters, the policing of the ships, and above all the space to be allotted each passenger and his baggage.[31]

France allowed a soldier two feet of space, and though the personal property of an Acadian exile consisted of only a bed and a trunk, nevertheless it was more than that of a French soldier. He thought, moreover, that the contract should fix the weight and volume of each passenger's baggage so as to leave some space for those who might have some pieces of furniture. Between decks he would permit only beds and trunks. Everything else must be stored in the holds of the ships. He would not permit overloading any of the ships. To do so would not only endanger the lives of all in the event of a storm at sea but also set the stage for any epidemic that could destroy the whole colonization effort. He would distribute the children evenly among the ships so that they would not crowd one ship more than another.[32]

D'Après expressed his fears to Aranda that the achievement of a satisfactory and economical contract would be a long-drawn-out argument. He foresaw daily useless discussions over details in absurd demands in each bid, the shirking of obligations to provide food in proper quantity and quality, the necessary adjustments in the "menu for 500 passengers," and the frozen condition of the Loire River at Mindin and Paimboeuf. As a result of such useless arguments, D'Après' first plan of removing the Acadians early in December, 1784, to Louisiana looked less and less possible of accomplishment every day. However, he tried at least to expedite matters. To that end he asked Aranda's permission to enlist the services of a man who had sixteen years of experience in consular work and shipping, and who knew every person of note in Nantes—his friend and fellow vice-consul, Luís Landaluze.[33] At the same time he availed himself of the services of Gaspar Lannux and Don Tomás De Laire, vice-consuls of Morlaix and of La Rochelle respectively, and of an old friend, Don Juan Quesnel.[34]

With the aid of the vice-consuls of Morlaix, St. Malo, and La Rochelle, D'Après worked out an economical menu on the rations that the king of France granted 500 of his troops traveling overseas. He called it "provisions necessary for 500 men traveling by sea for three months, or ninety days of a simple menu totalling 45,000 rations." He computed the entire cost at $5,377.71.[35]

Aranda gave D'Après full approval. But he again pointed out the importance of achieving "the most economical transportation possible for His Catholic Majesty," as that success meant so much to their future ambitions. He also offered a few suggestions whereby he thought D'Après could save time and money. First, there were 173 Acadian exiles enrolled for Louisiana in St. Malo and Morlaix. Of these, 92 were scheduled to depart on the first ship and 81 on the second. Could D'Asprès reach an agreement with one of the ship companies to call for these volunteers at their respective ports instead of asking the exiles to travel overland first to Nantes and then to either Mindin or Paimboeuf? The cost of transporting these passengers from Nantes to either Mindin or Paimboeuf, as the case might be, would cancel the cost of a ship's traveling directly from either one of those ports to St. Malo and Morlaix. Otherwise he thought that those two groups would encounter great difficulties and hardships in departing on time. His second suggestion aimed to facilitate the removal of the exiles from those ports on schedule. He thought that the vice-consuls of St. Malo and Morlaix should use the assistance of Peyroux in checking each family and its destination. They should also arrange with him the removal of the exiles from Belle-Ile-en-Mer to their port of embarkation. And he told him that His Majesty had ordered continuation of the pay to all Acadian volunteers, and moderate help to the extremely poor who would have to travel.[36]

D'Asprès really went to work. He met no difficulties on the part of French officials in Nantes. When the intendant, subdelegate, and chief of police saw his credentials, they did everything in their power to help him work out an early departure of the Acadians. They paid him their respects as an official body. The subdelegate even gave him all data he had on Acadians under his charge, namely, that he had paid each one three cents up to the end of June; that he did not pay anything to those born in Nantes, as they had no claim to any pay; and that he was under order to inform him that from the first of July, the pay would become Spain's duty.[37]

Next, D'Asprès called a meeting of the ship companies for October 28, 1784. Each company expressed a willingness to lower its terms, to employ only the ships necessary, to attend to all demands in its bids as soon as they knew the exact number of passengers. The lowest bid, however, to which he was able to reduce

any of them was $30.00 for each adult. That implied a longer
voyage by twenty days, which in turn, meant a greater expense
in provisions. One of the companies bluntly stated that it could
not transport the Acadians for $30.00 unless the Spanish govern-
ment permitted it to bring back a cargo of produce from one of
its island possessions.

D'Asprès ran into some unforeseen expenses. There was the
cost of $60.00 to notarize the contract. And the removal of the
Acadians from Nantes, St. Nazaire, Gabarras, Belle-Ile-en-Mer,
La Rochelle, Rochefort, and Bordeaux to the most convenient
port of either Paimboeuf or Mindin, and provisions for at least
two days involved a considerable sum of money.[38] Then the vice-
consuls of St. Malo and Morlaix were not able to get any definite
bids from the ship companies in those cities.[39]

Peyroux had succeeded in canvassing only 1,508 signatures.
D'Asprès was hoping to enlist at least 2,000.[40] He knew that
Spain was anxious to secure as many of the Acadians as possible
for their agricultural skill and their numerical strength in hold-
ing Louisiana against the encroachments of the Americans on the
east bank of the Mississippi. The latter threat was very real to
Spain, for as early as 1783, the Americans were flooding Louisiana
with their lumber to the point that Spain could hardly sell her
own wood.[41] D'Asprès, aware that his country's hold on Louisiana was precarious, strove to gather the largest number of colonists possible from among the Acadians. "I am paying 2,000 Acadians without distinctions because I think it is better to pay all
who intimate any desire to go to Louisiana, as such kindness will
tend to win for us the greatest number of volunteers among
them. . . . The pay of 2,000 for 123 days at 3 cents (*i.e.* from the
end of June to the end of October) amounted to $7,380.00 . . . .
Tell me if I should do otherwise," he wrote to Aranda.[42]

D'Asprès was also hoping to balance unforeseen expenses. He
got many Acadians to pay at least part of the cost of their estab-

lishments in Louisiana. With that saving he might still be able
to achieve "the most economical transportation possible." That
was one reason why he was so interested in an early departure
of the Acadians. Since he had already given them their pay for
four months (June to October), if he delayed their departure
much longer he would not get any contributions from them.[43]

Finally, on November 7, 1784, he could write to Aranda, "Sir,
I want you to see that I am doing my utmost to achieve a contract
with the ship companies on the most economical terms possible."[44] And in his letter he enclosed a contract, listing twenty-two
points to which he thought Aranda could agree. The contract
called for a charter of six ships to remove the Acadians from
France to Louisiana. D'Asprès had the promise of two ships from
Tourgouilhet and Rousseau, two from Marcorelles, one from
Juan Momeron Dupine, and another from Nicholas Viaud.[45] He
was also given the option by each company of an extra ship if
necessary.[46]

The contract D'Asprès sent Aranda stipulated that the six ships
would carry all passengers directly and without delay to New Orleans, Louisiana. But if some unforeseen circumstance should
force a disembarkation outside the Mississippi River, the ship
companies will bear the expense of transporting all passengers
and their baggage to New Orleans. All ships would be ready to
receive their passengers on the day contracted. A ship of 300 tons
would carry 225 passengers, but one of smaller tonnage, less.[47] If
delay in sailing was the company's fault, the company would pay
every registered passenger three cents daily up to the moment of
embarkation and would also feed them.[48] If bad weather delayed
the ships, the king of Spain would pay the shipowners two cents
a passenger for meals. But if Spain detained the ships for any
other reason than bad weather, that country would indemnify the
ship companies thirty-eight cents a day. The companies, however,
reserved the right to permit embarkation only on such days as

they judged the weather favorable for sailing. His Catholic Majesty was to defray the cost both of embarkation at Paimboeuf and of disembarkation at New Orleans.

The trip to New Orleans would last at least three months. It would be the duty of the ship companies to stock the ships with adequate and wholesome foods. His Majesty's agents were to make a thorough inspection of quantity and quality of foods, passenger equipment, and seaworthiness of the ships. Should a ship be forced to seek refuge in any port belonging to Spain, it would be the duty of the governor of that port not only to supply the provisions for all passengers during their forced stay but also to exempt that ship from all duties. But if a ship should be forced to anchor in a foreign port because of a storm, or pirates, or because of repairs, the shipowner would assume the duty of feeding its passengers. Later, however, His Majesty was to reimburse him for that forced delay at twelve cents a day per passenger. It was further agreed that all surplus food after arrival in New Orleans would remain on the ships. Passengers were to leave the ships within ten days after their arrival at New Orleans. If circumstances should force them to stay aboard any ship longer, the king would be obliged to indemnify the shipowner twelve cents per passenger and twenty dollars per ship per day.

The shipping companies contracted not to include infants of a few days age in the number of passengers. Women in childbirth and every sick person were to be cared for properly and fed a diet that included poultry. Two Acadian leaders with distinctive rank would be appointed for every one hundred passengers and authorized to decide the rations for the sick. Only in case of the outbreak of a contagious disease might the captain allow passengers to land in a foreign port.[49]

His Catholic Majesty was to pay the expense of the contract. He would also pay the ship companies on the day of embarkation for all registered passengers whether present or absent. And he would indemnify any chartered ship that carried only a third of its freight. He was to pay each ship company by bills of exchange in four payments on Le Couteulx Company of Paris as soon as he received notice that the ships had sailed for New Orleans.[50]

With the contract, D'Asprès also sent Aranda the final revision of his menu for the three meals during the voyage, entitled, "Rations of provisions which the shipowners will load on each ship for the maintenance of the Acadians."[51] He generously provided nine lumps of coal as firewood for each hundred persons, vinegar for sprinkling the ship, and double for preparation of meals, and at least one cask of water per person. On October 23, 1784, he received word from Aranda that he could sign the contract as soon as he thought that all matters were in order.

With the conditions of the contract and the menu for the voyage out of the way, D'Asprès next move was to get shipping companies to sign the contract and begin the immediate removal of the Acadians to Louisiana. Aranda was urging D'Asprès in every letter to hasten their departure so as not to abuse the kindness of the French court.[52] Moreover, early in October he had received a note from Floridablanca, asking when he would forward the new contract to José de Gálvez. Gálvez had intimated to the prime minister that he would allow the Acadians to depart as soon as he was in possession of the new contract.[53] No one was more anxious than D'Asprès to see the Acadians depart early so as to achieve the "most economic transportation possible" and the reward not only for himself but also for his associates.[54] Peyroux likewise was anxious to see the Acadians depart early so that he could claim his promised commission as commandant and captain in Spain's royal army.[55] But D'Asprès had written Aranda that he could close the contract and ship the Acadians to Louisiana only after he had the exact number of passengers. He thought that the most efficient method of learning the exact number of passengers was to demand a written statement of intention and acceptance from every family head.[56] But just when he imagined that he had corralled all the laggards there arose among them such fears that not only the success of their immediate removal but of any future removal to Louisiana was threatened.

On discovering that the ships were ready in November of 1784, many Acadians had become restive and suspicious. They wanted to know when they would be going, if at all, to Louisiana.[57] Because D'Asprès had not yet received the "conventional instructions," he could only tell them that they would know that on the day of departure itself, but that at present His Catholic Majesty must consult his own interests also. Others wanted to know before signing any statement what treatment Spanish officials would give them in Louisiana. They had heard rumors that many of their people in Louisiana were unable to work on lands assigned to them because food rations were insufficient,[58] rains and hurricanes had caused much sickness among them,[59] and some had been sold into slavery.[60] Though D'Asprès reminded them of the general happiness and prosperity of the Acadians in Louisiana, his answers did not seem to allay their fears at all. "The life we must live in France is hard enough," they retorted, "without taking a blind chance on that in Louisiana." [61] The Acadians took nothing for granted anymore. Others wanted to know definitely whether His Catholic Majesty would continue the pay after the king of France discontinued granting it to them. To which D'Asprès could only answer that he was "awaiting orders." Others again objected to traveling in December, because they would be exposed to the cruelty of winter, which might cause the death of many of their women and children. Large numbers favored a departure in spring or early autumn of 1785. Groups of fishermen refused to leave until the French government had paid them what it owed them, for otherwise they could not pay their own debts. Many groups refused to leave at all unless Spain would give them some assurance that she would continue the pay.[62]

There were in Nantes and St. Malo many Acadians who from the very beginning opposed Peyroux's plan of migration to Louisiana because necessity did not press them.[63] Moreover, Vergennes had failed to send D'Asprès a prompt decision, whether or not he would permit the French married to Acadians to go to Louisiana.[64] Aranda had written D'Asprès that "without the conventional instructions" from Madrid he also could do nothing to help him calm the fears of the Acadians.[65] D'Asprès was experiencing the blight of Madrid's vacillating policy.

D'Asprès saw himself beset by problems that threatened in the last moment to deprive him of successs in achieving in autumn of 1784 "the most economical transportation possible." With such great dissension among the Acadians, he thought of postponing their removal from autumn of 1784 to that of 1785. But immediately the shipowners confronted him with the agreement in Article 8 of the contract, awarding them twelve cents a passenger for every day of delay. Moreover, bad weather also might increase his expenses, they cautioned him.

D'Asprès, worried lest he disappoint Aranda, now thought of another plan of achieving a most economical removal of the exiles. What of embarking the greater part of the women and boys first? But these vigorously objected to that proposal. Some feared the severity of the winter and others, the storms on the ocean and gulf which might drive them to demand a forced landing. If granted, possible family separations might result.

Seeing no solution to his problems, D'Asprès on November 13, 1784, finally wrote to Aranda: "I am in favor of what could well succeed in the summer. Therefore, in duty to my superior, I suggest that you postpone the removal of the Acadians to Louisiana until next year, when you can accomplish it with ease and without fear. Of course, I realize that for them this postponement means an extension of the pay, and for you, six months more of expenses. But if you add the influence of that extra expense to the advantages of a voyage in either summer or early fall, you will succeed in getting all of them to go." [66]

Aranda wrote a letter of thanks to D'Asprès for his suggestions. He heartily agreed with the consul that his reasons for postponing the removal were well founded. He again cautioned him to use the utmost discretion until he had received "the conventional instructions from Madrid." Until then he urged D'Asprès to use copies of the two letters he had received to bolster the sagging spirits of the Acadians and thereby stimulate an early migration to Louisiana. [67]

The first of the two letters was from Vergennes, who forwarded De Calonne's regret at cutting off the pay to the Acadians. [68] Thinking that the departure of the Acadians was "very near" after the royal permit of April 27, 1784, De Calonne ordered the immediate cessation of their pay. But on being informed that the removal had been postponed, he ordered that "nothing must be changed in arrangements. The pay will continue until the Acadians depart." [69]

The other letter enclosed by Aranda was from the public treasury. It dealt with the decision of Charles III of Spain to grant the Acadians their pay until the day of departure. [70] But the public treasurer's letter was very unsatisfactory. What the Acadians wanted to know before signing D'Asprès' questionnaire was Spain's attitude towards their pay after January 1, 1785. Seeing that any departure in the fall of 1784 was out of question, would Spain grant them the pay after the first of January? As the public treasurer's answer was ambiguous, the majority of Acadians again refused to migrate from France until Spain gave them definite assurance in regard to their pay after the first of the year 1785. [71] Then, when Floridablanca began to present "such great difficulties in accomplishing the removal on time," Aranda replied on November 19, 1784, that he had ordered D'Asprès to suspend

all negotiations with the Acadians until he got a definite answer
to five questions he was submitting to Charles III:

1. In view of the reasons presented by D'Après, will it not
be better to postpone the removal of the Acadians until next
summer?

2. Does the king prefer a new contract of the French ship
companies or does he want Señor D'Après to seek other bids
in the port of Cadiz?

3. Since the Spanish court decreed the continuation of pay
to the Acadians upon belief of their early departure, does His
Majesty wish to continue the same after the first of the year
1785? In that event the Spanish court should give new orders
to the exchequer, since Señor Don José de Gálvez has given
different instructions to Señor Conde de Gausa in Paris.

4. If the pay is granted after the first of the year 1785, will
it apply to all the Louisiana volunteers or only to those Acadians to whom the Spanish court has already granted it?
D'Après claims that granting the pay to all Acadians will be
a very efficient way to coax all to depart, and the cost will not
be very much more.

5. Naturally, every Acadian volunteer has made many inquiries about his lot and destination in Louisiana. A general
idea of what Spain intends to do with them and for them
will be a cogent means not only of calming their fears, but of
hastening also their removal.[72]

Besides these five problems, Aranda was also awaiting an
answer to a persistent request of the ship companies. It was
an adjustment permission for which he had applied many months
ago. Should the removal of the Acadians be postponed would the
king of Spain permit them to bring back a cargo of wood on their
return trip from Louisiana? D'Après was urging official consent
to the request since it would enable him to secure the only sea-
worthy ship at St. Malo. He was assured by the ship companies
that the loaded ships would not meet any difficulties in the chan-

nel at Balize. On a prompt official answer, Aranda pointed out, depended the success of adjustments.[73]

But Madrid did not return such an answer. The delay clearly worried Aranda. He was haunted by the failure of past attempts at colonization in Europe and in America. He realized that those attempts had failed in part or in whole, because proper preparations had not been made to secure a permanent and prosperous establishment of the nascent colonies.[74] He saw clearly too that Spain's attempt to settle over 1,600 Acadians in Louisiana ran the risk of an even greater failure and expense, unless he first determined the approximate number of colonists, the day of departure, the number of houses for the colonists, the amount of tools needed, and the possible number of deaths.[75]

Back in Paris Aranda feared for the worst. Had he not filled the king's mind with doubt in regard to Spain's ability to keep Louisiana? After he had signed the peace treaty between England and Spain in Paris, 1783, did not Charles ask him whether he thought Spain could hold Louisiana against the Americans or should she return the province to France? And was it not he, Aranda, who had written to Charles that he thought both Spain and France had made a great mistake in aiding the Americans in their war of independence, and that American independence filled his own mind with great fears for the future of Louisiana? The Americans, he thought, would stop at nothing to wrest Louisiana, and maybe California as well, from Spain. "This federal republic," he had once written to His Majesty, "is born a pygmy . . . The day will come when she will be a giant, a colossus formidable even to France and Spain." [76] Nevertheless, despite Aranda's prophecy, and other unfavorable indications, Charles III decided to hold Louisiana and to accept Peyroux de la Coudrenière's scheme for removing the Acadian exiles in France thither, and on October 22, 1783, had issued his royal decree of acceptance. But Aranda likewise knew that Charles was never completely convinced that the Acadian colonization of Louisiana could hold that province for Spain, and he feared lest Charles in the last moment might cancel the entire project as hopeless and useless. Finally, on March 5 (?), 1785, Aranda received a letter from Madrid. Nervously he scanned its contents—the full royal approbation on each of his five inquiries.[77] In the letter Charles III gave Aranda his approval to postpone the departure of the Acadians until spring or early summer of 1785. His only stipulation was that D'Asprès should adjust the contracts with the French ship companies.[78] Next he cautioned Aranda to give a duplicate contract to each one of the captains so that on arrival of any one of the ships in Louisiana or in any other port belonging to Spain, the governor in that port would know his duties.[79] He also decreed that Aranda should grant the pay of three cents from January 1, 1785, up to the day of departure to all Acadians, even to those who had not received it from France, but were enrolled for Louisiana. In doing so, Charles agreed that granting the pay to all exiles would be an effective inducement to win over those who were still hesitant.

He also answered the Acadians' inquiry in regard to their lot and destination in Louisiana by disclosing to them the royal orders to Bernardo de Gálvez, the captain-general of that province. Those orders directed Gálvez to provide every Acadian family with good farm lands, to build them homes, to supply them with all necessary farming implements as quickly as possible, and to continue royal subsidy to the Acadians until they became self-supporting, so "that His Catholic Majesty's intention to populate the fertile province of Louisiana might not fail." [80] Charles III also generously granted permission to the shipowners to load a cargo of Louisiana wood on their return trip, subject of course to the restrictions in the duplicate of the royal decree sent to Bernardo de Gálvez.[81] And he urged that D'Asprès should secure some sort of adjustment in the cost of transporting trunks, furniture, and boxes belonging to the Acadians.[82] The king placed unlimited funds at Aranda's disposal in Spain's Bank of San Carlos in Paris. But he warned the ambassador to render an exact account of all expenses in order to receive from the ministry of the Indies royal sanction from the public treasury of Spain.[83] When Aranda had read the letter, he was filled with joy. Charles III had taken a long time to come to a final decision, but when he did arrive at one, he did so magnanimously.

Aranda sent immediate notice to Vergennes that from January 1, 1785, Spain would assume the obligation of paying the Acadian colonists for Louisiana.[84] He also lost no time in proving himself worthy of the confidence Charles III placed in him to accomplish the removal of the Acadians from France "with exactitude and with the greatest economy possible." [85]

Posthaste he sent word to D'Asprès of the favorable answers he had received from the king to his six queries. He urged him to double his efforts to achieve the speedy removal of the Acadians to Louisiana, to select reliable sailors familiar with the seas of Europe and America, and to pick appropriate ports for departure and arrival. Enclosed, he also sent papers authorizing D'Asprès to sign the contracts before a notary public. And finally he instructed him to give Peyroux a full account of the royal intention to subsidize the Acadians until they became self-supporting.[86]

You will convince the Acadians [Aranda's message concluded] of His Majesty's kindness. That knowledge should be a great stimulus to win the good will of those who are indifferent. His Majesty, moreover, has approved all the transactions of your office. He will also accept all Acadians who had expressed a desire after January 1, 1784, to go to Louisiana. You will advise me what you think is best—both for the good of the Acadians and the interest of His Majesty. Let me know the amount of money you will need so that I may have it delivered to you through the House of Le Couteulx. I have already given them orders to grant you whatever funds you should deem necessary.[87]

On April 4, 1785, Aranda reported to Madrid that Manuel d'Asprès had completed registering all Acadian volunteers for Louisiana in the port of Nantes. He had paid each one three cents daily during the months of January and February, and he had set their removal for the first days of May.[88] And on Sunday, May 10, 1785, after twenty-nine years of aimless exile, punctuated by frustrated dreams[89] and unscrupulous abuse of their gentle character,[90] the first group of 156 Acadians left king and France for Louisiana in the frigate *Le Bon Papa*.[91]

CHAPTER TEN

The Seven Acadian Expeditions to Louisiana

T HROUGH the "loyal and efficient services" of the consul of St. Malo, Manuel d'Asprès and his co-workers Luís Landaluze, Gaspar Lannux, Don Juan Quesnel, Tomás de Laire, Oliver Terrio, and Peyroux, Count de Aranda was able to achieve the removal of the 1,596 Acadian exiles in seven divisions.[1] To D'Asprès they were "Royal Expeditions";[2] to Aranda, "Acadian Expeditions."[3] In organizing these expeditions, D'Asprès tried to be as humane as possible and kept related groups of families and old friends together.[4] An important item for each expedition was the list of registration which he sent to the governor of New Orleans. In it he specified the number of families, individuals of each family, the total number of persons comprising each expedition, and the age and trade of each emigrant.[5]

Of the seven Acadian expeditions that of *Le Bon Papa* was the first.[6] D'Asprès had assigned to her 39 families of 165 members. Three families, however, numbers 37, 38, and 39, failed to report on the day of departure,[7] and *Le Bon Papa* left Paimboeuf on the tenth of May without them.[8] Each of the three families was small. Death from grief and misery had taken most of its members while in France. Don Luís Monreal had with him only his two nephews, Juan and Pedro. With Don Augustin Legay was his wife Josepha and a close friend, Manuel Antoma Landry. In Don Miguél Mallet's family were his wife María, and her sister Margarita Segolio.[9] Though they missed *Le Bon Papa* on Sunday, May 10, 1785, they eventually got to Louisiana through the kindness of Manuel d'Asprès.

130

Captain Pelletier of *Le Bon Papa* made the voyage across the Atlantic in eighty-one days.[10] He arrived on July 29, 1785 at New Orleans.[11] The voyage was a success in its freedom from storms, and from epidemics and sickness of any kind. And the exiles thanked God for that blessing upon arrival. Only one death, that of Rosa el Joven, infant daughter of Eustaquis el Joven and Juana Chiquet, marred an otherwise perfect voyage. Though the child held passport No. 19, her name was officially removed from the list of registrations.[12] Otherwise, the first expedition of 36 Acadian families, comprising 156 persons, arrived in a healthy condition.[13]

Both Aranda and D'Asprès had sent copies of the royal order of October 22, 1783, to Estevan Miró, the provisional governor of New Orleans, and to Count de Gálvez of Mexico City.[14] This cedula ordered the officials of Louisiana to welcome the Acadian exiles from France, settle them with the greatest possible speed, attend to all their needs as agriculturists, grant them tillable lands, good homes, farming tools, and a financial subsidy until they were able to support themselves. No one realized better than did Charles III that the failure of all colonization projects, whether in Europe or in America, had been caused by a lack of proper preparation. He was therefore determined to make the Acadians useful colonists and, with their help, not only hold Louisiana but also increase its internal and foreign commerce.[15]

By virtue of that royal decree, Count de Aranda on June 24, 1785, also notified Martín Navarro, intendant of Louisiana, of his duties in making proper provisions for the Acadians.[16] New Orleans legally had no governor at the time, for Estevan Miró did not receive confirmation of his appointment until July 20, 1785.[17] And Navarro received his orders later,[18] because he was absent first in Mexico and then in Havana.[19] But he came home posthaste. Acting upon the authority of the passports and letters D'Asprès had sent to the provisional governor of New Orleans,[20]

Navarro's first step was to appoint Anselmo Blanchard Acadian commissioner. He authorized him not only to welcome the exiles to New Orleans in the name of Spanish Louisiana but also to grant them entry into the province. He charged the commissioner to care for their immediate needs, to assist them in the choice of suitable lands, to guide them in the building of their new homes,[21] and in every way to show the Acadians that it was the wish of the Spanish government that they should have full liberty in the selection of their future abodes.[22] As compensation for this work, he appointed Blanchard a salary of $500 a year with duties of adviser and overseer of Acadians.[23]

Anselmo Blanchard began his new duties by going aboard *Le Bon Papa* and extending Spanish Louisiana's welcome to the Acadians. Then he made an official registration of the thirty-six families in the order in which they left *Le Bon Papa*.[24]

Spanish Louisiana began her naturalization of the new colonists by Hispanicizing their names. French names were difficult for Spaniards to pronounce. Thus Joseph LeBlanc became in Louisiana José Blanco; Marguerite, Margarita; Paul, Pablo; and Jeanne, Juana. And where family names offered difficulties in pronunciation and spelling, they were written out euphonically, e.g., Babin to Vaben or Vaven, LeJeune to El Joven, and so on.[25] In some cases the Spanish form of the French name is difficult to recognize. Nevertheless, Blanchard and his aides did their best to adhere as closely as possible to the French enunciation of names.

Navarro's next step was financial aid to the Acadians. Acting upon the royal cedula of October 22, 1783, he granted a subsidy of ten cents to every family head, whether man or woman, seven and a half cents to every adult, and two and a half cents to every child. The exiles felt happy and secure.[26] "With this money," Navarro informed the minister of the Indies, "they can buy the little things so necessary to life, such as wood, tools, and so forth. Moreover, I am preparing two hospitals, one for women and another in the royal stables for men. In spite of their successful voyage with only one death of an infant, the change in climate is now causing much sickness among them."[27]

The expedition of *Le Bon Papa* remained about a month recuperating in New Orleans. During that time there were some shuffles in its membership. It picked up twelve new members, three through births and nine through new adherents. But it also lost twelve members, ten through deaths and three through desertions.[28] Among the new adherents were Miguél Léger and Simon Babin, who were related to this expedition, the former through his mother Angella Pinel, and the latter through his sister, Maria Terriot.[29] Then with the aid of an old Acadian who had come to Louisiana in the year 1766, Anselmo Blanchard showed their leaders the choice farm lands in the vicinity of Manchac.[30] Of the thirty-eight families now forming the expedition of *Le Bon Papa,* thirty-seven voted to settle in Manchac on the banks of the Mississippi, and one family of two members chose La Fourche.[31]

As soon as the exiles had recovered from the effects of changes of food and climate, Navarro ordered Juan Prieto, custodian of the royal warehouses, to supply each family with meat cleavers, axes, hatchets, hoes, spades, and knives according to the number of active workers in each family.[32]

Navarro lost no time in getting the exiles settled on their farms.[33] On August 25 he hired the launches of Andrés Chiloque and Arnaldo Magnon at four dollars a day, two guides and twelve river hands,[34] and two barges of Estevan Plauche at two dollars and a half to transport the baggage of the exiles to Manchac.[35] Finally, he notified José de Gálvez that he had settled the expedition *Le Bon Papa* at Manchac "now a wilderness, but an excellent site for the exportation of fruit."[36]

Elated by the success of the expedition *Le Bon Papa,* and anxious to win a reputation for economical efficiency, D'Asprès planned a larger expedition on the ship *La Bergere*. He was partly pushed to the decision by the hundreds of applications from Acadians who now were carried away by enthusiasm and were besieging his office for permission to leave at the earliest possible date.[37] He wrote Aranda that Spain's kindness in guaranteeing good lands, houses, and the continuation of the pay had convinced every Acadian of the sincerity of her aims. The indifference and even hostility that had marked the first Acadian response to Spain's appeal for colonists gave way to wholehearted enthusiasm. Had the French government not interfered, Spain would have won all of the 2,370 Acadians for Louisiana. "I have sufficient information," he remarked, "to assure you that all want to go to Louisiana."[38] A few days later, he wrote Aranda and Count de Gálvez that he hoped "to achieve the removal of all before the end of May."[39] Consequently, he selected the frigate *La Bergere,* a much larger ship than *Le Bon Papa*. He explained to his superiors that he would have to use some larger ships in the following expeditions and that they might have some difficulty in navigating the channel at Balize.[40] Nevertheless, he would attempt their use, because he had so many pressing requests.

On May 7, therefore, just prior to the departure of *Le Bon Papa,* he booked 273 passengers[41] representing 73 families for *La Bergere*.[42] He then called a meeting at his home of the 73 family heads for the purpose of electing leaders, whose duty it would be to police the ship and distribute rations.[43] Despite D'Asprès' supervision there was some tension among the members of this expedition. D'Asprès had organized it in haste, and he unknowingly included members of the two groups that had split Acadian unity over Second Corsica. To preserve peace aboard ship, he bade the 73 family heads to elect their own leaders and to promise obedience under punishment of expulsion on arrival at New Orleans. The 73 heads elected five leaders, prominent among whom was Oliver Terrio, onetime manager of Peyroux and unselfish

Acadian patriot. They also decided at this meeting that the five leaders would have the privilege of sitting at table with Captain Deslandes of *La Bergere*.[44] According to Oliver Terrio, of the five leaders in this expedition, Charles Dugas, Charles Aucoin, and Simon Dugas were "well fixed financially"; but Étienne Dupuy, he wrote, was "as poor as myself."[45] Nevertheless the passengers accepted these leaders and promised obedience to them, to the rules of conduct, and to the captain's orders. D'Asprès then gave Captain Deslandes a duplicate of the contract as commanded by His Catholic Majesty.[46] *La Bergere* pulled up anchor on May 12 and amid a tumultuous roar of "adieu" and "bon voyage," D'Asprès waved *La Bergere* from the harbor of Paimboeuf.[47]

Besides the Acadian exiles, *La Bergere* carried five French passengers: Monsieur Mahyer and wife, Monsieur Leyay,[48] and Doctor Estevan Fouginet and wife.[49] Martín Navarro, intendant of Louisiana, had informed the king of the great need of a surgeon in New Orleans. Moreover, Aranda was seeking a doctor to accompany the expedition of *La Bergere*. Through the services of Squire Macarty Mactuque of Bordeaux, Aranda learned that Dr. Fouginet de Pellegrue wished to migrate to New Orleans.[50] Navarro recognized the ability of Dr. Fouginet, but in the absence of a royal order could not grant him a salary in keeping with his rank. He offered him the disappointing sum of $600 a year and the deep appreciation of all the citizens of New Orleans.[51]

The expedition of *La Bergere* arrived in New Orleans on August 15, and fortunately without any mishap.[52] Dr. Fouginet reported seven births, and six deaths of elderly people.[53] The expedition, like that of *Le Bon Papa,* remained encamped until October 4 at New Orleans.[54] During its sojourn in the city the size of expedition was increased by the addition of twelve births (including the seven aboard ship), five new adherents, and four marriages. But it also sustained a loss of fifteen deaths, including the six during the voyage, and one desertion.[55]

Navarro was watching the project of Acadian colonization with deep interest. He was convinced that if Spain was to hold Louisiana she would have to do so through population. He was happy, therefore, when a month later he could inform José de Gálvez of the first marriages in Louisiana among the Acadians of the seven expeditions.[56]

But Navarro was worried that D'Asprès had sent the expedition *La Bergere* without its trunks and important pieces of baggage. He therefore was detaining the expedition in New Orleans until the arrival on September 22 of the third ship, *Le Beaumont.* D'Asprès had promised to send the trunks and baggage of the *La Bergere* expedition with *Le Beaumont.*[57] But when the trunks did not arrive even with the fourth expedition he ordered Juan Prieto to equip the exiles of *La Bergere* immediately with all necessary farming tools.[58]

Navarro then appointed Juan Cambeau at the cost of forty cents to guide the Acadian surveyors of the expedition *La Bergere* up the Mississippi River.[59] When the Acadian surveyors could not come to any decision on a site for their village he dispatched Pedro Aragon y Villegas to counsel them.[60] With the aid of this veteran Louisianian's advice, the surveyors selected La Fourche in the district of Valenzuela.[61] In the meantime, the size of the expedition had grown to seventy-four families.

On October 4, Navarro began the local transportation of 74 families of 268 persons to La Fourche. He hired the combined service of His Majesty's goleta (or schooner), *San José,* and the launches of Arnaldo Magnon and Andrés Chiloque with a proportionate complement of guides and riverhands.[62] Six families of 23 people, who had chosen Atacapas,[63] however, remained several weeks longer in New Orleans. Many members in these families were sick.[64] But on November 13, Pedro Aragon y

Villegas conducted them to Atacapas on the goleta *San José,* via the Plaquemine Brulé River. One family of three persons went to Manchac.

On October 8, 1785, Navarro closed his books on the expedition *La Bergere:* "That they might have the greatest liberty in choosing the sites of their future homes, we allowed them to elect their own surveyors . . . We did everything to give them good roads that would help them expedite their first harvest . . . I am confident that not one of them can say that he was given a task greater than his strength."[65]

D'Après encountered little trouble in organizing the third expedition of *Le Beaumont.* He selected for this expedition 180 persons,[66] or 45 families.[67] The greater part of this group was made up of small families and newly married couples.[68] So anxious were the Acadians to leave France that when one family of four individuals dropped out just before departure of *Le Beaumont,* D'Après immediately had hundreds of substitutes.[69] The principal leader of this expedition was the father of the whole scheme of removing the Acadians to Louisiana, Peyroux de la Coudrenière. He was accompanied by his wife, his niece, and a friend, LeCat.[70] "I am authorized by the court," Aranda informed Floridablanca, "to send Monsieur Peyroux to Louisiana to take part in the first settlements of the Acadians."[71]

Le Beaumont was a medium-sized frigate, of late construction and speedy. D'Après had set her departure for May 27,[72] but contrary winds forced him to delay her sailing for fifteen days until June 11.[73] Her captain, Daniel,[74] crossed the Atlantic in record time for any of the expeditions, seventy days. He slipped throught the channel of Balize,[75] and arrived on August 19, 1785, at New Orleans.[76] Though there were no births, there was some sickness and two deaths aboard ship.[77]

Miró, who had become governor of New Orleans on July 20, 1785, appointed Pedro Aragon y Villegas in the place of Anselmo

Blanchard to welcome the expedition *Le Beaumont* and to serve
as its commissioner,[78] while Navarro, with the aid of Blanchard,
prepared its camping quarters in New Orleans.[79] There were
conflicting reports on the exact number of exiles in this expedition. Two reports on it, one of Count de Gálvez and the other an
unsigned letter to Josef Petely stated "170 passengers of more
than 34 families." [80] The report of Heredia to Floridablanca
spoke of 178 exiles.[81] D'Asprès' message to Miró announced 180
colonists.[82] And Aragon y Villegas, in his official registration,
recorded 174 Acadians arrived at New Orleans.[83] The confusion
seemed to have arisen from the sudden and speedy arrival of *Le
Beaumont* in the wake of *La Bergere*. Even Navarro had to lend
a hand in preparing camping quarters. New Orleans was beginning to hum with Acadians.

On September 4, 1785, Navarro again ordered Juan Prieto to
supply the expedition of *Le Beaumont* with all necessary farming
equipment.[84] And on September 5, while the expedition *Le Beaumont* was still recuperating in New Orleans, he arranged three
marriages to Acadian girls—those of Francisco Betancourt, an
immigrant, to Victoria La Vergne; Joseph Costa, immigrant, to
Margarita Trahan; and Juan García, a passenger on *Le Beaumont,* to Francisca Courtin.[85] He also noted that the family of
Carlos Henrique had paid its way on *Le Beaumont.*

The surveyors of this group lost no time in determining the
sites for their future homes. After two weeks of reconnoitering
they decided upon Baton Rouge. This selection pleased 41 families with a following of 145 members; 8 families of 28 persons
dissented, however, and 3 families of 8 persons went to La Fourche and 5 families of 20 members to Atacapas.

Though it stayed in New Orleans a shorter time than any
other, this expedition lost 6 more of its members—4 by death and
2 by desertion—but acquired 7 new additions—1 by birth, 3 by
new adherents, and 3 by marriages.[86]

By September 9, 1785, Navarro could report to his superior: "I gave everyone the necessary tools his trade demanded. I also provided them with a surgeon and medical supplies. Moreover, I placed grinding stones, and a big saw at intervals along the road. These tools should facilitate the work of logging trees to build their homes." [87]

Undoubtedly, the least successful of the seven royal expeditions was that of the *St. Remy*. D'Asprès had overreached himself in his anxiety to remove all the exiles before the end of June, and in that way accommodate all petitions and calm all fears among them.[88] So he packed the eager Acadians aboard the frigate *St. Remy,* regardless of health conditions. In doing so he reversed himself, because in drawing up the contracts he had fought the shipowners on the question of overcrowding and had promised Aranda that he would not sign any contract until he had a definite agreement with them on that point.[89] True, the *St. Remy* was a larger frigate than either *Le Bon Papa, La Bergere,* or *Le Beaumont;* but it was not big enough to accommodate comfortably all the passengers that D'Asprès booked for her.

On June 19, D'Asprès called a convocation of the 81 family heads of the expedition *St. Remy*.[90] They chose leaders and decided on rules of conduct and distribution of rations. On the day before departure every member of the expedition promised to obey his leader and the captain of the ship, Nicholas Baudin, under penalty of punishment on arrival at New Orleans. The *St. Remy* left St. Malo[91] on June 20, 1785,[92] with her human cargo of 341 passengers.[93]

The arrival of the *St. Remy* on September 9 caused much excitement in New Orleans.[94] She was the largest so far of the royal expeditions. Besides the huge complement of 325 passengers and 16 stowaways,[95] she carried a great load of baggage, furniture, and trunks.[96] As a result of that unhealthy congestion, smallpox broke out during the voyage and carried away twelve children.

Scurvy caused the deaths of three women.[97] On her arrival small-pox claimed sixteen more victims and caused much sickness in their camp at New Orleans.[98]

Navarro was alarmed and immediately notified D'Asprès that "the voyage of the *St. Remy* was dangerous, because she was overloaded. She had to seek the shelter of an island, and when she arrived at Balize, she got stranded in the channel. In the future, I would suggest the use of smaller ships of less than 12 feet draft, as that is the maximum depth of the channel." [99] While the *St. Remy* lay helplessly stranded in the channel, Josef Petely used every means at his disposal to check the spread of smallpox. He succeeded after a few days in getting it under control.[100] In New Orleans, when Navarro saw the dead, he reported to José de Gálvez, that "the *St. Remy* had taken a great risk at the mouth of the Mississippi." [101]

New Orleans in 1785 was poorly prepared to care for the sudden influx of any large number of immigrants, and Navarro had had great difficulty in accommodating the 155 exiled colonists from *Le Bon Papa*. To meet the housing shortage, he turned the customhouse into a camp village.[102] But his troubles had only begun. In August the city was crowded to overflowing, first, from the 441 exiles of the combined expeditions of *La Bergere* and *Le Beaumont,* and later in October from the 609 of the expeditions *St. Remy* and *La Amistad*.[103] To help the Acadians, he hastily erected a wooden hall 200 by 26 feet, capable of housing 800 people.[104]

As with the expedition *La Bergere,* so with that of the *St. Remy,* many of her members fell sick from the change of food and climate.[105] As a general precaution, to care for the sick among the new colonists, Navarro had built two small hospitals, one for women and another in the royal stables for men.[106] But with the great increase in the number of sick exiles, especially among women of the expedition *St. Remy,* he had to enlarge the hospi-

tal for women to forty-five beds.[107] To please the sick, he called
this enlarged hospital "Community House," and made it independent of the city hospital, since the Acadians in general, especially the women, had such "a great repugnance for French hospitals." [108] Smallpox, the hardships of a long voyage, and the change
of climate carried off many Acadian mothers. Navarro, in his
solicitude for the Acadians, hired wet-nurses to care for their
motherless babies.[109] In the grief and fear that seized the expedition *St. Remy* at the loss of so many young mothers, few paid
any attention to the needs of the sick old men. But their comfort
did not escape the eye of Navarro, who saw to it that they were
provided with orderlies.[110]

Navarro wrote José de Gálvez how joyfully the Acadians welcomed him when he first volunteered to be godfather for seven
of their babies. His kindness made the exiles very happy. But
when he consented to be godfather for all Acadian babies whether
born aboard ship or in camp at New Orleans, or during the trip
up the Mississippi River, he won the heart of every one of the
exiles. From that time on the Acadians loved him as a member
of "their nation." In his report to the Marqués de Sonora, he
remarked, "The Acadians of the *St. Remy* are in need of good
treatment and human kindness." [111] Sonora replied that the king
was edified by his charity and hoped that he would be godfather
many times more.[112]

As soon as the exiles of the *St. Remy* expedition had recovered
somewhat from their sickness, Navarro called a meeting in which
he disclosed to them his plans for their future homes. The royal
order of October 22, 1783, he announced, assured them of good
lands, houses, tools, and a subsidy until they became self-supporting and able to repay His Catholic Majesty the capital he had
expended on them.[113] But in view of the vagueness of the royal
orders he would have to use his own judgment as to how to fulfill its guarantees until José de Gálvez sent him more specific

instructions. Navarro explained that he had heard that many Acadians were good carpenters. Since that was so, he proposed that they should build their own houses, and he would support their efforts with a subsidy of $100 a house.[114] Because they were an honest people, he told them, he was confident that they would build their homes with thrift, avoid waste of time, and use only the best materials. To show his appreciation of their co-operation, he would grant them permission to apply any savings in time and material to purchase cattle for their farms.[115] The Acadians of the *St. Remy* expedition were delighted with his plan. And the Marqués de Sonora sent him his personal congratulations.[116]

Navarro did all in his power to reunite families and relatives. Many Acadians became separated from one another in their haste to be among the first to leave for Louisiana. When Spain's humane treatment of the exiles in Louisiana was learned abroad, family heads would make any sacrifice to leave France as fast as possible in order to be among the first to receive Spain's grant of arable land in Louisiana. As a consequence D'Aprés reported that there was considerable confusion at times among the Acadians awaiting transportation. They knew that ultimately they would find their respective families, but until then the loneliness was heavy, and eagerness to get settled made it all the more so. To heal all wounds Navarro granted these lonesome persons the rights of family head, which meant a subsidy of ten cents instead of seven and a half cents.[117]

Early in October the major part of the *St. Remy* expedition had regained good health. The camp bustled again with activity: elections of surveyors, discussions on future settlements, the admission of nineteen new adherents, and the celebration of eight births and five marriages.[118] Navarro, of course, was godfather and was feted in Acadian style. The marriages performed on October 3 united Francisco Couleur, immigrant, and María Hébert (48th family disembarked, *St. Remy*); and Maturino

Caummeau (52nd family disembarked) and Sofía Hébert (also of *St. Remy*).[119]

On October 4 Navarro informed Count de Gálvez that the expedition *St. Remy* was still "in its village camp on the other side of the river, but eager to depart as soon as its surveyors would return from their survey of suitable lands." [120] After a few days the surveyors of the expedition *St. Remy* arrived in New Orleans. They announced an almost unanimous decision for La Fourche. A majority of 85 families with 303 members welcomed that decision. But two families of 13 persons chose the villages of Atacapas and Opelousas, while two other individuals preferred Nueva Gálvez and Baton Rouge respectively.[121] In thus granting absolute freedom of choice to everyone, Navarro succeeded in pleasing all of them.

Navarro entrusted the local transportation of the expedition *St. Remy* to Anselmo Blanchard. The day after the Acadians had received their farming tools, Blanchard assembled them on the levee where His Majesty's goleta, *San José,* the launches of Arnaldo Magnon and Andrés Chiloque, and a boat of Josef de la Puente were awaiting them. In his meticulous supervision, Navarro overlooked no details. He left specific orders for transportation with Blanchard. For instance, Josef de la Puente might dispense with his river pilot, since he had an excellent one in his river hand, Josef de Flores, but Magnon and Chiloque must keep their sixteen river hands, add those of Bernardo Rosales and Vincente Gonzales, and also the service of the river pilot, José Callobre. On December 16, Blanchard began removal of all members of the *St. Remy* expedition who could endure the river trip to La Fourche de Chetimachas.[122]

Navarro proved that his interest in the Acadians was far deeper than merely currying their favor by being godfather for their babies or winning compliments from Marqués de Sonora by balancing the budget of his building schemes. He longed to see

Spain master of Louisiana through an industrious and loyal population of agriculturists. He knew that with the Acadians Spain
could advance to that goal. To help them attain that end he took
it upon himself to appoint Anselmo Blanchard as their commandant at La Fourche. He even presumed Spain's consent in granting him a salary of $500.

To the Acadians of La Fourche, Blanchard not only showed
himself a deeply interested commandant and advisor in the successful establishment of the colony, but also a kind, sympathetic,
and able administrator. In his patronage of the Acadians he
was next to Martin Navarro as a promoter and colonizer of
Louisiana.[123]

The fifth expedition, *La Amistad,* D'Asprés entrusted to the
direction of his friend, the vice-consul Luís Landaluze.[124] He had
scheduled her departure for late in June. But when Landaluze
took over, he postponed it still later until August 12, because he
had received forty applications from Acadians who could not
leave from St. Malo on the sixth expedition, *La Villa de Arcangel,* and he suspected that the number of "left-overs" might
grow to one hunderd or more.[125] Moreover, he did not favor
D'Asprès' concession to the shipowners of *La Amistad* which
resulted in crowding the ship with more than three hundred
passengers. In his judgment, the frigate was too small to carry
such a load without danger. He consequently reduced her quota
to 260 adults and 10 children,[126] making a total of 270 passengers
or 68 families.[127]

He permitted some non-Acadians to travel on *La Amistad* as
distinguished passengers. Those were Peyroux's brother-in-law,
Celestino Rodríguez, and three other near relatives of Peyroux:
María Adriana, María Luis, and Pedro Benjamin Coiunard. Because of their education, he also allowed them better quarters
aboard ship. And to accommodate Peyroux, he wrote a letter to
Governor Miró that he should use his influence with the French

consul in New Orleans to grant some sort of honorary visa, using as a pretext for their landing sickness or some other excuse.[128]

Captain of *La Amistad* was Joseph Beltremieux.[129] He brought the expedition on November 7, 1785, to New Orleans.[130] Though this expedition was smaller than that of *La Bergere,* it was as successful. There was, however, much sickness during the voyage in spite of Landaluze's precautions to avoid overcrowding. Six died aboard ship,[131] and twenty-seven were very sick.[132] But once they landed they recovered rapidly. Sixty-eight families formed the expedition *La Amistad.*[133]

When Navarro had looked over the expeditions *St. Remy* and *La Amistad,* he was surprised at the large number of single girls of marriageable age.[134] He had no specific instructions from Madrid on what to do about such a situation, but he did know of the royal wishes to populate Louisiana. He knew of sixteen stowaways on the *St. Remy*[135] and of twelve on *La Amistad,*[136] and that several of them had risked the fortune of a stowaway, because they could not bear the pain of separation from their sweethearts.[137] He knew also that among the sailors there were several young men who wished to marry Acadian girls, but feared that in so doing they would only deprive their wives of the financial subsidy from the government.[138] So he inaugurated his own marriage campaign. To encourage all bachelor immigrants to enter marriage with Acadian girls, he published two guarantees: first, to the stowaways and sailors, the right to settle in Louisiana; and second, to any local bachelor, the right of family head with a continuation of the usual subsidy from the government.[139]

> Though I have not received any instructions from the court [he wrote to Count de Gálvez of Mexico], nevertheless I know the royal wishes to populate and hold this province. I have, therefore, made a public announcement that any bachelor who marries an Acadian girl will enjoy the right of family head from the first day of his marriage. Thus

I have arranged twenty-three marriages. The bishop has not only approved my arrangements, but has even granted the prospective couples a dispensation from the banns of marriage. As a result I have won the goodwill of all Acadians, so much so that they have asked me to be godfather for all their babies born since they left France.[140]

From November 20 to December 19, 1785, there was much festivity among the Acadians. Back in Acadia a marriage was an event of communal celebration. And the Acadians clung tenaciously to their "national" traditions. The occasion of a marriage called for dancing, games, and a rehearsal of their national history, accompanied with the usual drink of beer, cider, or "café noir." And this was a special occasion.[141]

The expedition *La Amistad* also won the distinction of having the largest number of families, ninety-three, though not of persons. Beginning with sixty-eight families in Paimboeuf, it grew through its seventeen marriages, ten births, and twenty-four new adherents. It also won the additional distinction of being the only expedition that did not lose any of its members through death while in New Orleans.[142] On December 15, Navarro ordered Juan Prieto to equip it with all essential farming tools. From Prieto's list the reader can reconstruct the official registration of the ninety-three families that formed this expedition.[143]

As soon as Juan Prieto had completed the equipment of the expedition *La Amistad,* Navarro began its removal in two divisions from New Orleans. The first division, comprising 71 families of 224 members, he settled immediately at La Fourche in Valenzuela.[144] As a supplement to His Majesty's goleta *San José,* he again employed the launches of Arnaldo Magnon and Andrés Chiloque at four dollars a day. He also appointed as guides Miguél Romero, Josef Callobre, and Josef de la Puente, and as experienced river hands, Antonio Gutiérrez, Bernardo Migueles, and Josef Flores.[145] In the meantime the second division of twenty families picked up an additional family, and one bachelor. Prieto had equipped fourteen of these families on December 15, 1785. The remainder he fitted out on January 15, 1786.[146] But as this group had so many of the newlyweds, Navarro permitted them a longer sojourn in New Orleans. A few days later, Navarro informed José de Gálvez that he had happily established the bachelor at Baton Rouge, the newlywed couple at Bayou des Écores, three families of ten at Atacapas, and seventeen families of fifty-four persons at Nueva Gálvez.

D'Asprès at first had entrusted the organizing of the sixth expedition, *La Villa de Arcangel,* at St. Malo, to Luís Landaluze, but later took over himself.[147] As consul of St. Malo, he felt that this expedition should be his own special work.[148] He had received so many applications again that he decided to use a larger ship than usual to satisfy as many of the petitioners as possible. But of the 378 requests the most that he could conveniently accommodate on the frigate *La Villa de Arcangel* was 309 passengers of 53 families. The families of the exiles in St. Malo were large, and he had to refuse passage to 69 applicants.[149] In spite of congestion on *La Villa de Arcangel,* he did squeeze in an extra applicant, a non-Acadian and a distinguished French colonist, Duhamel Deschenais.[150]

La Villa de Arcangel was a large frigate under the command of Captain LeGoaster.[151] D'Asprès had the expedition prepared to leave St. Malo early in July,[152] but contrary winds detained her until mid-August.[153] She naturally traveled slowly, being large and overcrowded, and did not arrive at Balize until November 4. There like the *St. Remy* she went aground.[154] In addition, she had been out of provisions for some days, and had thirty-eight very sick passengers.[155]

Navarro promptly rushed water, provisions, medical supplies, and extra help so that by November 11, *La Villa de Arcangel* was able to enter the Mississippi River. Lazily she ploughed her way upstream for 110 miles to New Orleans and hove into sight of the city on December 3.[156] "As soon as the expedition *La Villa de Arcangel* arrived," Navarro informed Count de Gálvez, "I went on board to check the number of passengers. I gave them a speech of welcome in which I reminded them of His Majesty's plan in removing them from France to Louisiana. I stressed their obligation to him, and I did my best to impress on them the humanity of the Spanish nation. Personally I treated them with the utmost kindness. . . . Aside from the thirty-eight sick among them, all the other passengers were in good health." [157]

Then he explained to them his majesty's plan of Acadian colonization in Louisiana. The king had graciously sent instructions to his ministers in Louisiana to help the Acadians in all things until they could support themselves. But ultimately he expected them to repay him for his investment. Navarro then told them why he was personally delivering the "solde," that is, their pay. First, it was to avoid cheating; and second, it was to give him an exact knowledge of the cost of their support, excluding such extraordinary expenses as their transportation from France and those due to sickness.[158]

Next Navarro showed them some of the difficulties he had had in issuing correct orders for their monthly rations to Pedro Aragon y Villegas, commissioner for Acadians in New Orleans. He pointed out the confusion many Acadians of the other expeditions had created in going to the hospital without permission of the commissioner. Such conduct also led to financial confusion, since the commissioner, not wishing to slight or hurt anyone, was awarding to all members of the expeditions the usual rations. But Juan Ventura Morales, the royal treasurer, was alarmed at the rise of expenses and had written him a letter of complaint. Navarro told the Acadians that he was depending on the co-operation of each one, and he assured them of his gratitude for their good will.[159]

The leaders of the expedition *La Villa de Arcangel* thanked Navarro graciously for his welcome and instructions. They told him that the expedition was unanimous in its belief that "at long last" it had found "its day of peace and prosperity." They promised him as chiefs of the expedition faithfully to fulfill to the best of their ability all matters he had outlined in his speech. They assured him that everyone was eager to begin the work of colonization as soon as he would permit possession of the land their surveyors had chosen.[160]

After that exchange of speeches and courtesies, Navarro ordered Aragon y Villegas to lead the expedition to its quarters in the Acadian village camp. He placed the thirty-eight sick ones not in the royal hospital of the city but in the "Community House," which he had specially built for the sick of the *St. Remy* expedition. As noted before, he kept this hospital strictly independent of the city hospital, since he could not wean the Acadians "from their repugnance for French hospitals." [161]

While their elected surveyors were inspecting the country between Pointe Coupée and New Orleans, Navarro was looking over the possibilities of increasing the number of families in the *La Villa de Arcangel* expedition. When a couple of Acadians asked him to be godfather for two of their babies,[162] he used the opportunity to arrange some additional marriages.[163] In the meantime the surveyors for this expedition had returned from their reconnaissance of the banks of the Mississippi River. Two localities appealed to them as excellent: Bayou des Écores and Costa de la Fourche.[164]

Through the exertions of Navarro, the expedition had also grown in membership and number of families. It rose from 50 to 60 families representing 299 members. But it ranked next to the expedition *St. Remy* in its loss of 15 members by death and 2 by desertion, though those losses were partially balanced by its gains of 2 births, 11 new adherents, and 7 marriages.[165]

The expedition *La Villa de Arcangel* recovered its health by December 22, 1785, and lost no time lingering in New Orleans. For the sixth time Navarro issued his usual orders to Juan Prieto to equip the Acadians of this expedition with all necessary axes, hatchets, shovels, hoes, meat cleavers, and knives.[166] On January 17, 1786, Navarro once more hired the launches and services of Francisco Broutin, Andrés Chiloque, and Baptista Anstive and a boat from Santiago Mather and a barge from Luis Demarest, at four dollars a day for the boat and one dollar for the barge.[167] With the assistance of the usual guides and river hands, Navarro completed without any mishap on February 8 the removal of the expedition *La Villa de Arcangel*. He notified the Marqués de Sonora on February 22 that he had established fifty-three families of 271 members at Bayou des Écores,[168] six families of twenty-one members at La Fourche, and one family of seven at New Orleans.[169]

Navarro expected much from the Acadians as colonists. More than once he expressed to José de Gálvez his faith in them. "I can assure you," he wrote, "that after four years these Acadians will be America's most prosperous and sturdiest colonists, because they love their new home, and are determined to give Louisiana in 1786 its best harvest." [170]

All the ships of the first six royal expeditions were frigates. *La Carolina* was a brig. She was the smallest but speediest of the expeditions. She sailed directly from Nantes on October 15, under the care of *St. Remy*'s veteran skipper, Nicolas Baudin, and crossed the Atlantic in sixty-four days. On December 12, Josef Petely reported her arrival at Balize.[171] There she took on a pilot, sailed up the Mississippi in five days, discharged her cargo of trunks and twenty-eight families of eighty persons, and immediately started back to Nantes with a cargo of wood.[172]

The expedition enjoyed good health throughout the entire trip, losing only one member. Accompanying the emigrants was a distinguished passenger and chaplain, the non-Acadian priest, Father Juan León, whose destination was New Orleans.[173]

During the month spent in New Orleans, the expedition *La Carolina* had an increment of three births, five new adherents, and two marriages. Its losses were one death and one desertion.[174]

The good health of the groups of Acadians still encamped in New Orleans and their enthusiasm to begin work immediately pleased Navarro. He thereupon decided to bring to a successful close, and at the earliest date possible, all Acadian expeditions to Louisiana. Early in January he equipped six families of the expedition *La Carolina* ahead of the others, and commissioned Francisco Broutin to remove them conjointly with families of *La Amistad* to Nueva Gálvez.[175] Then, on January 17, he ordered Juan Prieto for the last time to dispense the necessary farm tools to the remaining eighteen families of the *La Carolina* expedition according to the number of able persons in each family.[176] And on the same day he removed these eighteen families of fifty-four members to La Fourche. At the last moment he permitted two other families of five persons to unite with the expedition *La Villa de Arcangel,* which was leaving New Orleans at the same time for Bayou des Écores.[177]

Owing to the influx of the Acadian exiles, the district of Valenzuela, of which La Fourche was the main town, grew by leaps and bounds. Navarro appointed Lieutenant Nicolas Verret on September 20, 1785, with a salary of $400 a year, to help guide the new colonists in their building program.[178] He acquitted himself so well in that duty that on May 8, 1786, Count de Gálvez appointed him commandant of the district of Valenzuela.[179]

By February 8, 1786, Martín Navarro had successfully supervised and completed his part in the project of establishing 1,587 Acadian exiles in villages of their own choice. The Marqués de Sonora complimented him in the name of the king on the excellent work.[180]

Back in France, the French authorities were watching the six royal expeditions with mingled astonishment and chagrin. D'Asprès had organized hastily yet quietly the expedition *La Carolina* with the prospect of securing three hundred more exiles for Louisiana. But as soon as the department of emigration in Paris learned of the Spanish success in establishing the Acadian exiles in Louisiana, it became alarmed and forbade further Acadian departures from France. D'Asprès knew that his work had come to an end. He had hoped to spring the *La Carolina* expedition as a surprise on Aranda. Consequently, when the French government foiled his plan, he was forced to use *La Carolina* as a supplement to the *La Villa de Arcangel* and *La Bergere* expeditions. With her he could ship to New Orleans only sixty-nine Acadians left over from the expedition *La Villa de Arcangel*, sixty-two trunks belonging to passengers of *La Bergere*, and a few last minute volunteers.[181] His disappointment was keen. He had come to love the Acadian exiles, their honesty, gentleness, and sincerity, and he ardently strove to better their lot.

> Within a very few days [he wrote to Aranda] we expect at the ports of La Rochelle and St. Malo some 250 Acadians from Miquelon. They had been removed to that island at the expense of the French court, but they are now returning because they were wasting away there.
>
> I have sufficient information to assure you that all of them want to go to Louisiana. But I also know that the court of France does not wish to grant them that permission. Seventy of them who have arrived with the governor of the island told me that ever since their arrival at La Rochelle, they have been begging that permission from the French court.[182]

With the expedition *La Carolina,* Count de Aranda brought to a close his work of removing 1,596 Acadian exiles from France to Louisiana.[183] As an integral attempt, the Acadian colonization in Louisiana surpassed by many hundreds kindred attempts such as that by the Pilgrim fathers in 1620 and the Massachusetts Bay Company in 1629. Spain and Louisiana share the unique distinction of having staged the world's largest trans-Atlantic colonization project on the North American continent.

CHAPTER ELEVEN

A New Acadia in Louisiana

Aranda had expected at least 1,700 volunteers among the Acadians in France to emigrate to Louisiana. His failure to secure that quota of colonists was one reason for his postponing their removal from December, 1784, to May, 1785.[1] Officially he reported 1,596 as the maximum number of volunteers[2] he had removed to Louisiana at the cost of "305,743 libras tornessas y 8 sueldos," that is, about $61,148.68.[3] But some last minute withdrawals and failure of others to appear reduced his official registration to 1,574 colonists,[4] representing 375 families. The total was further reduced by a loss of 85 through death and of 12 through desertions—a loss, however, partially balanced in the gain of 39 births and 15 immigrants.[5]

Aranda was not only deeply interested in the general project of colonization, but he also personally supervised each one of the seven royal expeditions after D'Asprès had organized them. In January, 1786, he sent a report to the Spanish court:

Consul d'Asprès and I have dispatched the Acadians to Louisiana. We have observed as closely as possible the instructions in your letter of February 19, 1785. And we have notified the governor of Louisiana to make all necessary preparations to facilitate settling each expedition after its arrival.

I have informed the personnel of this embassy of the contents of your letter. I am now preparing in the form of a ledger a very minute account of all facts and expenses. I am also enclosing a general plan, which shows the number of colonists of both sexes, their ages, family names, nicknames, trades, the original contracts and all receipts.[6]

Working from his own reports and from those of D'Asprès, Heredia, José de Gálvez, Count Bernardo de Gálvez, Navarro, and Governor Miró, Aranda summarized the settlements of the Acadians. There are, however, provoking variations in different official reports on the exact number of families and passengers in each expedition, and on the dates of departure from France and of arrival in New Orleans of some expeditions. For instance, in giving the number of passengers on *La Bergere,* D'Asprès stated 273, while Navarro reported 265 arrived. In his chart, Navarro wrote 267, whereas Count de Gálvez informed Governor Miró that the number of passengers on *La Bergere* was 275.[7] On July 20, 1785, the council of the Indies had appointed Estevan Miró as governor of Louisiana.[8] In December of the same year Governor Miró sent Count de Gálvez his record of the Acadian expeditions, families, and passengers that came to New Orleans between July 29, 1785, and December 12, 1785. His record is in sharp conflict with other official reports, except in the total of passenger colonists.[9]

To the official total of 1,596, which Aranda reported as final to His Catholic Majesty, the twenty-eight stowaways must be added. This makes a grand total of 1,624 Acadian colonists Spain transported from France to Louisiana "at the expense of the Spanish King." Sixteen of these stowaways were on the *St. Remy* and twelve on *La Amistad.*[10] When the ships were out on the ocean, the stowaways came out of hiding and demanded support until their arrival at New Orleans. Some were Frenchmen engaged to Acadian girls. Navarro admitted them as Acadians when they married their fiancées.[11]

Messieurs Pellier, Carrier, and Company presented Aranda with a supplementary bill of $480 for eighty-two days of rations and transportation for the sixteen stowaways on the *St. Remy.*[12] Aranda wrote Floridablanca that since it was the duty of the captain to detect all stowaways on his ship before departure, the government should not pay the ship company more than $157.44. That would be the cost of their rations at twelve cents a person as agreed upon in the contract.[13] And for the twelve stowaways on *La Amistad,* he advised that the government should pay Martineau and Brothers of La Rochelle at the same rate, that is, $118.[14] As he had already sent the financial statement to the king, and as he did not wish to disturb him any more, Aranda suggested to Floridablanca the recording of this extra expense of $275.44 under the heading of extraordinary expenses.[15] Adding those extraordinary expenses to the general expense, Aranda closed his books on the removal of 1,624 colonists at $61,424.12. Peyroux had realized his dream—"the removal of the Acadians from France to Louisiana at the expense of the King of Spain."[16]

Aranda presented his financial statement to Charles III with a preface. "It is to be noted," he wrote, "that our office has suspended the pay to the Acadians from the end of December, 1784, to the day of their departure. So also have we stopped other subsidies to them. All those savings the Acadians have offered in partial payment of their voyage. Their decision to do so, is due to the business attitude of our department. We have also kept an itemized account of our financial report. As a result of our economy, the removal and support of each passenger from France to New Orleans averages $30." [17]

Charles III expressed complete satisfaction in Aranda's financial report. He even praised the ambassador's efficiency in directing the seven royal expeditions and thanked him for his devotion to the royal service. He thereupon ordered the Marqués de Sonora to notify the royal treasury of his personal approval of Aranda's financial report and thereby excused him from any further investigation by its auditor.[18]

His Catholic Majesty also praised the efficient and loyal services of Manuel d'Asprès and his vice-consul, Luís Landaluze.[19] Of D'Asprès' activity, intelligence, and zeal, Aranda had often informed the king. There was no doubt that D'Après had executed his duty fully and excellently in spite of contradictions, and that he had watched carefully to save His Majesty any unnecessary expenses in the removal of the Acadians and in other related transactions.[20] "In all justice," Aranda reported, "I must recommend him highly"; and he suggested as a reward "the small cross of Charles III." [21] But His Majesty was not open to that hint and replied that "for the present the king has ordered a pecuniary reward." [22] He awarded D'Après faithful aide, Luís Landaluze, first $400 and then on July 2, 1786, the responsibility of making Nantes a terminus for Louisiana's foreign trade with France.[23]

But D'Après was anxious that His Majesty should also reward his other assistants, Gaspar Lannux of Morlaix, Don Juan Quesnel, and Tomás de Laire of La Rochelle. "Without their help," he explained to Aranda, "I would not have been able to execute all my duties in the various ports where the Acadians were living." [24] But by September 1, 1789, D'Après was still petitioning the Spanish court for a small distinction for each of his tireless co-workers. All that he asked was the rank of reviewing officer in the Spanish navy, "comisario de guerra de la marine," for their devoted and efficient services. But D'Après' pleas went unnoticed.[25]

And what of Peyroux's ambition? Did Charles III appreciate his plan and services? Did he honor and reward him? In March of 1784, Peyroux had written to Heredia, "If Spain intends to give me a reward, I beg you to obtain for me a commission of captain, and the command of one of the new Acadian posts that she will establish in Louisiana. In case his majesty will not give me that honor, I will always receive with gratitude whatever gratuities he should see fit to grant me." [26]

Spain rewarded Peyroux with two dollars a day from August, 1784, to May, 1785, for his services, besides compensating him with $292 for traveling expenses.[27] On the day of departure of the expedition *Le Beaumont,* she also honored him by putting him in charge of the Acadians on that transport and by allowing his wife, niece, and a friend, LeCat, to accompany him.[28]

Earlier, José de Gálvez had approved Peyroux's petition for a military and a political position in keeping with his ability and services.[29] Then in June, 1785, Bernardo de Gálvez wrote from Mexico City to the intendant of Louisiana, Martín Navarro, suggesting his appointment to such a military or political post as his merits, activities, prudence, and the advantage of circumstances in Louisiana might permit.[30]

Upon his arrival in New Orleans, however, Peyroux pleaded with Navarro for two rewards he thought were due to him—a military promotion and the position of commandant of the Acadian colony at Baton Rouge. It was there that the 145 Acadians of the expedition *Le Beaumont,* which he had commanded, settled. Navarro immediately inquired of Count de Gálvez what he should do in regard to Peyroux's demands. Gálvez authorized Governor Miró of Louisiana to honor Peyroux with the rank of captain in the royal army of Spain and of commandant of the non-Acadian post of St. Genevieve with an annual income of $600. That honor implied several minor duties, chief among which were the preservation of peace among the Indians and supervision of land grants in his area.[31]

Aranda gave no credit to Oliver Terrio, the Acadian shoemaker of Nantes. Yet to him, more than to anyone else, is due the credit for having animated the Acadians. For two years he neglected his shoeshop. His family suffered much from poverty, for he had gone bankrupt and could not meet his debts in order to leave France. His friends had to help him to migrate to Louisiana. His efforts were truly tireless, and without his unselfish devotion to the cause neither Peyroux nor D'Asprès would have registered 1,596 volunteers for Louisiana. In 1792 Terrio took Peyroux to court for having failed to keep his solemn promise of mutual assistance, "of sharing his last piece of bread with him."[32]

After the Acadian expeditions arrived in Louisiana Spain began spending large sums of money in rehabilitating her new colonists. She had given generously to their relief in New Orleans; had built a village camp and good hospitals for them; had equipped them with farm tools; had once more paid their transportation to the river settlements, and continued subsidizing them up to 1789.[33] Between August and December of 1785 alone, she had expended a total of $40,000 in aid to the impoverished Acadians.[34]

Shortly after the Acadians had begun work on their new farms, a grave problem arose. They could not feed and clothe their children on the allowance of two and a half cents a day. They realized that Spain had done much for them and generously so. True, some were sharp in their criticisms, but the majority were enduring bitter privations rather than grumble about their sufferings to Martín Navarro. But on a visit to one of their settlements, the beloved godfather of Acadian children quickly saw the needs of his godchildren, and opened a way for their parents to present their petition without embarrassment. He presented their needs with a favorable recommendation to Count de Gálvez. Having won the consent of his superior, he granted every Acadian, irrespective of age or sex, seven and a half cents. That arrangement was also better for him. It simplified bookkeeping and eliminated all confusion that might arise in granting one sum for adults and another for children.[35] The Acadians had come to regard Navarro as "un santo."

Navarro had told the Acadians on their arival that he wished them to realize the humanity of the Spanish people. Subsequent relief to these poor exiles in the form of merchandise, medical supplies, construction of homes, and financial aid bore out his words. Early in 1786 he instructed every commandant of the respective villages of Nueva Gálvez, Cabahannocer, Bayou de la Fourche, Costa de Manchac, Baton Rouge, Bayou des Écores, Atacapas, and Opelousas to settle the Acadians "with the greatest possible speed, attention to their needs, and also their usefulness to the province," and of course to notify him. In doing this, Spain spent an additional $2,062.90.[36]

Even the inhabitants of Arkansas appreciated the worth of the Acadians as farmers and colonists. Through their agent, Jacobo Dubreuil, they petitioned Navarro on October 28, 1785, to consider their village of Carlos Tercero de Arkansas as a suitable location for an Acadian colony. Navarro promised to consider their petition favorably,[37] but by April he was succeeded as intendant by Juan Ventura Morales, and consequently could not act on their request.[38]

On September 6, 1785, Navarro had written to Count de Gálvez: "I have received your letter of June 24, in which you have enclosed the Royal Order of February 4, pertaining to the settlement of the Acadians in Louisiana. I will accomplish it and I will inform you of all my success in this matter."[39] He was faithful to his promise. His chart of June 15, 1786, with an appended note, to be transmitted through the count to Charles III, was his last act in regard to Acadian settlements in Louisiana. "My dear Sir: Enclosed you will find a record of the number of Acadian families that have left France during the past year to settle Louisiana. This record tells of those born, died, aggregated, deserted, expelled, parishes of destination, and of total persons landed until the end of May. You will kindly give the record your attention."[40] With these few lines Navarro wrote the end to the Acadian odyssey. On August 6, 1786, Sonora replied in the name of Charles III of Spain, "The king knows of the number of individuals and Acadian families that have arrived on the seven expeditions to settle in Louisiana. He is happy to learn that they are all settled in the most advantageous places in the colony."[41]

In the meantime, Miró also, as governor of Louisiana, sent his official report of the end of the Acadian odyssey to Count de Gálvez in Mexico. "I am happy to inform you," the governor stated, "that with the exception of a small number of families that went to Atacapas and some other twelve that located themselves at Neuva Gálvez under Marigny, we have settled the majority of the Acadians at the posts of Valenzuela, Costa de Manchac, Baton Rouge, and Bayou des Écores, called by the English Thompson's Creek. The enthusiasm, industry, and loyalty of these new colonists will boost the prosperity of our province and increase its local and foreign trade."[42]

Through the humanity of the Spanish nation, the Acadians at last found a home, arable lands, and a new Acadia in Louisiana.[43] There, their descendants today enjoy the right to live in peace and freedom, possess the fruits of their labors, and worship God as did their ancestors in old Acadia.

The seven expeditions formed but half of Acadian immigration to the state of Louisiana. For these Acadians and those other three or four thousand who, between 1755 and 1776, filtered from the American colonies and the West Indies into Louisiana, the cruel expulsions of 1755 were gone with the clouds of the Seven Years' War. So also were their homes and farms in old Acadia gone. But their love of country and religion remained, and because of that love all Acadians suffered a bitter exile, indescribable poverty, sickness, anguish of soul, separations, and the death of cherished ones by the thousands.[44] That same love for country and religion distinguishes the Acadians of Louisiana today— that love which in the days of adversity strengthened them to sacrifice everything dear to life they have merely transferred to their beloved state of Louisiana. Today it shines forth gloriously in their spendid contributions politically, religiously, and economically.[45]

In service of country, church, and state many Acadians of

Louisiana occupied and still do occupy exalted positions. Louisiana points with pride to Joseph Breaux, once chief justice of the state Supreme Court, and to Archbishop Anthony Blanc, once spiritual head of the Archdiocese of New Orleans, and today to Bishop Jules Jeanmard, to Congressman Edward Hébert, and many others.

Economically, the Acadians of Louisiana have also made their noteworthy contributions. To them Louisiana owes its special breed of ponies, its nationally famous perique tobacco, and its delectable pralines. Indeed the Acadians of Louisiana hold a respectable place in America's laboring and agricultural classes.

Socially the Acadians of Louisiana still preserve the beautiful yet simple manners, customs, and languages of old Acadia. One has but to visit their neat settlements in St. Martinville, Lafourche, St. Landry, Iberville, and others that stretch along the bayous of south Louisiana to appreciate the beauty and simplicity of their present life. From these communities have come a host of American priests, educators, soldiers, merchants, and professional men and women.

To the Acadians of the seven expeditions, France could offer only "the most sterile lands" in gratitude for unique patriotism. However, as an example does not die with the passing of the producer but continues to live on in the minds and hearts of men, so their patriotism continues to live after them as one of the noblest examples in history of unswerving loyalty to God and country. The state of Louisiana can point with pride to the Acadians of the seven expeditions and to their brother exiles who have given and continue to give so vitally to her political, religious, and economic prestige in the American Union.

NOTES

The following abbreviations are used in the footnotes of this work to indicate archival locations:

A. A. É. Archives du Ministère des Affaires Étrangères (Paris)

A. D. V. Archives Départementales de la Vienne (Poitiers)

A. G. I. Archivo General de Indias (Seville)

A. H. N. Archivo Historico Nacional (Madrid)

A. M. Archives Morbihan (Vannes)

A. M. C. Archives du Ministère des Colonies (Paris)

A. N. Archives Nationales (Paris)

A. S. V. Archivo Segreto Vaticano (Vatican City)

B. A. R. Biblioteca de Palacio Antigua Real (Madrid)

B. M. Mss. British Museum, Manuscript Department (London)

B. N. Mss. Bibliothèque Nationale, Manuscript Department (Paris)

N.S.A. Nova Scotia Archives (Halifax)

P. A. C. Public Archives of Canada (Ottawa)

INTRODUCTION

1. There are no exact statistics as to the number of Acadians in Nova Scotia and surrounding islands in 1755. It may have been between 18,000 and 22,000, but the smaller figure probably is more accurate.
2. Colonies, Serie B, CXVII, f. 405, A. N. On September 2, 1763, Étienne François, duc de Choiseul wrote to the intendant of Chanteloup, "There are in the various maritime ports of France between 3,000 and 4,000 Acadians."
3. Correspondance politique, Angleterre, February, 1763, CDXLIX, f. 343. A. A. É.
4. Colonies, Serie B, CXVII, f. 405, A. N.
5. *Ibid.*, f. 117. Wrote Choiseul: "Since it is important that we do not lose these 4,000 persons, and above all that they do not benefit the English, I beg you to study how we can make the best use of them either for their culture or for their skills."
6. "Bruyère blanche," that is, heath or heather; "la brande" is similar to "la bruyère blanche" but more difficult to root out and exterminate.

CHAPTER ONE

1. Throughout this work the terms "Acadian nation" and "Acadian people" will be used, since the Acadians considered themselves a slightly different people from the French nation. Neither term will imply the meaning of the modern national state. Both are used in the medieval sense of a family, though in France the feeling was that socially the Acadians were a degree lower than the native born French.

2. Charles Gayarré, *History of Louisiana* (New York, 1854-66), II, 117-23; George Bancroft, *History of the United States of America, from the discovery of the Continent* (New York, 1883), II, 434.

3. Émile Lauvrière, *La tragédie d'un peuple, histoire du peuple Acadien de ses origines à nos jours* (Paris, 1922), I, 3.

4. Justin Winsor (ed.), *Narrative and Critical History of America* (Boston, 1884), IV, 1-46. See William I. Morse, *Acadiensia Nova, 1598-1778, new and unpublished documents and other data relating to Acadia* (London, 1935), II, early maps.

5. Marc Lescarbot, *Nova Francia, a Description of Acadia,* (1606), tr. P. Erondelle (Paris, 1609), 1.

6. Arthur George Doughty, *The Acadian Exiles,* X, in George M. Wrong and H. H. Langton (eds.) *Chronicles of Canada.* See Morse, *Acadiensia Nova* (1598-1779), II, ch. 6 letter of Delabat describing the rivers Seine and Dauphin: *Public Archives of Canada,* "Nova Scotia," II, 186. Doughty, *Acadian Exiles* gives several Micmac words which imply the fertility of Nova Scotia's soil and from which the French could have derived the name Acadia. Thus Sunakade describes a place where the cranberry abounds; Tracakadie and Passamaquoddy imply fertile fields; and Seguboon-akade (Shuben-acadie) indicates a place where edible roots flourish. Francis Parkman, *Pioneers of France in the New World,* Part I, in *France and England in North America* (Boston 1880), 220, suggests a possible derivation from the Indian names of Aquoddianke or Aquoddie for the fish called a pollack. See Nicolas Denys, *The description and natural History of the Coasts of North America* (Acadia), tr. and ed. William F. Ganong (Toronto, 1908).

7. "Mémoire sur les Acadiens," in *Mèmoires et Documents, Angleterre,* June, 1778, XLVII, f. 18, A. A. É., states that the first colonization began with twenty-five couples. This was probably in the latter half of the sixteenth century.

8. William Lawson Grant (ed. and tr.) *Voyages of Samuel de Champlain,* 1604-1618 (New York, 1907), 34-44, 122-24, 40.

9. Philip H. Smith, *Acadia: A Lost Chapter in American History,* (Pawling, New York), 53-54.

10. Reuben G. Thwaites (ed.), *Jesuit Relations and Allied Documents* (Cleveland, 1896-1901), I, 199 ff. See also II, III, IV, and Samuel Purchas, *His Pilgrims* (New York, 1905), XIX, 181 ff.

11. Curtis P. Nettles, *The Roots of American Civilization; A History of American Colonial life* (New York, 1938), 118-20.

12. Henry Kirke, *The First English Conquest of Canada with some account of the earliest settlements in Nova Scotia and Newfoundland* (London, 1871), 61-67. See *Calendar of State Papers,* Colonial Series (London, 1860-), *America and West Indies,* I (1574-1660), 152 ff., V (1661-68), VII (1669-74).

13. Origines Françaises, Vol. 9281, B. N. Mss.

14. *Collection de Manuscrits contenants lettres, mémoires et autres documents historiques relatifs à la Nouvelle France,* (Quebec, 1883-85), I, 115-24; *ibid.,* II, 335.

15. *Lauvrière, La tragédie d'un peuple,* I, ch. 4; *id., Deux traîtres d'Acadie et leur victime; les Latour père et fils Charles d'Aulnay* (Paris, 1932); John Winthrop, *The History of New England from 1630-1649* (ed.) James Savage (Boston, 1825-26), II, 137-38; Azarie Couillard Després, *Histoire des seigneurs de la Rivière de Sud* (Paris, 1912), 65-78; *id., Observations sur l'histoire de l'Acadie française,* (Montreal, 1919), I, 115-24.

16. John MacGregor, *British America* (London, 1832), II, 193-99. Lescarbot, *Histoire de la Nouvelle France,* IV, V.

17. Thomas C. Haliburton, *An Historical and Statistical Account of Nova Scotia* (Halifax, 1829), I, 171-73. René Gautheron, *Le Patrimonie Acadien.* Nouvelle Écosse (Rennes, 1932), 3, 4.

18. Émile Lauvrière, "Le Peuple Acadien AU XVIIe Siècle," in *Revue Historique Colonies Française XIIe ann.,* (3e trimestre, 1924), 429-44. See John B. Brebner, *New England's Outpost, Acadia before the Conquest,* in Columbia University *Studies in History, Economics, and Public Law,* No. 293 (New York, 1927), 37-56.

19. Mémoire sur les Acadiens, in Correspondance politique Angleterre, 1763, CDXLIX, f. 350, A. A. É.

20. J. Baptiste Jego, *Le Drame du Peuple Acadien; Reconstitution historique en neuf tableaux et une pose plastique de la dispersion des acadiens, d'asprès, "La tragédie d'un peuple," Émile Lauvrière* (Paris, 1932), 116. See Narcisse E. Dionne, *Le parler populaire des Canadiens français, ou Lexique des canadianismes, acadianismes* (Quebec, 1909).

21. James Geddes, *Study of an Acadian-French Dialect* (Halle, 1908), 2. Jay K. Ditchy, *Les Acadiens louisianais et leur parler,* (Paris, 1932), 9.

22. "Négociationes pour la paix," in Correspondance politique Angleterre, 1762, CDXLVIII, ff. 218-20, A. A. É.

23. "Mémoire," in Correspondance politique Angleterre, 1763, XLVII, f. 19, A. A. É.

24. Colonies, 1713-1788, C^{11}D, Acadie, VIII, ff. 270-77, A. N.

25. MacGregor, *British America,* II, 192-93, 199. Jego, *Le Drame du Peuple Acadien,* 113.

26. M. De Ch-t-l-n (1775), tr. from original manuscript in library of L'Hôtel Dieu, Quebec; also quoted in MacGregor, *British America,* 215. Alexandre Barde, *Histoire des Comites de Vigilance Aux Attakapas* (Saint-Jean-Baptiste, 1861).

27. Edmé Rameau de St. Père, *Une Colonie Féodale en Amérique (L'Acadie, 1604-1881),* I, (Paris, 1877), 109-110.

28. William Lawson Grant, *History of Canada* (London, 1919), 86-88.

29. William D. Raymond, *The River St. John, . . .* (St. John, N. B., 1910), 44.

30. Correspondance Générale, C^{11}E, V, ff. 175-85, A. N. See also IV, V, and VI which contain manuscript history of Acadia before 1758.

31. James Hannay, *The History of Acadia from its first discovery to its surrender to England, by the treaty of Paris* (St. John, N. B., 1879), 231-33. Especially *Calendar of State Papers,* Colonial Series, *America and the West Indies,* IX-XL (1675-1733).

32. Rameau de St. Père, *Une Colonie Fèodale en Amérique,* I, 193.

33. Brebner, *New England's Outpost,* 54, 55.

34. Colonel Vetch to Lords of Trade, November 24, 1714, in *Selections from the Public Documents of the Province of Nova Scotia,* ed. Thomas B. Akins (Halifax, 1869), 5.
35. William D. Williamson, *The History of the State of Maine* (Hallowell, 1839), II, 294.
36. "Amérique du Nord, Acadie," Colonies, 1751, IV, A. N. "Memorial presented by His Majesty's Commissioners to the Commissioners of His Most Christian Majesty in answer to their Memorial of the 4th of October, 1751, concerning Nova Scotia or Acadie," (Paris, 1753), in Colonies V, 1-267.
37. Williamson, *The History of the State of Maine,* II, 294.
38. Governor W. Shirley's letter to Sir Thomas Robinson, Boston, May 23, 1754, in Nova Scotia Documents, 382.
39. "Papers relating to Nova Scotia, 1710-1757," in Dr. Andrew Brown's Collection, Add.19072, No. 32, causes of the war 1755-1756, B. M. Mss.
40. Shirley to Robinson, November 11, 1754, in Nova Scotia Documents, 382, 387.
41. Catherine Read Williams, *The Neutral French;* or *The Exiles of Nova Scotia* (Providence, 1841), 23, 40. See Hannay, *History of Acadia,* 262.
42. Haliburton, *Historical and Statistical Account,* I, 150-56, 173, 196.
43. Correspondance Générale, Serie ¹¹E, VI, ff. 186-260, A. N.
44. George M. Wrong, *The Conquest of New France; A Chronicle of the Colonial Wars,* X, in Allen Johnson (ed.) *The Chronicles of America* (New Haven, 1921), 147-48. John Fiske, *New France and New England* (Boston, 1902).
45. John D. Hicks, *The Federal Union, A History of the United States to 1865* (Boston, 1937), 103.
46. George Louis Beer, *The Old Colonial System,* 1660-1754, Pt. I (New York, 1912), 14-17.
47. Shirley to Lawrence, December 14, 1754, in Nova Scotia Documents, 389.
48. Édouard Richard, *Acadia; missing links of a lost chapter in American history by an Acadian* (New York, 1895), II, 348.
49. Nova Scotia Documents, 19, 31, 34, 43, 51, 101 give opinions of different governors of Nova Scotia. Up to the time of Lawrence, every governor intimated expulsion as the surest solution but ultimately yielded to compromise. See "Papers relating to Nova Scotia," in Brown Collection, Add. 19072, f. 30. Brebner, *New England's Outpost,* 190-92. Arthur W. H. Eaton, *The History of King's County, Nova Scotia, heart of the Acadian land, giving a sketch of the French and their expulsion; and a history of the New England planters, who came in their stead, with many genealogies,* 1604-1910 (Salem, Mass., 1910), 49-57.
50. Joly de Fleury, "Mémoire sur les Acadiens," 1722, I, in Commerce et Colonies, f. 187, B. N. Mss.
51. William D. Raymond, "Nova Scotia under English Rule," in *Proceedings and Transactions of the Royal Society of Canada,* 1910, 3d ser., IV (1911), 57.
52. C. E. Lart, "Notes on the Fate of the Acadians," in *Canadian Historical Review* (March, 1924), V, 108-17.
53. Placide Gaudet (ed.) *Annual Report on Canadian Archives* II (Ottawa, 1905), App. 3, p.6.
54. Hannay, *History of Acadia,* 303-304.

55. Doughty, *Acadian Exiles,* 104; Winsor (ed.), *Narrative and Critical History,* V, ch. 7.
56. Nova Scotia Documents, 247-55, 267-68, 278.
57. "Papers Relating to Nova Scotia," in Brown Collection, Add. 19075, f. 121, B. M. Mss. Nova Scotia Documents, 253, 259. Doughty, *Acadian Exiles,* 106.
58. *Nova Scotia,* B., I, 177, P. A. C. Nova Scotia Documents, 263.
59. Joly de Fleury, "Mémoire sur les Acadiens," in Commerce et Colonies, 1772, I, f. 187, B. N. Mss. Nova Scotia Documents, 233.
60. Doughty, *Acadian Exiles,* 108-12. Nova Scotia Documents, 247-56.
61. "Papers Relating to Nova Scotia," Letter 31 (1755), in Brown Collection, Add. 19072, B. M. Mss. Nova Scotia Documents, 278. This startling increase in population came about mainly as a result of large families, since migration to Acadia was negligible during this period. Families of eight, twelve, fifteen, or eighteen members were quite common. See "Proposed Capture of Nova Scotia by the Americans; treaty with the Indians; attitude and sufferings of the Acadians," (containing the report of Colonel John Allan), in *American Catholic Historical Research,* VII (October, 1911), 375-80.
62. Nova Scotia Documents, 249-50, 259, 270.
63. "Papers Relating to Nova Scotia," in Brown Collection, Add. 19073, ff. 42, 43, B. M. Mss. Nova Scotia Documents, 278.
64. "Papers Relating to Nova Scotia," in Brown Collection, Add. 19073, f. 64, B. M. Mss.
65. L. U. Fontaine, *Cent trente-cinq ans après ou la renaissance Acadienne* (Montreal, 1890), 32.
66. Herbert E. Bolton and Thomas M. Marshall, *The Colonization of North America* (New York, 1934), 81 ff.
67. "Amérique du Nord. Acadie, Règlement des Limites," in Colonies, C¹¹E, 1751, IV. "Memorial presented by His Majesty's commissioners in Acadie," V, 1-267, A. N.
68. Williamson, *The History of the State of Maine,* II, 291-94.
69. Winsor (ed.), *Narrative and Critical History,* IV, 135; V, 6, 150. *Ibid.,* "Maps and Bounds of Acadia," 472-82.
70. R. G. Thwaites, *France in America 1497-1763* (New York, 1905), Vol. VII, in *The American Nation Series,* 186.
71. Origines Françaises, Vol. 9281, f. 216, B. N. Mss.
72. Richard Hildreth, *History of the United States of America, . . .* (New York, 1849), II, 458.
73. "Notes sur l'Acadie et l'île Royale," in Origines Françaises, Vol. 9281, f. 1-134, B. N. Mss.
74. Collection de Manuscrits (Quebec, 1884), II, 40, B. N. Mss.
75. *Census of Canada,* IV, (1876), "Introduction."
76. Beamis Murdoch, *A History of Nova Scotia or Acadie* (Halifax, 1865-67), I, 337. See Azarie Couillard Després, *En marge de la tragédie d'un peuple de M. Émile Lauvrière; ou Erreurs sur l'histoire de l'Acadie refutées* (Bruges, 1925).
77. Shirley to Robinson, November 11, 1754, in Nova Scotia Documents, 387; Jeremy Belknap, *The History of New Hampshire, Comprehending the Events of One Complete Century from the Discovery of the River Pascataqua* (Boston, 1791-92), II, 225-316.
78. "Papers Relating to Nova Scotia," in Brown Collection, Add. 19073, f. 66, B. M. Mss.

79. Nova Scotia Documents, 5, 265. Vetch estimated the Acadian population in 1714 as 500 families, or 2,500 souls; George Patterson, "Honorable Samuel Vetch, First English Governor of Nova Scotia," in *Nova Scotia Historical Society Collections*, IV, (1885), 22 ff.

80. *Census of Canada*, IV, (1876); Rameau de St. Père, *Une Colonie Féodale en Amérique*, I, 357, accepted 16,000 as the population. Williams, *Neutral French*, 53, thought 18,000 more correct.

81. Winsor (ed.), *Narrative and Critical History*, V, 455.

82. Bancroft, *History of the United States*, II, 429-30.

83. Nova Scotia Documents, 256.

84. Bancroft, *History of the United States*, II, 434. Also Abijah Willard, "An Unwritten Chapter of Evangeline," in *Magazine of History*, IX (January, 1909), 10-12.

85. "John Winslow's Journal," in *Nova Scotia Historical Society Collections*, III (1879), 178. "He packed 1,100 exiles into four transports."

86. "Papers Relating to Nova Scotia," in Brown Collection, Add. 19071, B. M. Mss. On July 1, 1791, Brook Watson, one of the British officers supervising the expulsions in 1755, wrote from London to Dr. Andrew Brown of Halifax that 1,300 had perished in crossing the Atlantic Ocean.

87. MacGregor, *British America*, II, 197. W. I. Morse, *Gravestones of Acadie, and other essays on local history, genealogy and parish records of Annapolis county, Nova Scotia* (London, 1929).

88. Thomas Hutchinson, *History of the Colony and Province of Massachusetts Bay*, ed., John Hutchinson (Cambridge, 1936), III, 29-31.

89. Bancroft, *History of the United States*, II, 433.

90. Henri Raymond Casgrain, *Un Pèlerinage au Pays d'Évangéline* (3d ed., Paris, 1889), 154. See also Haliburton, *An Historical and Statistical Account*, 196, who writes, "Their expulsion was necessary."

91. Nova Scotia Documents, 297. Rameau de St. Père, *Une Colonie Féodale en Amérique*, I, 357.

92. Doughty, *Acadian Exiles*, 150, 160. W. I. Morse, *The Land of the New Adventure (the Georgian era in Nova Scotia)* (London, 1932), 147.

93. Raymond, *River St. John*, 119-122, 124, 126, 142.

94. "Acadian Genealogy and Notes," in *Annual Report on Canadian Archives* (Ottawa, 1873), II, (1905), pt. 3, App. A. XV, (ed. Placide Gaudet, Leon Ville, *En Acadie, Martyre d'un Peuple* (Paris, 1927), ch. 7.

95. *Canada Statistics* (Ottawa, 1941). Charles Douglas Roberts, "Echoes from Old Acadia," in *Canadian Leaves*, ed., G. M. Fairchild (New York, 1887), 145-73.

96. "Mémoire de M. de la Rochette au duc de Nivernois," in Correspondance politique Angleterre, 1762, CDXLVIII, ff. 216-18, A. A. É.

97. Casgrain, *Un Pèlerinage*, 154. Haliburton, *An Historical and Statistical Account*, 182, estimates 7,000 in the first dispersal; Rameau de St. Père, *Une Colonie Féodale*, I, 357, not more than 6,000; and Richard, *Acadia*, II, 125, between 6,500 and 7,500.

98. "Mémoire," in Mémoires et Documents Angleterre, June, 1778, XLVII, f. 22, A. A. É. Lauvrière, *La Tragédie d'un Peuple*, II, 101. The figures here given are an approximation, as no records have been found giving the exact number of deportees to the American colonies. Of great interest is Pascal Poirier, "Des Acadiens déportés à Boston en 1775," in *Proceedings and Transactions of the Royal Society of Canada*, 1908, II, 3d., ser., (1909), 132. The first load

of exiles came to Boston on the *Seaflower*. Boston reluctantly admitted them.

99. Correspondance politique Angleterre, 1763, DLI, ff. 123, 208, A. A. É.

100. So described by New York Legislature, July 6, 1756.

101. Richard, *Acadia*, II, 340.

102. The first shipload of 300 exiled Acadians came on November 19, 1755. On December 8, 1755, came the ships *Hannah*, with 135; *Swan*, with 161; and *Three Friends*, with 156 from Grand Pré and Piziquid. Those surviving the epidemic of smallpox settled on Pine Street in cabins called Neutral Huts. See Placide Gaudet, "Un épisode de l'expulsion des Acadiens," in *Bulletin des Recherches Historiques*, (Paris, February, 1908); William Reed, "The Acadian Exiles or French Neutrals in Pennsylvania," in *Historical Society of Pennsylvania Memoires*, VI (1858), 283-316; also "Mémoire," in Correspondance politique Angleterre, 1763, CDXLIX, f. 344. A. A. É.

103. Felix Voorhies, *"Acadian Reminiscences," with the true story of Evangeline* (Boston, 1907). "Mémoire," in Correspondance politique Angleterre, 1763, CDXLVIII, f. 219, A. A. É. A party of 200, headed by René Le Blanc camped for three years on the estate of Charles Smith and Henry Brent.

104. "Mémoire," in Correspondance politique Angleterre, 1763, CDXLIX, f. 344, A. A. É. Nova Scotia Documents, 280. The South Carolinians, anxious to rid themselves of the exiles, gave them two old, leaky boats and sent them back to Acadia. Stranded near Hampton, Virginia, the Irish colony there took them for pirates and forced them to buy an unseaworthy vessel "for 400 pieces of eight." When the magistrate of Hampton learned of this, he sent a boat to rescue them and punished the citizens.

105. William B. Stevens, *A History of Georgia* . . . (New York, 1847), I, 413-17. Governor Reynolds gave them permission to leave Savannah. The weary exiles built small tubs and sailed for Acadia. At Long Island many were arrested and their children apprenticed to merchants and farmers. See also Collegione Nunziatura di Fiandra, (Bruxelles), November 22, 1763, Leg. 135, f. 208, A. S. V. Timothy Shay Arthur, *The History of Georgia, from its earliest settlement to the present time* (Philadelphia, 1852).

106. Lauvrière, *La tragédie d'un peuple*, II, 112.

107. Doughty, *Acadian Exiles*, 154-55.

108. Bancroft, *History of the United States*, II, 434.

109. Rameau de St. Père, *Une Colonie Féodale*, II (Paris, 1889), 342.

110. Émile Dubois, *Chez nos frères les Acadiens* (Montreal, 1920), 121-22. Raymond, *The River St. John*, 126-27.

111. Henry W. Longfellow, *Evangeline* (Boston, 1896), 8, 80, 81. See *Acadiensis* (St. John, N. B., 1901——), Vols I-VIII; Berton E. Robinson, "Grand Pré of the Acadians," in *Canadian Geographical Journal*, XI, (August, 1935), 77-84. John Frederic Herbin, *The History of Grand Pré* (4th ed.) *the home of Longfellow's "Evangeline," by the only descendant of the exiled people now living in the Grand-Pré of the Acadians* (St. John, N. B., 1911).

112. "Memoire," in Correspondance politique Angleterre, 1763, CDXLIX, ff. 343, 443-53, A. A. É.; *ibid.*, CDXLVIII, f. 219.

113. "Papers Relating to Nova Scotia," Letter of Brook Watson, dated London, July 1, 1791, in Brown Collection, Add. 19071, B. M. Mss. Those who landed at Southampton were a different group from the 1,500 whom the Virginians had rejected. Possibly Watson referred to the losses of the *Violet* and the *Duke William* in his figure of 1,300 lost in mid-Atlantic.

CHAPTER TWO

1. The Archives du Ministère des affaires Étrangères provided the greater part of the material in this chapter and in Chapter Three.

2. Wolfgang Michael, "Great Britain, 1759-63," in *Cambridge Modern History,* (New York, 1909), VI, 393-478. See Francis Parkman, *Half Century of Conflict,* in *France and England in North America,* Pt. VI (Boston, 1891-1903); *ibid., Montcalm and Wolf,* Pt. VII (Boston, 1910); *id., The Old Regime in Canada* (Boston, 1902).

3. Joly de Fleury, Commerce et Colonies, vol. 1772, ff. 190-91, B. N. Mss. Chart shows all the Acadian families that arrived in France between 1758 and 1763 as 679 families of 2,542 members. See also "Families Acadiens," Correspondance politique Angleterre, 1763, XLVII, f. 15, A. A. É. Choiseul placed the number of Acadians in France between 3,000 and 4,000 persons. Colonies, Serie B, CXVII, f. 405, A. N.

4. "Mémoire sur les Acadiens," Correspondance politique Angleterre, 1763, CDXLIX, f. 353, A. A. É. placed the number in American colonies approximately at 10,000.

5. "Mémoire du duc de Nivernois," in Colonies, C^{11}D, VIII, f. 252, A. N. Some Acadians left for Santo Domingo and Martinique.

6. Rameau de St. Père, *Une Colonie Féodale,* II, 216, Lauvrière, "L'Acadie et l'Amérique latine," in *Revue Amérique Latine,* VII (March-April, 1924), 193-202, 316-27.

7. The writer spent several years in British Honduras. While there he came upon the graves of scores of Acadians who had once sought refuge on the shores between Monkey River and Point Diable. Also Basil Sollers, "Party of Acadians who sailed from the Potomac, bound for the Mississippi," in *Maryland Historical Magazine,* IV (September, 1909), 279-81.

8. Ignacio Heredia to Conde de Floridablanca, Paris, February 21, 1784, in Estado-Legajo, 3885 (13), Carta 6, A. H. N.

9. "Mémoire," Correspondance politique Angleterre, CDXLIX, f. 343-48, A. A. É.

10. *Ibid.,* 345.

11. "Mémoire," in Correspondance politique Angleterre, 1763, CDXLIX, f. 345, A. A. É.

12. *Ibid.,* f. 343.

13. *Ibid.,* f. 353.

14. *Ibid.,* f. 346. This manuscript speaks of six sols to adults, three sols to children, and five "chelin" for lodgment.

15. "Mémoire," Mémoires et documents Angleterre, June, 1778, XLVII, f. 22, A. A. É.

16. "Négociations pour la paix," in Correspondance politique Angleterre, 1762, Versailles, September 2, 1762, CDXLVII, f. 13, A. A. É.

17. *Ibid.,* f. 13, A. A. É.; see also "Mémoire sur les Acadiens," in Mémoires et Documents Angleterre June, 1778, XLVII, f. 22, A. A. É.

18. "Mémoire," in Correspondance politique Angleterre, 1763, London, February, 1763, CDXLIX, f. 347, A. A. É.

19. *Ibid.,* f. 347.

20. *Ibid.,* ff. 343, 344.

21. *Ibid.,* f. 344; Mémoires et Documents Angleterre, June, 1778, XLVII, f. 22.

22. Mémoires et Documents Angleterre, June, 1778, f. 22.

23. Réfugiés, "Mémoire du duc de Nivernois," in Colonies, Acadie C¹¹D, VIII, f. 245, A. N.
24. "Lettre à le duc de Nivernois," in Correspondance politique Angleterre, 1762, Versailles, December 11, 1762, CDXLVIII, f. 267-68, A. A. É.
25. "Letter of de la Rochette to Acadians in England," in Brown Collection Add. 19069, B. M. Mss.; Correspondance politique Angleterre, 1762, CDXL, ff. 208-20, A. A. É.
26. "Mémoire," in Correspondance politique Angleterre, 1763, CDXLIX, f. 344, A. A. É. On November 20, 1762, Nivernois reported the captivity of 300 Acadians in England to the French court, and asserted that the English were using pressure on them to change their religion (f. 68). The duke got a letter from the contrôleur général to work for their liberation. Correspondance politique Angleterre, 1763, CDXLVIII, ff. 68, 267, A. A. É.
27. "Mémoire," ibid., Angleterre, 1763, CDXLIX, f. 345.
28. Mémoires et Documents Angleterre, June, 1778, XLVII, f. 22, A. A. É.
29. "Mémoire," in Correspondance politique Angleterre, 1763, CDXLIX f. 345, A. A. É.
30. "Les négociations pour la paix," in Correspondance politique Angleterre, CDXLIX, ff. 151-55, A. A. É.
31. Ibid., 156; Correspondance politique Angleterre, 1763, CDXLVIII, ff. 151-54.
32. "Mémoire," in Correspondance politique Angleterre, CDXLIX, f. 353, A. A. É.
33. Joly de Fleury, Commerce et Colonies, vol. 1722, ff. 188-91, B. N. Mss.
34. Ibid., ff. 188-90; also "Acadiens en France, 1762-73," in Colonies Serie G, CDLXXXII, CDLXXXIII, and CDLXXXIV, A.M.C. The lost ships Violet and Duke William, and many Acadians from Prince Edward and Cape Breton islands; also Colonies, C¹¹D, VIII f. 252, A. N. One memoir reported the number of Acadians who went over to France after the surrender of Louisbourg in 1763 as 3,500. Of that number some 500 later left France for Santo Domingo, Martinique, and other French islands. Another 400 went to Belle-Ile-en-Mer, but 2,000 still remained in the seaports and were refusing to cross the ocean again because they had been promised good lands and work in France.
35. "Mémoire," in Correspondance politique Angleterre, 1763, London, February 1763, CDXLIX, f. 345, A. A. É.; "A Son Excélence, April 4, 1784, in Correspondance politique Espagne, 1784, DCXII, f. 287, A. A. É.
36. "Mémoire," in Correspondance politique Angleterre, 1763, CDXLIX f. 345.
37. Ibid., f. 346.
38. "Mémoire," in Mémoire et Documents Angleterre, June, 1778, XLVII, f. 22, A. A. É.; Colonies, C¹¹D, VIII, ff. 242-51, A. N.
39. "Mémoire," in Correspondance politique Angleterre, 1763, CDXLIX, f. 346, A. A. É.
40. "Mémoire," in Mémoires et Documents Angleterre, June, 1778, XLVII, f. 23.
41. Ibid.
42. "Mémoire," in Correspondance politique Angleterre, 1763, CDXLIX, f. 347.
43. Ibid.
44. Ibid., ff. 343-45. Of the 340 Acadians who left Virginia for Southampton, forty died from various causes such as old age, malnutrition, unsanitary conditions aboard ship, and grief.
45. Ibid.

46. *Ibid.,* f. 348.
47. "Mémoire" in Mémoire et Documents Angleterre, June, 1778, f. 22, two-hundred-fifty guineas. Twenty-one chelin were in a guinea. A chelin was worth about twenty-four cents.
48. "Mémoire," in Correspondance politique Angleterre, 1763, CDXLIX, f. 348, A. A. É.
49. *Ibid.*
50. *Ibid.,* f. 348; "Mémoire du Duc de Nivernois," in Colonies, C¹¹D, VIII, f. 242 *et seq.,* A. N.
51. "Mémoire," in Correspondance politique Angleterre, 1763, CDXLIX, f. 348, A. A. É.
52. *Ibid.*
53. *Ibid.,* f. 349; "Mémoire," in Colonies, C¹¹D, VIII, f. 243. A. N.
54. "Mémoire," in Correspondance politique Angleterre, 1763, CDXLIX, f. 350, A. A. É.
55. Réfugiés, "Mémoire du duc de Nivernois," in Colonies, Acadie C¹¹D, VIII, f. 245, A. N.: also "Nivernois au Praslin, in Correspondance politique Angleterre, 1763, CDL, ff. 83, 85, A. A. É.

CHAPTER THREE

1. "Nivernois au Praslin," in Correspondance politique Angleterre, 1763, London, March 14, 1763, CDL, f. 84, A. A. É.
2. "Mémoire sur les Acadiens, " in Correspondance politique Angleterre, 1763, London, February 1763, CDXLIX, f. 350, A. A. É.
3. "Mémoire sur les Acadiens," in Mémoires et Documents Angleterre, June, 1778, XLVII, f. 23., A. A. É.
4. "Nivernois au Praslin," in Correspondance politique Angleterre, 1763, CDL, f. 86.
5. *Ibid.,* ff. 83, 85.
6. *Ibid.,* ff. 86-87. Nivernois' figures were given in livres. The livre, an old French coin, was worth approximately 20 cents.
7. *Ibid.,* f. 87.
8. "Mémoire," in Correspondance politique Angleterre, 1763, CDXLIX, ff. 347, 348.
9. "Mémoire," in Mémories et Documents Angleterre, June, 1778, XLVII, f. 23.
10. *Ibid.;* also "Nivernois au Praslin," Correspondance politique Angleterre, 1763, CDL, f. 83.
11. "Mémoire," *ibid.,* CDXLIX, f. 352.
12. "Nivernois au Praslin," *ibid.,* CDL, f. 84.
13. "Papers relating to Nova Scotia," in Brown Collection, Add. 19069 (copia), B. M. Mss.
14. "Mémoire," in Mémoires et Documents Angleterre, June, 1778, XLVII, f. 23.
15. Colonies, Serie B. CXIX, f. 6; and CXX, ff. 47, 48, 85, 110, 113-16, 153, 343, 358, A. N., give a general idea of his schemes.
16. "Choiseul au Nivernois," in Mémoires et Documents Angleterre, Supplement, 1763, XLVII, ff. 11, 12, A. A. É.
17. "Instructions à donner au M. de la Rochette par le duc de Nivernois," in Mémoires et Documents Angleterre, April 18, 1763, XLVII, f. 10, A. A. É

18. "Choiseul au Nivernois," in Mémoires et Documents Angleterre, Supplement, 1763, XLVII, ff. 11-12, stated that 753 Acadians were to be removed. See also Mémoires et Documents Angleterre, 1763-1805, XLVII, ff. 11, 12, A. A. É. Statistics given.

19. "Instructions," in Mémoires et Documents Angleterre," 1763, XLVII ,f. 10.

20. *Ibid*.

21. Mémoires et Documents Angleterre, 1763-1805, XLVII, ff. 11-12, A. A. É. A denier equals a farthing, approximpately 1/12 of a penny; thus 50 livres, 13 sols, 4 deniers. The livre, sol, and denier had a much greater purchasing power in 1763 than they would have today.

22. *Ibid.*, 1763-1805, ff. 11-12, A. A. É.

23. Colonies, Serie B, CXVII, ff. 41-43, 83, 89, 106, 107, 120, 157, 257, 278, 454, A. N.

24. Mémoire et Documents Angleterre, June, 1778, XLVII, f. 23, A. A. É.

25. *Ibid*.

CHAPTER FOUR

1. "Choiseul au Comte de Guerchy," Versailles, November 22, 1763, Correspondance politique Angleterre, 1763, CDLII, f. 203, A. A. É.

2. *Ibid.*, f. 205. All charts are given as they stand in the original. Again, accents, spelling, and form may differ widely from modern usage.

3. Colonies, Serie B, CX, ff. 301-13; also CXVII, f. 117, A. N. The Acadians kept refusing the king's offer of settling in any of the tropical colonies, saying they could not live in hot climates.

4. Colonies, Serie B, CXV, f. 333, A. N.

5. "Mémoire remis au duc de Nivernois," in Colonies, Serie $C^{11}D$, VIII, f. 241; "Mémoire sur les Acadiens," in Correspondance politique Angleterre, 1778, XLVII, f. 242, A. A. É.

6. "Mémoire sur les Acadiens," in Correspondance politique Angleterre, XLVII, f. 252.

7. "Mémoire au duc de Nivernois," Colonies, Serie $C^{11}D$, VIII f. 252, A. N.; also Colonies, Serie B, CXVII, f. 405. A. N.; Richard, *Acadia*, II, 338, claimed that a total of 4,500 had entered France. See also Lauvrière, *La Tragédie d'un Peuple*, II, 162.

8. "Mémoire au duc de Praslin," in Correspondance politique Angleterre, 1763, March 4, 1763, CDL, f. 84, A. A. É.

9. "Mémoire Acadienne au Nivernois" *ibid.*, ff. 415-16. Another report records the letter sent on June 20, 1763. It was signed by Paul Loires, Joseph Bourg, Bruneau, Trahan, and Pierre Landry in the name of all the exiles in Philadelphia. See also "Mémoire," in Correspondance politique Angleterre, 1763, CDLII, f. 332, A. A. É.; and "The Acadians in Pennsylvania," in *American Catholic Historical Research,* VIII, (April, 1911), 108-11.

10. "Mémoire Acadienne au Nivernois," in Correspondance politique Angleterre, 1762, December 2, 1762, CDXLVIII, ff. 218-29, (copia), A. A. É.

11. "Mémoire Acadienne au Nivernois," *ibid.,* 1763, CDL, f. 438, A. A. É.

12. *Ibid.*, ff. 438-46. At Lower Marlborough were the Leroy, Brasseau, Lescun, Launné, L'Clemand, and David (f. 444); at Princess Ann were Saint Germain, Maffier, Elbert, Trahan, Thiar, and Babin families (f. 441); at Newton, the Boudrot, Daigle, Ríchard, Jeandin, Gautrot, and Hébert families (f. 440); at Upper Marlborough, the Babin, Rivette, Landry, Foray,

Broussard, Ríchard, Landré, Castille, Brasseux, and Brausard families (f. 444); at Georgetown and Fredericktown, the Hébert, Grangé, Babín, Le Blanc, and Brasseux families (f. 440); at Snowhill, the David, Déchamp, Forest, Mélanson, Grangér, Lucas, Le Blanc, Douilard, and Tibodot families (f. 441); at Baltimore, the Mellontant, Oling, Doiront, and Blanchard families (f. 446); at Annapolis, the Dufier, Mélanson, Bel'lisle, Manjeant, Cèlestin, Hébert, Sapin, LeBlanc, Braux, Meunier, Chamaux, and Baudit-Gonfant families (f. 443); at Port Tobacco, the Braux, Commost, Babín, Trahan, Gaídres, Satiér, Broussard, Duprés, Ríchard, Benoist, Landry, Cloatre, and Poufard families (f. 442); and at Oxford the Bigeos, Braux, Simones, and Babein families (f. 445). Many of these names were badly spelled.

13. "Mémoire," in Correspondance politique Angleterre, 1763, CDLI, ff. 63-76, 123, A. A. É.

14. *Ibid.,* 206-208.

15. "Mémoire Acadienne au Nivernois," *ibid.,* CDL f. 440.

16. *Ibid.,* f. 441. See also Vol. 451, ff. 62-64, 124-25. The Acadians in South Carolina claimed that the English had taken some of their babies against the will of the parents under the pretext that those infants were in need of wet nurses. Only a royal decree could restore those children to their lawful parents. In the Carolinas were the Landry, Bernard, Babineau, Deraux, Commau, Bourgois, Girouard, Cormier (f. 64), Porier, Bourg, Babín, Hébert, Guillebeau, Bro, and Girouard families (f. 125). Their letter of appeal to Nivernois was signed by Balthazard Come, Marian LeBlanc, and Jacques Hugond, and dated August 13, 1763.

17. *Ibid.,* ff. 123, 124, 438.

18. Stevens, *A History of Georgia,* I, 413-18.

19. "Mémoire Acadienne au Nivernois," in Correspondance politique Angleterre, 1763, CDLI, f. 438.

20. *Ibid.,* CDLI, f. 439.

21. Colonies, Serie B, CXVI, f. 66, A. N. See George Francis Dow, "The French Acadians in Topsfield and Their Life in Exile," in *Topsfield Historical Society Collection,* XIV (1909), 137-47; *id.,* "The French Acadians in Essex County and Their Life in Exile," in *Essex Institute Historical Collections,* XLV (October, 1909), 293-307; Sara Swan Griffin, "The Acadian Exiles," in *Lowell Historical Society Contributions,* II, No. I, 89-107.

22. Colonies, Serie B, CXVII, ff. 454, 471, 472, 477.

23. "Choiseul au Guerchy," in Correspondance politique Angleterre, 1763, CDLII, ff. 203-204. Choiseul expressed to Guerchy deep satisfaction with La Rochette's devotion to France. His efficiency in executing the tasks the Duke of Nivernois had entrusted to him and his tireless efforts to reassemble the Acadian exiles in France deserved a reward, and Choiseul asked the ambassador to suggest an appropriate remuneration for such services.

24. "Guerchy au Choiseul," in Correspondance politique Angleterre, 1763, CDLII, ff. 322-23, A. A. É.

25. Wilmot to Halifax, January 28, 1764, in Nova Scotia Documents, 341.

26. Halifax to Wilmot, June 9, 1764, in Nova Scotia Documents, 348. See also Montague Wilmot, "Proclamation aux Acadiens de M. Wilmot, Gouveneur de la Nouvelle-Écosse," in *Revue Historique Colonies Françaises,* XVI, November, 1928, ff. 703-704. Halifax emphasized to Wilmot that it was England's policy to treat the French Acadians like other English Catholic subjects in

America. If the exiles were willing to take the oath of allegiance they would have the right to settle any place in the English empire, which was agreeable to themselves and at the same time consistent with public peace and national security.

27. "Papers Relating to Nova Scotia, 1749-1790," in Brown Collection, Add. 19073, f. 69, B. M. Mss.

28. Nova Scotia Documents, 352.

29. "Papers Relating to Nova Scotia" (An enumeration of the Acadian families resident in Nova Scotia given unto the Secretary's office, 1771), in Brown Collection, Add. 19071, ff. 125-26, B. M. Mss. See also Wilmot to Board of Trade, June 19, 1764, in W. L. Grant (ed.) *Acts of the Privy Council of England,* Colonial Series, 1745-66 (London, 1911), IV, 671-72.

30. *Ibid.*

31. Richard, *Acadia,* II, 312; also "Addresse des Acadiens du Fort Cumberland au duc de Choiseul, Ministre du roi, du 24 août 1763," in *Revue Historique Colonies Françaises,* XVI, November, 1928, 701-704. "Letter from Acadians in Halifax to Nivernois, August 13, 1763," in Correspondance politique Angleterre, 1763, CDLI, ff. 57-61, A. A. É. "Your letter was for us like the rays of the morning after a stormy night; it announced the approaching day of our delivery. Long have we wished for that fortunate day that would unite us to our confrères." On the River St. John were 87 exiles of the Bergeron, Régisport, Brun, Saindon, Bourguinion, Bourg, Beliveau, Gaudet, Dechofour, Sourriez, Lamoutin, and other families. In Halifax were 692 members of the Saunaie, Cerau, Richar, Eber, Lelende, Pitre, Poirie, Terijo, Bourgue, Cibaudo, Gaudet, Cormaie, Mambrou, Melanson, Savois, LeGere, Bourgois, Galan, Dugas, Bergeron, Parc, Blanchard, Trahan, Robicho, Baben, Bernar, and many other families. The names were badly spelled.

32. Halifax to Wilmot, June 9, 1764, in Nova Scotia Documents, f. 348.

33. "Papers Relating to Nova Scotia Collection," in Brown Collection, Add. 19073, f. 69.

34. W. A. Calnek, *History of the County Annapolis, Including Old Port Royal and Acadia,* ed. A. W. Savary (Toronto, 1897); John Clarence Webster, *Acadia at the End of the Seventeenth Century,* (St. John, N. B., 1934); Lèonce de Grandmaison, "L'histoire pathétique du peuple Acadien," in

35. "Papers Relating to Nova Scotia," in Brown Collection, Add. 19071, ff. 125-26, B. N. Mss. The records for Nova Scotia after 1763 show that the catastrophe of the expulsion did not change the simplicity of Acadian manners and way of life, their custom of early marriages, or their exemplary and virtuous lives. Their descendants in the Gaspé peninsula and New Brunswick today are still attached "à la glèbe," raise cattle, build their own houses, and "leave the evils of tomorrow until tomorrow brings them." Their increase in population has been phenomenal. Among the happiest of the inhabitants of the Western Hemisphere, they are still in a great measure a separate people.

36. Martín Navarro to José de Gálvez, New Orleans, September 9, 1785, in Cuba 633 (copia 330), A. G. I.

CHAPTER FIVE

1. Joly de Fleury, "Memoir on the Acadians, submitted to Louis XVI immediately after his coronation," in Commerce et Colonies, 1722, I, f. 187, B. N. Mss.
2. "Mémoire sur les Acadians," in Mémoire et Document Angleterre, June, 1778, XLVII, f. 23, A. A. É. He was commissaire de la marine from 1766-74.
3. Lemoine asked for 100,000 écus. The écu, or crown, now an obsolete French coin, once was worth about three francs.
4. Mémoire et Documents Angleterre, June, 1778, XLVII, f. 23, A. A. É.
5. *Ibid.*, f. 24.
6. "Mémoire sur les Acadiens," in Correspondance politique Angleterre, 1763, London, February, 1763, CDXLIX, f. 350, A. A. É.
7. The *landes* were moors, heath, wastelands, or other sterile areas (see map of western France). This was the age when the influence of the Physiocrats was supreme in France. According to Jethro Tull (1674-1741) "the earth is only source of wealth." See his work entitled, *The Horse-hoing Husbandry* . . . (London, 1733); also Victor de Riquetti, Marquis de Mirabeau, *L'Ami des hommes, ou Traité de la population.* (Rouxel edition, 1883); also Philippe de Cantillon, *Essai sur la nature du commerce en général* (Paris, 1754). Choiseul, Nivernois, Turgot, Necker, and the Marquis de Pérusse des Cars were all deeply influenced by the doctrines of the eighteenth century Physiocrats.
8. Correspondance politique Angleterre, 1763, CDXLIX, f. 351, A. A. É.
9. *Ibid.* Sardines were an essential article among French exports to England, and the English were re-exporting a great quantity of sardines and other fish caught off the coasts of Cornwall.
10. *Ibid.*, ff. 351, 352. The island of Bouin is known today as Isle de Noirmoutier. From the enthusiastic report of the Duke of Nivernois to Choiseul, the author expected to find it a pleasant spot when he visited the island in April, 1948. But the island is no more than a bleak, marshy sandbar whose beaches have some possibilities for people who specialize in sunbathing. The Acadians must have been fortunate to have escaped its colonization.
11. *Ibid.*, f. 352. Nivernois thought that the French ought to imitate the later English system of building colonies and subsidize the colonists through a program of outright grants of food, seed, and tools, and of tax exemption.
12. "Choiseul à M. le duc de Nivernois," Colonies, Serie B, Versailles, March 11, 1763, CXVII, f. 83, A. N.; *ibid.*, Versailles, March 17, 1763, f. 89.
13. Cs 3, No. 245, A. D. V.
14. Mémoire et Documents Angleterre, June, 1778, f. 23. Also Colonies, Serie B. CXX, f. 195, A. N. One high official, Berton, even proposed sending the Acadians to work in the French mines. Choiseul, otherwise self-centered, rejected the plan as brutal and cruel to a people who had lived in comparative ease and who had shown such love and attachment to France.
15. See works on the disastrous colonization of French Guiana under the Chevalier Étienne François Turgot, governor; and Tibault de Chanvalon, intendant for the years 1763-64, in Colonies, Serie B, CXVII, ff. 40, 41, 159, 196, 206, 313, 360-63; CXIX, f. 6; and CXX, ff. 47, 86, 110-16,

153, 225, 343-58, A. N. Alfred Zimmermann, *Die Europäischen Kolonien* (Berlin, 1901), IV, 220-27. Louis Marie Prudhomme, *Voyage à la Guiane et à Cayenne,* (Paris, 1789); Charles G. Vergennes, *Mémoire, Historique et Politique sur La Louisiana,* . . . (Paris, 1802), 56-181; Gabriel Hanotaux and Alfred Martineau, *Histoire des colonies Françaises et de l'expansion de la France dans le monde* (Paris, 1929), I, 587-97.

16. Eugéne Théodor Daubigny, *Choiseul et La France d'Outre-Mer après le traité de Paris* (Paris, 1892), 32-39.

17. W. R. Shepherd, "The Cession of Louisiana to Spain," in *Political Science Quarterly,* XIX (1904), 439-58.

18. Quoted in Frederic Austin Ogg, *The Opening of the Mississippi,* . . . (New York, 1904), 291.

19. Colonies, Serie B, Cayenne, CXIX, f. 6; CXVII, ff. 116, 117, A. N.

20. Colonies, C¹⁴, XXVIII, A. M. C. Also for a detailed account, see Lauvrière, *La tragédie d'un peuple,* II, 181-89.

21. Daubigny, *Choiseul et La France d'Outre-mer après le traité de Paris* (Paris, 1892), 338-40; and Alfred Zimmermann, *Die Kolonial-politik Frankreichs* (Berlin, 1901), 224-26; See also Colonies, Serie B, CXIX, f. 177, A. N. The king's intention was that the Acadians should not be compelled to go to Cayenne, but only invited and told of the advantages offered there. A kind Providence, however, filled them with a great fear of Guiana. See "Mémoire" in Colonies, C¹¹D, VIII, f. 242 ff., A. N.

22. Lauvrière, *La tragédie d'un peuple,* II, 185-86.

23. Ernest Martin, *Les exilés Acadiens en France au XVIIIᵉ siècle et leur établissement en Poitou* (Paris, 1936), 60-61.

24. Colonies, Serie B, CXVII, Serie B, f. 405, A. N.

25. *Ibid.,* CXXII, ff. 181-82, A. N.

26. *Ibid.,* CXVII, ff. 229-340, 426; also CXX, ff. 270-75, 323, A. N.

27. *Ibid.,* CXVII, f. 367, A. N.

28. "Registres des Acadiens de Belle-Ile-en-Mer," in Canada Français, II, (1889), and III (1890), 1-60 in A. M. V.; also Norman McLeod Rogers, "Acadian Exiles in France," in *Dalhousie Review,* V (April, 1925), 10-22.

29. Colonies, Serie B, CXXII, f. 397, A. N.

30. Letter, August 5, 1765, Correspondance de l'abbé Le Loutre avec M. le Baron de Warren, in *Les Acadiens à Belle-Ile-en-Mer,* ed., Joseph M. Lanco (Josselin, 1924), 13. Le Loutre was referring to Choiseul's estate of Chanteloup.

31. Colonies C¹¹D, (1713-1788), VIII, f. 304, A. N.

32. *Ibid.,* VIII, f. 305-13, A. N.

33. *Ibid.,* Serie B, CXXII, f. 278, A. N.

34. Richard, *Acadia,* II, 239.

35. Léandre Le Gallen, *Belle-Ile-en-Mer, histoire politique religieuse et militaire* (Vannes, 1903), 239. This is a detailed account of the settlement.

36. *Ibid.,* 238.

37. Canada Français, (1888), C, I, A. M. V.

38. Colonies, Serie B, CXLIII, f. 672; *ibid.,* CXXXI, 326-30, A. N.

39. L. LeMay, *Histoire de Belle-Ile,* quoted in Le Gallen, *Histoire de Belle-Ile,* 238. See also "Mémoire sur les Acadiens presenté à Nos Seigneurs du Clergé en France, assemblés à Paris en juillet 1775," in *Revue de l'Aunis* (1867).

40. Finances, 15-3.495, A. N.; also Colonies, Serie B, vol. 131, ff. 327-29, A. N.
41. Correspondance de M. l'Abbé Le Lautre, in Lanco (ed.), *Les Acadiens à Belle-Ile-en-Mer*, 30. *Ibid.*, 39.
42. Ibid., 39.
43. The writer, visiting Belle-Ile-en-Mer in 1948, saw few fertile spots and much desert land. He was surprised that people could make a living there at all. As a summer resort the island is attractive, though it is very cold there during the winter. As a farming project, Belle-Ile would be poor.
44. Colonies, Serie B, CXXV, ff. 195-99, A. N.
45. *Ibid.*, CXLIII, f. 127 ff., A. N.
46. *Ibid.*, CXXII, f. 23, A. N.
47. Correspondance de M. l'Abbé Le Loutre, in Lanco (ed.), *Les Acadiens à Belle-Ile-en-mer*, 30.
48. Colonies, Serie B, CXVII, f. 117, A. N.
49. *Ibid.*, CXVI, ff. 12-15; CXVII, ff. 389-391; CXX, ff. 16-17; CXXI, ff. 1-18, A. N. See also Correspondance politique Angleterre, 1763, CDL, f. 4, A. A. É.; also Réfugiés, 1765, in Canada, I, 122, G1, 458, ff. 27-39, A. M. C.
50. Réfugiés in Colonies, Serie G1, CXXII, ff. 3, 5, 27-29, 50, 88, A. N.; and Lauvrière, *La tragédie d'un peuple*, II, 203-25.
51. Colonies, Serie B, CXXXIV, ff. 154-160, A. N.
52. See Martin, *Les exilés Acadiens en France*, 84-85, for a detailed report.
53. Colonies, Serie B, CXLIII, ff. 349, 648, A. N.
54. Mémoires et Documents Angleterre, June, 1778, f. 23, A. A. É.
55. *Ibid.*
56. *Ibid.*
57. *Ibid.*, f. 24.
58. Joly de Fleury, Commerce et Colonies, 1722, f. 188, B. N.
59. Mémoire et Documents Angleterre, 1763, June, 1778, XLVII, f. 24, A. A. É.
60. "A Son Excélence, Monseigneur Le Comte De Vergennes," in Correspondance politique Espagne, April 4, 1784, DCXII, f. 287, A. A. É.
61. Joly de Fleury, Commerce et Colonies, f. 188.
62. "Mémoire sur les Acadiens" in Correspondance politique Angleterre, 1763, CDXLIX, f. 349, A. A. É.
63. Mémoires et Documents Angleterre, June, 1778, f. 23.
64. Joly de Fleury, Commerce et Colonies, f. 187, B. N.
65. Alexis Papuchon, *La Colonie acadienne du Poitou, in Bulletins de La Société des Antiquaires de L'Ouest* (2e trimestre, Poitiers, 1908), 18.
66. Joly de Fleury, Commerce et Colonies, f. 187, B. N.
67. Manuel Danvila y Collado, *Reinado de Carlos*, III (Madrid 1893-96), IV, 3-71; Joseph Addison, *Charles the Third of Spain* (Oxford, 1900).
68. Mémoires et Documents Angleterre, June, 1778, f. 23, A. A. É.
69. Joly de Fleury, Commerce et Colonies, 1722, f. 187, B. N.
70. Mémoires et Documents Angleterre, June, 1778, f. 230.
71. Papuchon, *La Colonie Acadienne du Poitou*, 18; also Lauvrière, *La tragédie d'un peuple*, II, 173; and Martin, *Les Exilés Acadiens en France*, 91.
72. "Mémoire," in Correspondance politique Angleterre, 1763, CDXLIX, f. 344, A. A. É.; also La Rochette's letter, March 18, 1763, in "Papers Relating to Nova Scotia," Ad. 19069 (copia), Brown Collection, B. M. Mss.; also Finances, 15-3.495, A. N.
73. Joly de Fleury, Commerce et Colonies, f. 188.

CHAPTER SIX

1. "A Son Excélence, Monseigneur le Comte Vergennes, April 4, 1784, in Correspondance politique Espagne, 1784, DCXII, f. 287, A. A. É.
2. For an excellent and detailed account of this project see Papuchon, *La Colonie Acadienne;* and Martin, *Les Exilés Acadiens*. Berton's figure was 20,000 arpents. An arpent Châtellerault was about .6593 of an acre.
3. Charles Claude LaLanne, *Histoire de Châtelleraud et du Châtelleraudais* (Châtellerault, 1859), 250.
4. Dépôt 22, Liasse 89, 98, A. D. V.
5. Lalanne, *Histoire de Châtelleraud,* 250.
6. Colonies, C^{11}D, VIII, f. 303, A. N. Lemoine was commissioner of the admiralty at Bordeaux 1766-74. Part of the fields selected was situated in the baronies of D'Angles and Chauvigny belonging to the Bishop of Poitiers; 110 arpents belonged to the abbey de l'Etoile of the Order of St. Bernard, and some 980 arpents to the Order of Fontevristes of La Puye. But the major part of the settlement was on the state of the Marquis de Pérusse des Cars.
7. "Mémoire," in Mémoires et Documents Angleterre, June, 1778, XLVII, f. 24.
8. Colonies, C^{11}D, 1713-88, VIII, ff. 299-303, A. N.
9. Joly de Fleury, Commerce et Colonies, I, f. 188, B. N. Mss., claims that in 1773 there were 679 families of 2,542 members. Of these 1,154 had been born in France; 366 families had mother and father alive; 26 families had fathers who were widowers, and 120 widowed mothers; 167 families with one or two orphans. See also Colonies, C^{11}D, 1713-88, VIII, f. 299, A. N.; also Mémoires et Documents Angleterre, June, 1778, f. 15, A. A. É.; also Report, 1905, in Canada Archives, II Appendix G, 148, 157.
10. Colonies, C^{11}D, VIII, F. 303.
11. *Ibid.,* f. 299.
12. "Mémoire: Familles Acadiennes," 1777 in Mémoires et Documents Angleterre, f. 15, A. A. É. The marquis' grant to Acadians was 7,110 arpents to be divided into 5 equal parts of 1,422 arpents per village—900 to the village farmers at 30 arpents per cabin; and the remaining 522 arpents to be distributed among mechanics at 3 arpents per person.
13. Colonies, C^{11}D, VIII, f. 299. The 1,023 mechanics represent the combined classes of 153 and 870 mechanics in the second and third classes respectively. Lemoine favored the plan of allowing the 153 mechanics of the second class to return to the seaports to seek employment in their trades if they did not care to work on the farms after the colony was well established.
14. *Ibid.,* f. 300.
15. "Mémoire: Familles Acadienns," 1777, in Mémoires et Documents Angleterre, f. 16. Lemoine calculated that one full payment to the Marquis de Pérusse des Cars would assure the appropriation of necessary funds and at the same time protect the government, which could easily stop all payments if the marquis failed to keep the contract.
16. Colonies, C^{11}D, 1713-88, VIII, f. 302, A. N.
17. *Ibid.,* 300; also Finances, F15-3.495, A. N. That rate of revenue did not include the state's perquisites.
18. Papuchon, *La Colonie Acadienne,* 32.
19. Colonies, C^{11}D, 1713-88, VIII, f. 297, A. N; also "Mémoire sur les Acadiens," in Mémoires et Documents Angleterre, XLVII, f. 24, A. A. É.

20. Mémoire et Documents Angleterre, June, 1778, f. 24.
21. Papuchon, *La Colonie Acadienne,* 44-51. The writer visited this area in 1948 and met many of the Acadians, descendants of the first colonists. He dug into the ground in many places and came upon a hard, stony subsoil impervious to water. During the past century the French government had spent great sums of money to reclaim huge tracts of this region. The sagebrush and broom plant to a great measure have been destroyed; the stony strata of subsoil ploughed up, and much fertilizer distributed. Today thousands of acres in this once sterile plateau are very productive in cereals.
22. *Ibid.* See Charles Seignobos, *A History of the French People,* tr. Catherine Alison Phillips (London, 1933).
23. Mémoires et Documents Angleterre, June, 1778, f. 24.
24. Colonies, Serie B, CXLIV, f. 307, A. N.
25. Art. 2, "Observations," in Colonies, $C^{11}D$, 1713-88, VIII, f. 296, A. N.; also Mémoires et Documents Angleterre, June, 1778, f. 24.
26. Colonies, $C^{11}D$, 1713-88, VIII, ff. 296-97, A. N.
27. "Memoire: Familles Acadiennes," in Mémoires et Documents Angleterre, 1777, f. 17.
28. *Ibid.,* f. 24.
29. *Ibid.,* f. 17.
30. *Ibid.*
31. Papuchon, *La Colonie Acadienne,* 45-46; Lalanne *Histoire de Châtelleraud,* 252. These facts might explain the offer of the merchants in Nantes to buy in 1784 the uncultivated estate of the Marquis de Pérusse des Cars. The business firms of the maritime towns had been advertising to unsuspecting emigrants the great advantages of a farm in Normandy or Brittany.
32. When the author visited the site of La Colonie du Poitou in 1948, he met descendants of those 160 exiles who clung to "La Grand' Ligne." From them he gathered many of the facts narrated in this and the following chapter.
33. Mémoires et Documents Angleterre, June, 1778, f. 24.
34. Finances, F15-3.495, A. N.
35. Mémoires et Documents Angleterre, June, 1778, f. 25, A. A. É.
36. Finances, F15-3.495, A. N.

CHAPTER SEVEN

1. "Mémoire sur les Acadiens," in Mémoires et Documents Angleterre, June, 1778, XLVII, f. 25, A. A. É. This chapter follows the account given in the memoir very closely.
2. *Ibid.,* f. 25, Finances, F15-3.495, A. N. His plan resembled the plan for the Grecian colony of 120 families who formed the Marquisate de Marbeuf near Ajaccio. According to one census of Lemoine there were 2,566 Acadians in France in 1773. "Recueil de pièces relatif aux Acadiens," MS. 1480, in Bibliothèque de Bordeaux. Elsewhere the Acadian population in France was given as 2,542 and 2,370.
3. Mémoires et Documents Angleterre, June, 1778, XLVII, f. 25, A. A. É.
4. *Ibid.,* f. 25. When Necker got the report that the cost of establishing the Acadians in Corsica would come to approximately $360,000, he rejected the plan. Finances, F15-3.495, A. N.

5. "Mémoire sur les Acadiens," in Mémoires et Documents Angleterre, June, 1778, XLVII, f. 26.

6. *Ibid*. Throughout this chapter and subsequent chapters the terms "Acadian nation, Acadian people, national honor, national unity," are used in the sense in which the Acadians themselves used those terms, as an indication that they regarded themselves as a people apart from the French, and just a little different from the mother country.

7. *Ibid*.

8. *Ibid*.

9. *Ibid*.

10. *Ibid*., f. 27. The French government had always recognized that each Acadian had undeniable claims (based on the promises of Louis XV) to the legal title to arable lands and to a state support of six cents a day until self-supporting. In the meeting of November 10, 1777, the government reaffirmed the Acadian claims and at the same time held that the state had a sovereign right to abolish those claims, though it did not know by what means. It realized that the rump assembly could extinguish the claims of only the members of its eighty families.

11. *Ibid*.

12. *Ibid.*, Finances, F15-3.495, A. N.

13. Mémoires et Documents Angleterre, June, 1778, f. 27.

14. *Ibid*.

15. *Ibid*.

16. *Ibid*.

17. Oliver Terrio, 1783-1792, "Précis des faits qui ont precedé, effectué et suivi l'Émigration de dix-sept-cents Acadiens des provinces de France à la Colonie de la Louisiane, en mil-sept-cents quatre vingt cinq," with twenty-three letters attached, in Cuba, 197, ff. 1-2, A. G. I.

18. Joly de Fleury, Commerce et Colonies, I, f. 188, B. N. Ms. Elsewhere stated as 2,370 persons, chapter VI, fn. 9. Another census of Lemoine gave 2,556. "Recueil de pièces relatifs aux Acadiens." MS. 1480 in Bibliotheque de Bordeaux.

19. Colonies, C¹¹D (1713-88), VIII, f. 292, A. N.

20. Mémoires et Documents Angleterre, June, 1778, f. 28.

21. Terrio, "Précis des faits," in Cuba, 197, ff. 1-2.

22. Mémoires et Documents Angleterre, June, 1778, f. 28.

23. Finances, F15-3.495, A. N.

24. "A Son Excélence, Monseigneur le Comte de Vergennes," in Correspondance politique Espagne, April 4, 1784, DCXII, f. 287, A. A. É.

25. Colonies, C¹¹D (1713-88), VIII, f. 292, A. N.

26. *Ibid.*, Serie B, CXVII, f. 405, A. N.

27. "A Son Excélence," in Correspondance politique Espagne, April 4, 1784, DCXII, f. 287.

28. Finances, F15-3.492, -93, -94, -95; F15-3.331B; F15-3.52A, Côtes du Nord; F15-3.356A, La Manche; and F¹ et F⁴, F¹⁵, are full of statistics on government aid and pensions given the Acadians and refugees from Prince Edward and Cape Breton islands. There is no doubt that the French government was generous when possible towards the Acadians; but on the other hand, it failed miserably to use efficient means to settle them on good arable lands. Also "Lettres," in Correspondance politique Espagne, 1785, DCXX, ff. 55-100.

29. Joly de Fleury, Commerce et Colonies, f. 188.

30. "A Son Excélence," in Correspondance politique Espagne, April 4, 1784, f. 287.

31. Terrio, "Précis des faits," in Cuba, 197, f. 2.

CHAPTER EIGHT

1. Terrio, "Précis des faits," in Cuba, 197, A. G. I.; Correspondance politique Espagne, 1783, DCX, f. 7, A. A. É. Aranda was authorized to sign the preliminaries of peace as offered by England. See letter for preliminary articles of peace, Versailles, January 20, 1783, in Cuba 594 and 1375, A. G. I.

2. Terrio, Précis des faits," in Cuba, 197, A. G. I.

3. Peyroux to Heredia, Nantes, March 7, 1784, in Estado-Legajo 3885 (13), carta 11, A. H. N. Peyroux's wife was a Portuguese woman named Rodriquez. See that portion of Chapter Ten relating to the expedition of *La Armistad*.

4. Heredia to Floridablanca, Paris, February 21, 1784, *ibid.*, carta 6, A. H. N.

5. Peyroux to Heredia, Nantes, March 7, 1784, *ibid.*, carta 11.

6. Heredia to Floridablanca, Paris, February 21, 1784, *ibid.*, carta 6.

7. *Ibid.* The expectation of royal reward is intimated in many of the letters, especially in numbers 39, 45, 49, 70, 72, and 73.

8. Correspondance politique Angleterre, 1777, DCX, f. 6 ff., A. A. É.

9. Peyroux to Heredia, Nantes, March 7, 1784, in Estado-Legajo, 3885 (13), cartas 6 and 11, A. H. N.

10. Heredia to Floridablanca, Paris, February 21, 1784, *ibid.*, carta 6.

11. Terrio, "Précis des faits," in Cuba, 197, f. 2, A. G. I.

12. *Ibid.*

13. Mémoire et Documents Angleterre, XLVII, ff. 24, 25, A. A. É.

14. *Ibid.*, f. 22.

15. "Recueil de Pièces relatif aux Acadiens," Ms. 1480, in Bibliothèque de Bordeaux, f. 70.

16. Finances, F15-3.495, f. 29, A. N.; Terrio, "Précis des faits," in Cuba, 197, A. G. I.

17. Nettels, *Roots of American Civilization,* 705.

18. Finances, 15-3.495, f. 29, A. N.

19. *Ibid.*

20. *Ibid.*, f. 30,; also Colonies, C¹¹D, VIII, f. 292 (copia).

21. Mémoire et Documents Angleterre, XLVII, f. 23, A. A. É.; Terrio, "Précis des faits," in Cuba, 197, f. 2, A. G. I.

22. Finances, 15-3.495, f. 30, A. N.

23. Heredia to Floridablanca, January 3, 1783, in Estado-Legajo 3885 (13), carta 1, A. H. N.

24. Terrio, "Précis de faits," in Cuba, 197, f. 2, A. G. I.

25. *Ibid.*

26. Correspondance politique Espagne, DCXI, f. 34, A. A. É.

27. Terrio, "Précis des faits," in Cuba, 197, f. 3. In October of 1777, Count de Aranda had sent two Acadian families of twenty-two members to Cabahannocer at the expense of Spain. After the collapse of second Corsica, Necker hoped that Aranda would continue his transportations of Acadians to populate Louisiana. It would relieve the French treasury of "an expense and care to which there seemed no end." But Aranda dropped the idea until

Peyroux appeared on the scene. Besides the French subdelegates in the maritime towns, influenced by the merchants, saw to it that Acadian petitions to go to Louisiana did not reach Aranda.

28. Peyroux to Terrio, Paris, August 8, 1783, *ibid.*, carta 1.
29. *Id.*, "Memoir," in Estado-Legajo 3885 (13), carta 3, No. 1782, A. H. N.
30. *Ibid.*
31. *Ibid.* Also Navarro to Baylio Antonio Valdés, "Matters of Government from 13th to 30th of September, 1783," December 19, 1787, in Cuba, 594, carta 26, A. G. I.
32. Peyroux, "Mémoire," in Estado-Legajo 3885 (13), carta 3, A. H. N.
33. José de Gálvez to Floridablanca, August 21, 24, 1783, San Ildefonso, *ibid.*, cartas 2, 5. Also conde de Gálvez to Navarro, June 24, 1875, in Cuba, 594, A. G. I.
34. Peyroux to Terrio, Paris, January 21, 1784, "Précis des faits," in Cuba, 197, carta 2, A. G. I.
35. Heredia to Floridablanca, Paris, February 21, 1784, in Estado-Legajo 3885 (13), carta 6, A. H. N.
36. Colonies, C¹¹D, VIII, ff. 317-20, A. N. Heredia to Floridablanca, Paris, February 21, 1784, in Estado-Legajo 3885 (13), carta 6, A. H. N.
37. Peyroux to Terrio, Paris, January 21, 1784, "Précis des faits," in Cuba, 197, carta 2, A. G. I.
38. Peyroux to Heredia, Nantes, March 22, 1784, in Estado-Legajo 3885 (13), carta 9 (copia), A. H. N.
39. José de Gálvez to Floridablanca, El Pardo, March 27, 1784, in Estado-Legajo 3885 (13), carta 7, A. H. N. Heredia to *id.*, Paris, March 26, 1784, *ibid.*, carta 8.
40. Peyroux to Heredia, Nantes, March 7, 1784, *ibid.*, carta 11 (copia).
41. *Ibid.*, carta 21.
42. Heredia to Floridablanca, Paris, March 26, 1784, in Estado-Legajo 3885 (13), carta 8, A. H. N.
43. Correspondance politique Espagne, 1784, DCX, f. 6, A. A. É.; Peyroux to Heredia, Nantes, March 22, 1784 in Estado-Legajo 3885 (13), carta 9, A. H. N.
44. Heredia to Floridablanca, Paris, March 26, 1784, *ibid.*, carta 8 (copia 4).
45. *Id.* to Vergennes, Paris, March 24, 1784, *ibid.*, carta 10 (copia), A. H. N.
46. Colonies, C¹¹D, VIII, f. 316, A. N.
47. Heredia to Peyroux, March 26, 1784 in Estado-Legajo 3885 (13), carta 11 (copia 3), A. H. N.
48. Colonies, C¹¹D, VIII, f. 316, A. N.
49. Heredia to Peyroux, Paris, March 26, 1784, in Estado-Legajo 3885 (13), carta 11 (copia 3), A. H. N.
50. Peyroux to Heredia, Nantes, April 8, 1784, *ibid.*, carta 13 (copia), A. H. N.
51. Correspondance politique Espagne, DCXII, ff. 287-88, A. A. É. Finances, F15-3.495, A. N., and Acadians(?) to Count de Vergennes, Nantes, April 4, 1784, in Cuba, 197, carta 6, A. G. I.
52. Correspondance politique Espagne, DCXII, f. 367, A. A. É.
53. Vergennes to Aranda, May 11, 1784, in Estado-Legajo 3885 (13), carta 15 (copia), A. H. N.; also *id* to *id.*, Versailles, May 11, 1784, "Précis des faits," in Cuba, 197, carta 7.
54. Correspondance politique Espagne, 1783, DCX, f. 14 ff. A. A. É.
55. Terrio, "Précis des faits," in Cuba, 197, f. 3.

56. Terrio to Heredia, Nantes, May 27, 1784, *ibid.*, carta 9.
57. *Ibid.*
58. *Ibid.*, f. 3.
59. Gàlvez to Aranda, Aranjuez, May 28, 1784, in Estado-Legajo 3885 (13), cartas 18, 19, A. H. N.
60. Aranda to Peyroux, July 8, 1784, "Précis des faits," in Cuba, 197, carta 11, A. G. I.
61. Peyroux to Terrio, Paris, July 18, 1784, *ibid.*, carta 12.
62. *Id.* to *id.*, Nantes, August 1, 1784, *ibid.*, carta 13, f. 14.
63. Terrio, "Précis des faits," in Cuba, 197, f. 3.
64. *Ibid.*, ff. 3, 4.
65. Peyroux to Aranda (?), Nantes, August 10, 1784, in Estado-Legajo 3885 (13), carta 23 (copia).
66. The term "family head" is used because in many cases the eldest son assumed the responsibility of the dead or lost father.
67. Peyroux to Aranda (?), August 16, 1784, in Estado-Legajo 3885 (13), carta 25 (copia).
68. *Id.* to *id.*, Nantes, August 10, 1784, *ibid.*, carta 23.
69. Aranda to Peyroux, Paris, August 20, 1784, *ibid.*, carta 24. *Id.* to Floridablanca, *ibid.*, carta 22.
70. Peyroux to Heredia, Nantes, March 22, 1784, *ibid.*, carta 9 (copia).
71. *Id.* to Aranda (?), August 16, 1784, *ibid.*, carta 25 (copia).
72. *Id.* to *id.* (?), Paris, July 17, 1784, *ibid.*, carta 21. José de Gálvez, to Bernardo de Gàlvez, September 1, 1784, in Cuba, 149 [a] and 594, A. G. I.
73. Peyroux to ———, Paris, July 17, 1784, in Estado-Legajo 3885 (13), carta 21, A. H. N.; José de Gálvez to Floridablanca, San Ildefonso, September 1, 1784, in Estado-Legajo 3885 (13), carta 28, A. H. N.
74. José de Gálvez to Floridablanca, San Lorenzo, October 8, 1784, *ibid.*, carta 38.
75. Peyroux to ———, Paris, July 17, 1784, *ibid.*, carta 21. Also Aranda to Floridablanca, Paris, April 4, 1785, *ibid.*, carta 52 gives list of these foreigners. There were three families consisting of John Bernard, a Russian, master tailor; Juana Richard, his French wife; and Marlin and Ana, his son and daughter; Pedro Laurenay, a German master cabinetmaker; Maria Bidet, his French wife, and Pedro, his son; Pedro Juan Jacques, a German carpenter; Ana Drapeau, his French wife, and his five children.
76. José de Gálvez to Floridablanca, San Ildefonso, September 1, 1784, *ibid.*, carta 28, transmits answer to each of Peyroux's eight questions.
77. Peyroux to Aranda (?), August 16, 1784, *ibid.*, carta 25.
78. *Ibid.*
79. José de Gálvez to Floridablanca, San Ildefonso, September 6, 1784, *ibid.*, carta 30.
80. Peyroux to Aranda, Paris, September 13, 1784, *ibid.*, carta 34 (copia); also Réfugiés, in Canada, II, G¹, 459, f. 123, A. M. C.
81. Peyroux to Aranda, Paris, September 13, 1784, in Estado-Legajo 3885 (13), carta 34; also ——— to José de Gálvez, San Ildefonso, September 27, 1784, *ibid.*, carta 36.
82. Peyroux to Aranda, Paris, September 13, 1784, *ibid.*, carta 34. On October 8, 1784 at San Lorenzo, José de Gálvez wrote Floridablanca that there must not be any separation of husbands and wives. *Ibid.*, carta 38.

83. Peyroux to Aranda, Paris, September 13, 1784, *ibid.,* carta 34; Correspondance politique Espagne, 1784, DCXII ff. 334, 367; DCXIII, f. 185, A. A. É.
84. Peyroux to Aranda, Paris, September 13, 1784, in Estado-Legajo 3885 (13), carta 34. Gálvez to Floridablanca, San Lorenzo, October 8, 1784, *ibid.,* carta 38, A. H. N.
85. Peyroux to Aranda, Paris, September 13, 1784, *ibid.,* carta 34. Gálvez approved the presence of one surgeon on each ship but stipulated that he must pay his own passage. He also consented to send one chaplain on every ship.
86. *Ibid.* See also Gálvez to Floridablanca, San Lorenzo, October 8, 1874, *ibid.,* carta 38, granting him the rank of captain general "de referida Provincia" and providing that he should be honored according to his ability and conduct.
87. Aranda to Floridablanca, Paris, September 13, 1784, *ibid.,* carta 33; and Peyroux to Aranda, Paris, September 13, 1784, *ibid.,* carta 34, A. H. N.

CHAPTER NINE

1. José de Gálvez to Floridablanca, Aranjuez, May 28, 1784, in Estado-Legajo 3885 (13), carta 18, A. H. N.; *id.* to *id.,* Aranjuez, May 31, 1784, *ibid.,* carta 19; Ministry of the Indies to Aranda, San Ildefonso, September 13, 1784, *ibid.,* carta 32, A. H. N.
2. Gálvez to Floridablanca, El Pardo, February 4, 1785, *ibid.,* carta 47.
3. *Ibid.*
4. Aranda to Floridablanca, Paris, March 14, 1785, *ibid.,* carta 49.
5. *Id.* to *id.,* Paris, November 19, 1784, *ibid.,* carta 39.
6. Heredia to Floridablanca, Paris, February 21, 1784, *ibid.,* carta 6; Peyroux to Heredia, Nantes, March 7, 1784, *ibid.,* carta 11 (copia).
7. *Id* to *id.,* Nantes, March 7, 1784, *ibid.,* carta 11 (copia 1).
8. *Ibid.*
9. Peyroux to Aranda, Paris, September 13, 1784, *ibid.,* carta 34 (copia).
10. *Id.* to Heredia, Paris, March 7, 1784, *ibid.,* 3885 (13), carta 11 (copia 2).
11. *Ibid.*
12. *Ibid.,* carta 11 (copia 1), A. H. N. Michel estimated hammocks at $1.20; Peyroux proposed to supply them at $.80 including the ropes. He would hire the ships, secure the riggings, the barrels for water, attend to quantity and quality of provisions, and serve healthy meals. He would do all for less than Michel. He would hire very few sailors because he could find good sailors among the Acadians. That his offer went unheeded was probably due to the powerful influence of the business interests in Nantes and St. Malo at the Spanish embassy in Paris. See Aranda to Floridablanca, Paris, September 6, 1784, *ibid.,* carta 31.
13. *Id* to *id.,* Nantes, April 8, 1784, *ibid.,* carta 13 (copia).
14. *Id.* to ——, Nantes, April 27, 1784, *ibid.,* carta 16 (copia 2).
15. Heredia to Floridablanca, Paris, May 14, 1784, *ibid.,* carta 14.
16. Peyroux to Heredia, Paris, April 27, 1784, *ibid.,* carta 16 (copia 2).
17. *Ibid.*
18. Tourgouilhet and Rousseau to Aranda, Nantes, August 21, 1784, *ibid.,* carta 27.
19. *Ibid.* Roughly speaking the trans-Atlantic fare for one Acadian was $36.00.

20. Aranda to Floridablanca, Paris, August 30, 1784, *ibid.,* carta 26.
21. José de Gálvez to *id.,* San Ildefonso, September 6, 1784, *ibid.,* carta 30.
22. Peyroux to Aranda, Paris., September 13, 1784, *ibid.,* carta 34 (copia). Peyroux's enthusiasm for Tourgouilhet and Rousseau may have been influenced by the fact that his older brother was partner with them in a company which they had recently formed to trade in Louisiana woods and peltries. He thought, moreover, that through his contacts in Louisiana he could organize a stock company that would be very advantageous to the colony.
23. Aranda to Floridablanca, Paris, September 6, 1784, *ibid.,* carta 31.
24. Ministerio de Indias to Aranda, El Pardo, February 19, 1785, *ibid.*
25. Aranda to D'Asprès, Paris, September 27, 1784, *ibid.,* carta 40 (copia).
26. D'Asprès to Aranda, Nantes, October 10, 1784, *ibid.,* carta 41.
27. Tourgouilhet and Rousseau to Spanish Embassy, Nantes, October 8, 1784, *ibid.,* carta 51 B. See B. F. French (ed.), *Historical Collections of Louisiana* . . . (New York, 1846-53), V, 29-30, on the Balize.
28. Antonio Marcorelles to Spanish Embassy, Nantes, October 9, 1784, in Estado-Legajo 3885 (13), carta 51C.
29. D'Asprès to Aranda, Nantes, October 10, 1784, *ibid.,* carta 41.
30. *Ibid.* D'Asprès argued that placing the contract in the hands of one company with no more than two ships would force it to charter four or six other ships. The cost of chartering extra ships would absorb its profits. One result would be the delaying of transportation, and another would be the use of poorly equipped ships for a long voyage. He had no criticism of the provisions with which Tourgouilhet and Rousseau promised to stock their ships.
31. *Ibid.* D'Asprès did not neglect any details. He even insisted on a gangplank four to eight feet long to facilitate the landing of steerage passengers.
32. *Ibid.,* D'Asprès to ——, in Cuba, 597, A. G. I.
33. D'Asprès to Aranda, Nantes, October 10, 1784, *ibid.,* carta 41.
34. Aranda to Floridablanca, Paris, December 5, 1785, *ibid.,* carta 66; *id* to *id.,* November 29, 1785, *ibid.,* carta 68; D'Après to Asanda, Paris, December 24, 1785, *ibid.,* carta 70.
35. D'Asprès to Aranda, Nantes, November 7, 1784, *ibid.,* carta 43B. However, the estimate did not include the cost of a barrel of water per capita ($1,800), nor the additional expense for the purchase of utensils needed for the distribution of meals. In the possible drop of food prices, D'Après saw an opportunity for making a considerable saving.
36. Aranda to D'Asprès, Paris, October 23, 1784, *ibid.,* carta 42.
37. D'Asprès to Aranda, Nantes, November 7, 1784, *ibid.,* carta 43 (copia 4).
38. *Ibid.* D'Asprès also wanted to know if he had authority to pay the ship companies on the day of departure. Cuba, 597, A. G. I.
39. *Ibid.*
40. Peyroux to Aranda, Paris, September 13, 1784, *ibid.,* carta 34 (copia).
41. José de Gálvez to Floridablanca, El Pardo, February 4, 1785, *ibid.,* carta 47; also Aranda to D'Asprès, Paris, November 17, 1784, *ibid.,* carta 45; M. Navarro to Don Baylio Antonio Valdés, "Matters of Government from the 13th to 30th September, 1783," December 19, 1787, in Cuba, 594, A.G.I.
42. D'Asprès to Aranda, Nantes, November 7, 1784, in Estado-Legajo (13), carta 43 (copia 4), A. H. N.

43. *Ibid.*
44. *Ibid.* (copia 3).
45. *Ibid.*
46. *Id.* to *id.*, November 8, 1784, *ibid.*, carta 43 (copia 4).
47. *Ibid.* An agreement was reached whereby the baggage of every passenger would be aboard ship on the day the contract was signed.
48. *Id* to *id.*, November 7, 1784, *ibid.*, carta 43 (copia 3).
49. *Id* to *id.*, November 9, 1784, *ibid.*, carta 43 (copia). D'Asprès here suggested the insertion of a clause which would forbid the ship companies and the captains of the respective ships to make a "forced landing" in a foreign port against the will of the passengers. The shipowners and captains opposed a clause of that nature but D'Asprès did not necessarily suspect them, since he had known them for many years.
50. D'Asprès told Aranda that this condition was of the greatest importance, and that he should confirm his authority by a letter written in French so that everyone would understand it. D'Asprès to Aranda, Nantes, November 7, 1784, *ibid.*, carta 43 (copia 4). Also "Contract of shipowners with Spanish government to transport Acadian families from St. Malo to New Orleans," Cuba, 597, A. G. I.
51. *Ibid.*, in Cuba, 597.
52. Aranda to D'Asprès, Paris, November 17, 1784, in Estado-Legajo 3885 (13), carta 45 (copia 6), A. H. N.
53. Gálvez to Floridablanca, San Lorenzo, October 8, 1784, *ibid.*, carta 38.
54. D'Asprès to Aranda, Nantes, November 7, 1784, *ibid.*, carta 43 (copia 4); *id.* to *id.*, Paris, December 24, 1784, *ibid.*, carta 70 (copia). D'Asprès to ———, Madrid, September 1, 1789, *ibid.*, carta 72.
55. Peyroux to Heredia, Nantes, March 7, 1784, *ibid.*, carta 11 (copia 1).
56. D'Asprès to Aranda, Nantes, November 7, 1784, *ibid.*, carta 43 (copia 4). D'Asprès issued such a request to every family head on March 23, 1785.
57. *Id.* to *id.*, Nantes, November 13, 1784, *ibid.*, carta 44 (copia 5).
58. J. Orieta to A. Ulloa, San Gabriel, September 7, 1767, in Cuba, 109, A. G. I.
59. *Id* to *id.*, September 23, 1767.
60. "Mémoire des habitans et négociants de la Louisiane sur l'événement du October 29, 1768," in Colonies, C 13 A, XLVIII, 245-55, A. N.
61. D'Asprés to Aranda, Nantes, November 13, 1784, in Estado-Legajo 3885 (13), carta 44 (copia 5), A. N. N.
62. *Id.* to *id.*, *ibid.*, carta 44 (copia 5).
63. *Id.* to *id.*, Paris, December 24, 1785, *ibid.*, carta 70 (copia).
64. *Id* to *id.*, Paris, November 7, 1784, *ibid.*, carta 43 (copia 4).
65. Aranda to D'Asprès, Paris, November 17, 1784, *ibid.*, carta 45.
66. D'Asprès to Aranda, Nantes, November 13, 1784, *ibid.*, carta 44. In the event that the proposed postponement would increase expenses too much, D'Asprès suggested that Aranda give the contract for removal of the Acadians to the ship companies of Cadiz. They had a royal cédula to carry merchandise direct from the ports of France to Louisiana. In that way he could meet the extra expense involved in extension of the pay for six months.
67. Aranda to D'Asprès, Paris, November 17, 1784, *ibid.*, carta 45 (copia 6). On November 14, 1784, D'Après had sent Aranda a tentative census of Aca-

dians for Louisiana. He had visited Paimboeuf in person to recruit more volunteers. While there he inspected all ships chartered. D'Asprès to Aranda, Nantes, November 13, 1784, *ibid.,* carta 44.

68. Vergennes to Aranda, Versailles, November 16, 1784, *ibid.,* carta 46 (copia 7).

69. De Calonne to Vergennes, Paris, September 6, 1784, *ibid.,* carta 46 (copia).

70. Comptroller General to Aranda, attached to Aranda's letter to D'Asprès, Madrid, November 16, 1784, *ibid.,* carta 45 (copia 6).

71. D'Asprès to Aranda, Nantes, November 13, 1784, *ibid.,* carta 44 (copia 5).

72. Aranda to Floridablanca, Paris, November 19, 1784, *ibid.,* carta 39, (No. 107).

73. *Id.* to *id.,* Paris, November 14, 1785, *ibid.,* carta 49, postscript. See "Copy of articles in letter of the Consul Don Manuel d'Asprès," March, 1785, *ibid.,* carta 51ᵃ.

74. *Id.* to *id.,* Paris, November 19, 1784, *ibid.,* carta 39.

75. *Ibid.*

76. *De Bow's Review* (May, 1847), 411, quoted in Gayarré, *History of Louisiana,* II, 393-94.

77. José de Gálvez to Floridablanca, El Pardo, February 4, 1785, in Estado-Legajo 3885 (13), carta 47, A. H. N. See unsigned copy of a letter to Floridablanca, March, 1785, *ibid.,* carta 50, containing Charles III's answer to Aranda's five questions, which the prime minister sent to Aranda to observe, and which in turn Aranda sent as his latest orders to D'Après.

78. *Ibid.*

79. José de Gálvez to Floridablanca, El Pardo, February 4, 1785, *ibid.,* carta 47.

80. *Ibid.,* See *id.* to Bernardo de Gálvez, El Pardo, February 4, 1785, in Cuba, 1375, A. G. I.; *id.* to E. Miró, Mexico, June 24, 1785, *ibid.,* 149A. José de Gálvez to Floridablanca, El Pardo, February 4, 1785, in Estado-Legajo 3885 (13), carta 47, A. H. N.

81. —— to José de Gálvez, Aranjuez, April 17, 1785, in Estado-Legajo 3885 (13), carta 54, A. H. N. *Id.* to Floridablanca, Aranjuez, April 20, 1785, *ibid.,* carta 55; José de Gálvez to Count de Gálvez, April 20, 1785, in Cuba, 626B, A.G.I.; D'Asprès to Miró, Nantes, May 27, 1785, *ibid.*

82. Aranda to Floridablanca, Paris, May 10, 1785, in Estado-Legajo 3885 (13), carta 56, A. H. N.

83. José de Gálvez to *id.,* El Pardo, February 4, 1785, *ibid.,* carta 47. Aranda rendered a most meticulous and methodical account of every penny and sent to José de Gálvez a "Register Book" in which he gave the name of every Acadian recruited for Louisiana, his age, and his trade.

84. Aranda to Vergennes, in Correspondance politique Espagne, DCXVI, ff. 269-70, A. A. É.

85. *Id.* to Floridablanca, Paris, March 4, 1785, in Estado-Legajo 3885 (13), carta 49, A. H. N.

86. —— to *id.,* March, 1785, *ibid.,* carta 50 (unsigned), which Aranda sent to D'Après.

87. *Ibid.*

88. Aranda to *id.,* Paris, April 4, 1785, *ibid.,* carta 52.

89. Acadian petition to Vergennes, in Correspondance politique Espagne, DCXLL, f. 287, A. A. É.

90. Terrio, "Précis des faits," in Cuba, 197, A. G. I.

91. Aranda to Floridablanca, Paris, May 13, 1785, in Estado-Legajo 3885 (13), carta 57, A. H. N.

CHAPTER TEN

In this chapter and the following many of the cartas found in the Cuban legajos (bundles) were copies without signature or addressee. In many cases the names of writer and addressee were evident from internal evidences either in the letter or from related letters, and in these cases the proper names were supplied for the sake of clarity. But wherever there was a grave doubt question marks or dashes were used.

Le Bon Papa

1. Aranda to Floridablanca, Paris, December 5, 1785, in Estado-Legajo 3885 (13), carta 66, A. H. N.; *id. to id.*, Paris, January 27, 1766, *ibid.*, carta 73, A. H. N.
2. D'Après to Aranda, Paris, December 24, 1785, *ibid.*, carta 70 (copia); *id.* to Miró, Nantes, September 30, 1785, in Cuba, 626B, A. G. I.
3. Aranda to Floridablanca, Paris, January 27, 1786, in Estado-Legajo 3885 (13), carta 73, A. H. N.
4. Register of each expedition. D'Après to Provisional Governor (in New Orleans). Nantes, May 27, 1785, in Cuba, 626B, A. G. I.
5. *Ibid.*, Nantes, May 8, 1785.
6. Aranda to Floridablanca, Paris, May 12, 1785 in Estado-Legajo 3885 (13), carta 57, A. H. N.
7. Anselmo Blanchard's registration list, New Orleans, July 29, 1785, in Cuba, 602B, A. G. I.
8. Aranda to Floridablanca, Paris, May 13, 1785, in Estado-Legajo 3885 (13), carta 57, A. H. N., gives May 10; so does Oliver Terrio, "Précis de faits," in Cuba, 197, A. G. I. But Blanchard's registration list made in New Orleans, July 29, 1785, *ibid.*, 602B, states May 8.
9. Registration list, New Orleans, July 29, 1785, in *ibid.*, 602B, A. G. I.
10. D'Après to Provisional Governor (in New Orleans), Nantes, May 8, 1785, in Cuba, 626B; also Navarro to El Conde de Gálvez, New Orleans, August 2, 1785, *ibid.*, 85.
11. Blanchard's registration list, New Orleans, July 29, 1785, *ibid.*, 602B.
12. Blanchard's report, New Orleans, July 29, 1785, *ibid.*, 602B; Navarro to José de Gálvez, New Orleans, August 15, 1785, *ibid.*, 633.
13. *Id.* to Count de Gálvez, New Orleans, August 2, 1785, *ibid.*, 85; *id*, to José de Gálvez, New Orleans, August 15, 1785, *ibid.*, 633, speaks of 37 families of 155 persons.
14. Count de Gálvez to *id.*, Mexico, June 24, 1785, *ibid.*, 594, A. G. I.
15. José de Gálvez to Count de Gálvez, El Pardo, February 4, 1785, *ibid.*, 604A, A. G. I.
16. Count de Gálvez to Navarro, Mexico, June 24, 1785, *ibid.*, 594.
17. *Id.* to Miró, Mexico, October 18, 1785, *ibid.*, 149A. He was granted a salary of 4,000 pesos a year and exempted from paying the king half the salary for the first year.
18. Navarro to Count de Gálvez, New Orleans, September 6, 1785, *ibid.*, 85.
19. *Id.* to José de Gálvez, New Orleans, September 9, 1785, *ibid.*, 633 (copia 326).

20. D'Asprès to Provisional Governor (in New Orleans), Nantes, March 8, 12, 1785, *ibid.,* 626B.
21. Navarro to ——, New Orleans, July 30, 1785, *ibid.,* 604A.
22. *Id.* to Count de Gálvez, New Orleans, August 2, October 4, 1785, *ibid.,* 85.
23. *Id.* to Morales, March 10, 1786, *ibid.,* 606; Sonora to Count de Gálvez, March 4, 1786, *ibid.,* 1375.
24. Blanchard's registration list, New Orleans, July 29, 1785, *ibid.,* 602B, A. G. I. The spelling of these names and of names throughout this work is given as they were found in the documents. There were great differences from modern usage in spelling and accents. See Appendix A.
25. See the official registration lists, and Josef V. Vahamonde to Miró, Baton Rouge, September 30, 1788, *ibid.,* 576.
26. Navarro to José Gálvez, New Orleans, August 15, 1785, *ibid.,* 633; *id.* to Count de Gálvez, New Orleans, August 2, 1785, *ibid.,* 85.
27. *Id.* to José Gálvez, New Orleans, August 15, 1785, *ibid.,* 633 (copia 306).
28. Navarro's chart, New Orleans, June 15, 1786, *ibid.,* 633; found also in 604A, 608B, and 626B.
29. Blanchard's report, New Orleans, August 26, 1785, *ibid.,* 602B.
30. Navarro to José de Gálvez, New Orleans, August 15, 1785, *ibid.,* 633 (copia 306).
31. *Id.* to Count de Gálvez, New Orleans, October 4, 1785, *ibid.,* 85.
32. Blanchard to Navarro, New Orleans, August 26, 1785, *ibid.,* 602B.
33. Navarro to José de Gálvez, New Orleans, September 9, 1785, *ibid.,* 633 (carta 332).
34. *Id.* to Morales, New Orleans, August 26, 1785, *ibid.,* 604A (carta 1).
35. *Id.* to *id.,* New Orleans, September 16, 1785, *ibid.,* 604A (carta 5).
36. *Id.* to José de Gálvez, New Orleans, August 15, 1785, *ibid.,* 633.

La Bergere

37. D'Asprès to Count de Gálvez, Nantes, May 12, 1785, *ibid.,* 626B.
38. *Id.* to Aranda, Paris, December 24, 1785 in Estado-Legajo, carta 70, A. H. N.
39. Aranda to Floridablanca, Paris, May 13, 1785, *ibid.,* carta 57.
40. D'Asprès to Count de Gálvez (in Havana), Nantes, May 12, 1785, in Cuba, 626B, A. G. I.
41. *Ibid.; id.* to Provisional Governor (in New Orleans), Nantes, May 12, 1785, *ibid.,* 626B. Navarro to José de Gálvez, New Orleans, August 15, 1785, *ibid.,* 633 (copia 306); *id.* to Count de Gálvez, New Orleans, October 4, 1785, *ibid.,* 85, both give 265 passengers; but Count de Gálvez to Miró, Mexico, October 20, 1785, *ibid.,* 633, gives 275 passengers.
42. Navarro's chart, New Orleans, June 15, 1786, *ibid.,* 633.
43. Terrio, "Précis de faits" (Resolution), Nantes, May 12, 1785, *ibid.,* 197.
44. *Ibid.,* also Navarro to José Gálvez New Orleans, September 9, 1785, *ibid.,* 633 (copia 332). This was one of the conditions in the contract with the shipowners. See Chapter Nine.
45. Terrio, "Précis des faits" (Resolution), *ibid.,* 197.
46. D'Asprés to Count de Gálvez (in Havana), Nantes, May 12, 1785, in Cuba, 626B, A. G. I.
47. *Ibid.,* Miró to D'Asprès, New Orleans, September 9, 1785, *ibid.*
48. Count de Gálvez to Miró, Mexico, November 15, 1785, *ibid.,* 633.
49. D'Asprès to Provisional Governor (in New Orleans), Nantes, May 12, 1785, *ibid.,* 626B.

50. José de Gálvez to Count de Gálvez, El Prado, February 21, 1785, *ibid.*, 1375.
51. Navarro to José de Gálvez, New Orleans, October 8, 1785, *ibid.*, 593 (carta 337).
52. Navarro to José de Gálvez, New Orleans, August 15, 1785, *ibid.*, 633 (copia 316).
53. Navarro's chart, New Orleans, June 15, 1786, *ibid.*, 633.
54. *Id* to José de Gálvez, New Orleans, October 8, 1785, *ibid.*, carta 339.
55. Navarro's chart, New Orleans, June 15, 1786, *ibid.*, 633.
56. *Id.* to Morales, New Orleans, October 26, 1785, *ibid.*, 604A. The marriages were between Antonio Mollard, immigrant, and María Bourgue of the twenty-sixth family disembarked on September 19, 1785; Francisco Terruit, immigrant, and Isabel Bourgue of the fortieth family disembarked on September 19, 1785; and Joseph Dugats of the sixth family disembarked from the *St. Remy* and Isabel Landry, of the sixtieth family of the *St. Remy* on October 23, 1785. The record of a fourth marriage is missing.
57. *Id.* to José de Gálvez, New Orleans, October 8, 1785, *ibid.*, 633 (copia 338).
58. Prieto to Navarro, New Orleans, September 22, 1785, *ibid.*, 567. The author could not find the list giving the order of the Acadian families as they disembarked at New Orleans from *La Bergere*. The same was true for the fourth, fifth, sixth, and seventh expeditions. However, the names of the families can be gathered easily from those given in Juan Prieto's list of tools with which he furnished those expeditions. See Appendix B.
59. Navarro to Morales, New Orleans, September 1, 1785, *ibid.*, 604A., carta 3.
60. *Id.* to *id.*, New Orleans, October 1, 1785, *ibid.*, 604A, carta 13.
61. *Id.* to José de Gálvez, New Orleans, October 8, 1785, *ibid.*, 633 (copia 339).
62. *Id.* to Morales, New Orleans, September 25, 1785, *ibid.*, 604A.
63. *Id.* to *id.*, New Orleans, November 13, 1785, *ibid.*
64. *Id* to *id.*, New Orleans, November 28, 1785, *ibid.*
65. *Id.* to José de Gálvez, New Orleans, October 8, 1785, *ibid.*, 633 (copia 339).

Le Beaumont

66. D'Après to Provisional Governor (in New Orleans), Nantes, May 27, 1785, in Cuba, 626B, A. G. I.
67. Navarro's chart, New Orleans, June 15, 1786, *ibid.*, 633; *id.* to José de Gálvez, New Orleans, September 9, 1785, *ibid.*, 633 (copia 332), reported 51 families.
68. See registration list of Pedro Aragon y Villegas, New Orleans, September 6, 1785, *ibid.*, 626A.
69. D'Après to Provisional Governor (in New Orleans), Nantes, May 27, 1785, *ibid.*, 626B.
70. *Ibid.*
71. Aranda to Floridablanca, Paris, November 19, 1784, in Estado-Legajo 3885 (13), carta 39, A. H. N.
72. D'Après to Provisional Governor (in New Orleans), Nantes, May 27, 1785, in Cuba, 626B; also Miró to D'Après, New Orleans, September 9, 1785, *ibid.*, A. G. I.
73. D'Après to Provisional Governor (in New Orleans), Nantes, May 27, 1785, *ibid.*; Heredia to Floridablanca, Paris, June 20, 1785, in Estado-Legajo (13), carta 59, A. H. N.
74. Navarro to José de Gálvez, New Orleans, September 9, 1785, in Cuba, 633, carta 332, A. G. I.

75. D'Après to Provisional Governor (in New Orleans), Nantes, May 27, 1785, *ibid., 626B.*
76. Navarro to Morales, New Orleans, September 4, 1785, *ibid.,* 576; Count de Gálvez to Miró, Mexico, October 20, 1785, *ibid.,* 633.
77. Navarro's chart, New Orleans, June 15, 1786, *ibid.*
78. Miró to ———, New Orleans, July 29, 1785, *ibid.,* 604A.
79. Navarro to José de Gálvez, New Orleans, September 9, 1785, *ibid.,* 633.
80. Count de Gálvez to Miró, Mexico, October 20, 1785, *ibid ;* ——— to Josef Petely, New Orleans, August 19, 1785, *ibid.,* 85 (copia).
81. Heredia to Floridablanca, Paris, June 20, 1785, in Estado-Legajo 3885 (13). carta 59, A. H. N.
82. D'Après to Provisional Governor (in New Orleans), Nantes, May 27, 1785 in Cuba, 626B, A. G. I.
83. Registration list of Pedro Aragon y Villegas, New Orleans, September 6, 1785, *ibid.,* 626A (copia). See Appendix C.
84. Prieto to Navarro, New Orleans, September 4, 1785, *ibid.,* 576.
85. Navarro to Morales, New Orleans, September 6, 1785, *ibid.,* 604A.
86. Navarro's chart, New Orleans, June 15, 1785, *ibid.,* 633.
87. *Id.* to José de Gálvez, New Orleans, September 9, 1785, *ibid.* (copia 332); Sonora to Navarro, El Pardo, March 2, 1786, *ibid.,* 560. This was the royal approval of Navarro's work.

St. Remy

88. Heredia to Floridablanca, Paris, June 20, 1785, in Estado-Legajo 3885 (13), carta 59, A. H. N.
89. D'Après to Aranda, Nantes, October 10, 1785, *ibid,* carta 41.
90. Report of D'Après, Nantes, June 23, 1785, in Cuba, 626B, A. G. I.; Navarro's chart, New Orleans, June 15, 1786, *ibid.,* 633, gives 77 families.
91. D'Après to Provincial Governor (in New Orleans), Nantes, June 29, 1785, *ibid., 626B.* In his report of June 23, D'Après implies that the *St. Remy* had sailed from Nantes.
92. Aranda to Floridablanca, Paris, July 31, 1785, carta 81, A. H. N.
93. D'Après to Provincial Governor (in New Orleans), Nantes, June 23, 1785, in Cuba, 626B, A. G. I.; Heredia to Floridablanca, Paris, July 4, 1785, in Estado-Legajo 3885 (13), carta 60, A. H. N. But Navarro to José de Gálvez, New Orleans, September 9, 1785, in Cuba, 633 (copia 335), A. G. I., reported that the "frigate *St. Remy* [had] just arrived from Nantes with 329 Acadians."
94. Miró to D'Après, New Orleans, September 9, 1785, in Cuba, 626B, A. G. I.
95. Aranda to Floridablanca, Paris, July 31, 1786, in Estado-Legajo 3885 (13), carta 81, A. H. N.
96. Miró to D'Aprés, New Orleans, September 9, 1785, in Cuba, 626B, A. G. I.
97. Navarro to ———, New Orleans, September 9, 1785, *ibid.,* 633 (carta 335).
98. *Id.* to ———, New Orleans, September 9, 1785, *ibid.,* 633.
99. *Id.* [?] to D'Après, New Orleans, September 9, 1785, *ibid., 626B.*
100. ——— to Petely, New Orleans, August 3, 1785, *ibid.,* 3.
101. Navarro [?] to José de Gálvez [?], New Orleans, September 9, 1785, *ibid.,* 633 (carta 336).
102. Navarro to Marqués de Sonora, New Orleans, April 15, 1786, *ibid.,* 593 (copia 377).

103. Count de Gálvez to Miró, Mexico, March 18, 1786, *ibid.,* 149A, gives 420 and 598 Acadians.
104. Navarro to José de Gálvez, New Orleans, September 9, 1785, *ibid.,* 633 (carta 329); Sonora to *id.,* El Pardo, March 2, 1786, *ibid.,* 560.
105. Navarro [?] to José de Gálvez, New Orleans, August 15, 1785, *ibid.,* 633 (copia).
106. *Ibid.*
107. Navarro to José de Gálvez, New Orleans, September 9, 1785, *ibid.* (carta 328).
108. Miró to ——, New Orleans, September 9, 1785, *ibid.*
109. Navarro to Count de Gálvez, New Orleans, December 12, 1785, *ibid.,* 85.
110. Miró to ——, New Orleans, September 9, 1785, *ibid.,* 633 (carta 328).
111. Navarro to José de Gálvez, New Orleans, September 9, 1785, *ibid.* (carta 330).
112. Sonora to Navarro, El Prado, March 2, 1786, *ibid.,* 560.
113. José de Gálvez to Count de Gálvez, El Pardo, February 4, 1785, *ibid.,* 604A; Count de Gálvez to Miró, Mexico, June 24, 1785, *ibid.,* 149A; Sonora to Floridablanca, El Pardo, February 4, 1786, *ibid.,* 592; *id.* to Count de Gálvez, El Pardo, March 2, 1786, *ibid.,* 1375.
114. Navarro to José de Gálvez, New Orleans, September 9, 1785, *ibid.,* 633 (copia 333). This was the same sum the government had allowed the isleños or Canary Islanders.
115. *Ibid.;* Navarro to Count de Gálvez, New Orleans, December 12, 1785, *ibid.,* 85.
116. Sonora to Navarro, El Prado, March 2, 1786, *ibid.,* 560.
117. Navarro to Morales, New Orleans, September 16, 1785, *ibid.,* 604A; New Orleans, October 25, 1785, in Cuba, 604B (carta 13); *ibid.,* New Orleans, November 7, 1785; Manuel Josef Rámos to Nicholas Verret, New Orleans, November 18, 1785, *ibid.,* 608B. The separated Acadians given such status were:

María Magdalene Durambourgue (wife of the absent Juan Lirret) and her daughters, María Juan and Rosa Adelaide, who were to join her brother Juan Baptista Durambourgue with privilege of family head until her husband arrived; María Boudreau (wife of the absent Francisco Avarat), Juan María, her infant, and Joseph Boudreau, her brother, who were to join her father, Juan Carlos Boudreau; Joseph Grandchè who was to join the family of his cousin, Simon Landry; Magdalena le Prince, wife of Ourdon Tomás Caligán, and Susan María, daughter of Tranquilo le Prince who were to join her brother with privilege of family head until her husband arrived; Joseph, "Chere Amis," his wife, Ana Thibodo, and her son, Pedro Bourgue, whom Navarro felt ought to form one family; Iber Rouseau and his wife Ana Aucoing, whom he felt ought to form one family; María Rosa Livoir, passenger on *La Bergere,* whom he felt ought to be united to the family of Gregorio Blanchard, her brother-in-law; María La Bouve, whom he felt ought to be united to her brother, Pedro La Bouve; Juan Liveret, 23 years of age (of expedition *La Amistad*), who was to join his family of Citania Boudreau; and Juan Buclose, 22 years of age (of expedition *La Amistad*), who was to join his mother María Magdalena Durambourgue.

118. The author was able to find the record of only two of these five marriages. Navarro to Morales, November 15, 1785, *ibid.,* 604B.

119. Navarro to Morales, New Orleans, November 15, 1785, *ibid.*
120. Navarro to Count de Gálvez, New Orleans, October 4, 1785, *ibid.,* 85; *id.* to *id.,* in Cuba, 3, A. G. I.
121. Navarro's chart, New Orleans, June 1786, *ibid.,* 633. The author was unsuccessful in finding the list of the 87 families Juan Prieto had equipped with the necessary farming tools early in December, 1785.
122. Navarro to Morales, New Orleans, October 13, 14, 1785, *ibid.,* 604A (cartas 7, 8); *id.* to *id.,* December 15, 1785, *ibid.* (carta 14); *id.* to *id.,* New Orleans, December 16, 1785, *ibid.* (carta 15).
123. *Id.* to José de Gálvez, New Orleans, September 9, 1785, *ibid.,* 633 (carta 331); *id.* to *id.,* New Orleans, October 4, 1785, *ibid.,* 85; Count de Gálvez to *id.,* Mexico, November 13, 1785, *ibid.,* 606 supports him; Sonora to Count de Gálvez, El Pardo, March 4, 1786, *ibid.,* 1375. This was royal approval of his conduct.

La Amistad

124. D'Asprès to Provisional Governor (in New Orleans), Nantes, June 29, 1785, Cuba, 626B, A. G. I.; Louis Landaluze to Miró, Nantes, July 26, 1785, *ibid.*
125. Heredia to Floridablanca, Paris, August 12, 1785, in Estado-Legajo 3885 (13), carta 61, A. H. N.; Landaluze to Miró, Nantes, July 26, 1785, in Cuba, 626B, A. G. I. The manuscripts are not clear as to the exact day of departure of *La Amistad,* but August 12, 1785, seems to be the probable date.
126. Landaluze to ——, Nantes, July 26, 1785, in Cuba, 626B, A. G. I.
127. Navarro to Count de Gálvez, New Orleans, December 1, 1785, *ibid.,* 85; Navarro's chart, New Orleans, June 15, 1786, *ibid.,* 633.
128. Landaluze to ——, Nantes, July 26, 1785, *ibid.,* 626B.
129. Navarro to Count de Gálvez, December 1, 1785, *ibid.,* 85.
130. *Id.* to Morales, New Orleans, November 28, 1785, *ibid.* 604B.
131. Navarro's chart, New Orleans, June 15, 1786, *ibid.,* 633.
132. *Id.* to José de Gálvez, New Orleans, November 14 [?], 1785, *ibid.,* 595 (copia 344). Manuscript illegible in places.
133. *Id.* to Morales, New Orleans, November 28, 1785, *ibid.,* 604B.
134. *Id.* to Count de Gálvez, New Orleans, December 12, 1785, *ibid.,* 85.
135. Aranda to Floridablanca, Paris, July 31, 1786, in Estado-Legajo 3885 (13), carta 81, A. H. N.
136. *Id.* to *id.,* Paris, September 22, 1786, *ibid.,* carta 82.
137. Navarro to José de Gálvez, New Orleans, September 9, 1785, in Cuba, 633 (carta 334), A. G. I.
138. Terrio, "Précis des faits," *ibid.,* 197, f. 3.
139. Navarro to José de Gálvez, New Orleans, September 9, 1785, *ibid.,* 633 (carta 334); Sonora to Navarro, El Pardo, March 2, 1786, *ibid.,* 560.
140. *Id.* to Count de Gálvez, New Orleans, December 12, 1785, *ibid.,* 85.
141. Henry E. Chambers, *Mississippi Valley Beginnings, an outline of the early history of the earlier West* (New York, 1922), 139-40. See Appendix D.
142. Navarro's chart, New Orleans, June 15, 1786, in Cuba, 633, A. G. I.
143. Prieto to Morales, New Orleans, December 15, 1785, *ibid.,* 576. See Appendix E.
144. Navarro's chart, New Orleans, June 15, 1786, *ibid.,* 633; *id.* to José de Gálvez, New Orleans, December 1, 1785, *ibid.,* 85; Prieto to Morales, New Orleans, December 15, 1785, *ibid.,* 576.

145. *Id.* to Morales, New Orleans, November 10, 18, 1785, *ibid.,* 604A (cartas 9, 11).

146. Prieto to Morales, New Orleans, December 15, 1785, and January 15, 1786, *ibid.,* 576.

La Ville de Arcangel

147. D'Asprès to Provisional Governor (in New Orleans), Nantes, June 29, 1785, *ibid.,* 626B.

148. Landaluze to Governor of New Orleans, Nantes, July 26, 1785, *ibid.*

149. D'Asprès to Governor of New Orleans, Nantes, July 12, 1785, *ibid.;* Aranda to Floridablanca, Paris, October 6, 1785, in Estado-Legajo 3885 (13), carta 64, A. H. N.; José de Gálvez to Floridablanca, San Lorenzo, October 29, 1785, *ibid.,* carta 65; Navarro to José de Gálvez, New Orleans, November 14, 1785 in Cuba, 633, A. G. I., states 307 passengers; *id.* to *id.,* New Orleans, December 12, 1785, *ibid.,* 85, gives 304 passengers.

150. D'Asprès to Governor of New Orleans, Nantes, July 12, 1785, *ibid.,* 626B.

151. D'Asprès to Governor of New Orleans, Nantes, July 12, 1785, *ibid.,* 626B.

152. *Ibid.*

153. Heredia to Floridablanca, Paris, August 12, 1785, in Estado-Legajo 3885 (13), carta 61, A. H. N.

154. Navarro to José de Gálvez, New Orleans, November 14, 1785, in Cuba, 633 (carta 345), A. G. I.

155. *Id.* to Count de Gálvez, New Orleans, December 12, 1785, *ibid.,* 85.

156. *Ibid. Id.* [?] to José de Gálvez, New Orleans, December 22, 1785, *ibid.,* 633 (carta 351).

157. *Id.* [?] to Count de Gálvez, New Orleans, December 12, 1785, *ibid.,* 85.

158. *Ibid.;* José de Gálvez to Floridablanca, El Pardo, February 4, 1785, *ibid.,* 594.

159. Morales to Navarro, New Orleans, February 7, 1786, *ibid.,* 606.

160. Navarro to Count de Gálvez, New Orleans, December 12, 1785, *ibid.,* 85; *id.* [?] to ——, New Orleans, December 22, 1785, *ibid.,* 633 (carta 351).

161. *Id.* to Count de Gálvez, New Orleans, December 12, 1785, *ibid.,* 85; *id.* to Sonora, New Orleans, April 15, 1786, *ibid.,* 593 (carta 377).

162. Navarro's chart, New Orleans, June 15, 1786, *ibid.,* 633.

163. *Id.* to Morales, New Orleans, January 15, 1786, *ibid.,* 604B.

The record of one marriage is missing, but available records show Nicolas Courtula, immigrant, was married to María Carlota Pitre (32nd family) on December 12, 1785; Juan Mapre, immigrant, to María Landry, on December 22, 1785; Francisco Hébert, Acadian (3rd family landed), to Angelica Henry, sister of Pedro Henry (38th family landed), on January 3, 1786; Alexo AuCoing (5th family), to Francisca Henry on January 3, 1786; Santiago Blanchard to Modesta Aimie (36th family) on January 5, 1786; and Pedro AuCoing (24th family), to María Hébert, on January 14, 1786.

164. *Id.* to ——, New Orleans, January 20, 1786, *ibid.,* 604B.

165. Navarro's chart, New Orleans, June 15, 1786, *ibid.,* 633.

166. Prieto to Morales, New Orleans, January 17, 1786, *ibid.,* 576. See Appendix F.

167. Navarro to Morales, New Orleans, January 10, 1786, *ibid.,* 604A (cartas 13, 18, 20).

168. *Id.* to Sonora, New Orleans, February 22, 1786, *ibid.,* 593 (carta 363).

169. *Id.* to Count de Gálvez, New Orleans, February 8, 1786, *ibid.,* 86; Navarro's chart, New Orleans, June 15, 1786, *ibid.,* 633.
170. *Id.* to Count de Gálvez, New Orleans, December 12, 1785, *ibid.,* 85.

La Carolina

171. Josef Petely to Miró, Balize, December 12, 1785, *ibid.,* 3 (carta 772).
172. D'Asprès to Miró, Nantes, September 20, 1785, *ibid.,* 626.
173. —— to D'Asprès, New Orleans, February 14, 1786, *ibid.,* 626.
174. Navarro's chart, New Orleans, June 15, 1786, *ibid.,* 633.
175. Navarro to ——, New Orleans, January 13, 1786, *ibid.,* 604A (carta 20); Prieto to Morales, New Orleans, December 15, 1785, *ibid.,* 576; Navarro's "Record of Acadian families of the expedition *La Amistad* that arrived on November 7, 1785," New Orleans, November 28, 1785, *ibid.,* 604B.
176. Prieto to Morales, New Orleans, January 17, 1786, *ibid.,* 576. One family was omitted from the list. See Appendix G.
177. Navarro to ——, New Orleans, January 13 and February 15, 1786, *ibid.,* 604A. (cartas 20, 21).
178. *Id.* to Count de Gálvez, New Orleans, February 8, 1786, *ibid.,* 86.
179. Count de Gálvez to Navarro, New Orleans, May 8, 1786, *ibid.,* 604A.
180. Sonora to Navarro, El Prado, March 2, 1786, *ibid.,* 560.
181. José de Gálvez to Floridablanca, San Lorenzo, October 29, 1785, in Estado-Legajo 3885 (13), carta 65, A. H. N.; D'Asprès to Miró, Nantes, September 30, 1785, in Cuba, 626, A. G. I.
182. D'Asprès to Aranda, Paris, December 24, 1785, in Estado-Legajo 3885 (13), carta 70, A. H. N.
183. Aranda to Floridablanca, Paris, December 5, 1785, *ibid.,* carta 66.

CHAPTER ELEVEN

1. Terrio, "Précis des faits," in Cuba, 197, f. 4, A. G. I.
2. Aranda to Floridablanca, Paris, December 5, 1785, in Estado-Legajo 3885 (13), carta 66, A. H. N. Sonora to *id.,* El Pardo, March 2, 1786, *ibid.,* carta 79.
3. Aranda to Floridablanca, Paris, January 27, 1786, in Estado-Legajo 3885 (13), carta 73, A. H. N.; Sonora to *id.,* El Pardo, March 2, 1786, *ibid.,* carta 79.
4. Aranda to *id.,* Paris, October 6, 1785, *ibid.,* carta 64; José de Gálvez to *id.,* San Lorenzo, October 29, 1785, *ibid.,* carta 65.
5. Navarro's chart, New Orleans, June 15, 1786, in Cuba 633, found also in *ibid.,* 604A, 608B, 626B, A. G. I.
6. Aranda to Floridablanca, Paris, January 27, 1786, in Estado-Legajo 3885 (13), carta 73, A. H. N.
7. Count de Gálvez to Miró, Mexico, October 20, 1785, in Cuba, 633, A. G. I.
8. *Id.* to *id.,* Mexico, October 18, 1785, *ibid.,* 149A.
9. Miró to Count de Gálvez, New Orleans, December 12, 1785, *ibid.,* 2360.
10. Aranda to Floridablanca, Paris, July 31, 1786, in Estado-Legajo 3885 (13), carta 81; *ibid.,* September 22, carta 82, A. H. N.
11. Navarro to José de Gálvez, New Orleans, September 9, 1785, in Cuba, 633 (carta 334), A. G. I.
12. Aranda to Floridablanca, Paris, July 31, 1786, in Estado-Legajo 3885 (13), carta 81, A. H. N.
13. D'Asprès to Aranda, Nantes, November 7, 1784, *ibid.,* carta 43 (copia 3).

14. Aranda to Floridablanca, Paris, September 22, 1786, *ibid.*, carta 82.
15. *Id.* to *id.*, Paris, July 31, 1786, *ibid.*, carta 81; Heredia to *id.*, Paris, October 28, 1786, *ibid.*, carta 83.
16. *Id.* to *id.*, Paris, February 21, 1784, *ibid.*, carta 6.
17. Aranda to *id.*, Paris, January 27, 1786, *ibid.*, carta 73.
18. Sonora to *id.*, El Pardo, March 2, 1786, *ibid.*, carta 79.
19. ——— to Aranda, El Prado, April 6, 1786, in Estado-Legajo 3885 (13), carta 80; unsigned, unaddressed letter, November 29, 1785, *ibid.*, carta 68.
20. Aranda to Floridablanca, Paris, January 27, 1786, *ibid.*, 3885 (13), carta 73.
21. *Id.* to *id.*, Paris, December 5, 1786, *ibid.*, 3885 (13), carta 66.
22. ——— to Aranda, El Pardo, April 6, 1786, *ibid.*, carta 80.
23. Sonora to Intendant of Louisiana, Aranjuez, July 2, 1786, in Cuba, 593, A. G. I.
24. D'Asprès to Aranda, Paris, December 24, 1785, in Estado-Legajo (13), carta 70, A. H. N.
25. *Id.* to ———, Madrid, September 1, 1789, *ibid.*, carta 72; Juan de la Plaza to Floridablanca, Dunkerque, November 14, 1785, *ibid.*, carta 67; Lineage of Manuel d'Asprès, September 1, 1789, *ibid.*, carta 69; Luis Landaluze to ———, Nantes, November 12, 1785, *ibid.*, carta 71.
26. Peyroux to Heredia, Nantes, March 7, 1784, *ibid.*, carta 11 (copia 1).
27. Aranda to Floridablanca, November 19, 1784, *ibid.*, carta 39.
28. D'Asprès to Miró, May 27, 1785, in Cuba, 626B, A. G. I.; José de Gálvez to Floridablanca, San Ildefonso, September 6, 1784 in Estado-Legajo 3885 (13), carta 30, A. H. N.
29. José de Gálvez to Floridablanca, El Pardo, February 4, 1785, in Estado-Legajo 3885 (13), carta 47, A. H. N.
30. Count de Gálvez to Navarro, Mexico, June 24, 1785, in Cuba, 594.
31. Count de Gálvez to Miró, Mexico, November 15, 1785, *ibid.*, 149A; Sonora to Navarro, El Pardo, March 2, 1786, *ibid.*, 560; Navarro to Morales, New Orleans, December 12, 1785, *ibid.*, 604A, carta 62. José de Gálvez had first granted Peyroux $500 a year, but when he complained vociferously about the reduction in his salary, Marqués de Sonora later raised it to $600, *ibid.*
32. Terrio, "Précis des faits," La Fourche, Louisiana, April 2, 1792, *ibid.*, 197, carta 22.
33. Miró to J. Orúe, New Orleans, June 20, 1789, *ibid.*, 705; Orúe to Miró, New Orleans, July 8, 1791, *ibid*, 576; Valdés to *id.*, May 6, 1789, *ibid.*
34. Morales to Navarro, New Orleans, January 31, 1786, *ibid.*, 606.
35. Navarro to Count de Gálvez, New Orleans, February 8, 1786, *ibid.*, 86; *id.* to *id.*, New Orleans, January 13, 1786, *ibid.*, 633 (carta 358), *ibid.*, 604A.
36. Count de Gálvez to Miró, Mexico, September 25, 1785, *ibid.*, 149A.
37. Navarro to Jacobo Dubreuil, New Orleans, December 23, 1785, *ibid.*, 85. ——— to Dubreuil, New Orleans, December 23, 1785, *ibid.*, 602A.
38. Sonora to Morales, El Pardo, April 5, 1785, *ibid.*, 597. In this letter, Sonora addressed Morales as "Intendant of Louisiana" in telling him that the king knew of the safe arrival of *La Carolina.*
39. Navarro to Count de Gálvez, New Orleans, September 6, 1785, *ibid.*, 85.
40. *Id.* to *id.*, New Orleans, August 23, 1786, *ibid.*, 633, carta 415 (copia). Original of Navarro's chart, New Orleans, June 15, 1786, is found in Legajo Cuba, 604A.
41. Sonora to *id.*, San Ildefonso, August 6, 1786, *ibid.*, 1375.
42. Miró to *id.*, New Orleans, February 7, 1786, *ibid.*, 2360.

43. José de Gálvez to Floridablanca, El Pardo, February 4, 1785, in Estado-Legajo 3885 (13), carta 47, A. H. N.

44. "Mémoire sur les Acadiens," in Angleterre 1763, CDXLIX, f. 343, A. A. É.; Foucault à M. Dobuq, February 28, 1765, in Colonies, C¹³A, XLV, A. N.; R. P. Riguad, *Vie De la Bonne Soeur Elizabeth* (Paris, 1867), 130-31; Antonio Huot, "Les Acadiens de la Louisiane," in *Revue Canadienne*, LVII (July, 1909), 32-47.

45. Chambers, *Mississippi Valley Beginnings*, 131-146.

APPENDIX A

Anselmo Blanchard's registration of Acadian families in the order in which they left *Le Bon Papa:* *

1st—Joseph Le Blanc; Ana Hébert, wife; Joseph, son; Simon, son; Blanca, daughter; María, daughter; Esther, mother-in-law and widow.

2nd—Andrés Trample; Margarita Le Blanc, wife; Juan, son; Carlos, son; Santiago, son; Servando, son; Olivier, son; Andrés, son; Isable, daughter; María Magdalena, daughter.

3rd—Joseph Henrique; Cecilia Breau, wife; Juan Lorenzo, son; Joseph, son; Pedro, son; María Josepha, daughter; Ana Fernanda, daughter; Magdalena Polonia, daughter.

4th—Carlos Landry; Margarita Boudeut, wife; Fermin, son; Sebastian, son; Luís, son; Juan, son; Carlos, son; Francisco, son; Margarita, daughter.

5th—Amable Hébert; Andrés, son; María, daughter; Genoveva, daughter; Isabel, daughter.

6th—Juan Carlos LeBlanc; Brigida Ebert, wife.

7th—Simon LeBlanc; María Trahan, wife; Joseph, son; Santiago, son; Ana, daughter.

8th—Juan LeBlanc; Teresa Ebert. wife; María, daughter, 15 months.

9th—Alesandro Douaison; Ursula Ebert, wife; Isaac, son; Maturino, son; Juan, son; Juan Baptista, son; María Rosa, daughter; Magdalena, daughter.

10th—Francisco Ebert.

11th—Ana Boudreau, widow Haché; Maria Haché, daughter, Margarita, daughter.

12th—Pedro Usé; María Kimin, wife.

13th—Cecilia Bourg, widow Usé; Carlos Usé, son; Juan Baptista, son; Gregorio, son; Ana María, daughter.

14th—Pedro Kimin; María Magdalena, wife; Ana, daughter; María, daughter; Victoria Francisca, daughter.

15th—Pablo Domingo Boudreaud; María Oliva Landry, wife; Pablo Marin, infant at the breast.

16th—Juan Baptista Dugats; María Closinet, wife; María, daughter, María Haché, daughter.

17th—Juan Baptista Dugats; Ana Bourg, wife; Ana, daughter; María Boudreaud, grand-daughter.

* Anselmo Blanchard's registration, New Orleans, July 29, 1785, in Cuba, 602 b, A. G. I.

199

18th—Joseph Aucoin; Isabel Henrique, wife; Juan Joseph, son; Francisco Santos, son; Isabel Juana, daughter; María Modesta, daughter; Victoria Clara, daughter.

19th—Eustachio el Joven; Juana Cliquet, wife; Servando, son; Francisco, son; María Magdalena, daughter; Pelagia Gotreau, niece.

20th—Juan Baptista Joven; Helena Dumont, wife; Gregorio, son; Julian, son; María, daughter; María, Genoveva Gotreau, niece.

21st—Anselmo Landry; Agata Vaciou, wife.

22nd—Juan Bautista Baudreau; María Modesta Traham, wife; Juan Constante, son; Maria Felicidad, daughter; Margarita, daughter.

23rd—Angela Pinel, widow Légere; Luís Légere, son; Juan, son.

24th—Juan Carlos Brousard; Euprasia Mariot, wife; Juan Carlos, son; Francisco, son; Pedro, son; Domingo, son; Pablo Baudreaud, stepson.

25th—Juan Traham.

26th—Daniel Benoit; Henriqueta Legendre, wife; Henriqueta, daughter.

27th—Pedro LeBlanc; Ana Josepha Hébert, wife; Joseph, son; Pedro, son; Juan, son; Vittorio, son.

28th—Juan Bautista Guédry; Margarita Hébert, wife; Pedro, son; Francisco, son; Margarita Felicidad, daughter; Margarita, daughter of Guédry.

29th—Luís Stivrin; María Babin, wife; Luís, son; Maria, daughter; one child not baptized.

30th—Francisco Babin.

31st—Helena Haché, unmarried; María Josepha, her sister; Isabel, her sister.

32nd—Carlos Daigre; Ana María Vincent, wife.

33rd—Francisca Boudreaud, widow Dugats; Pedro Dugats, son.

34th—Margarita Laveaux, widow Legendre; Luís Legendre, son; Ides, daughter.

35th—Juan Bautista Legenire; María Rose Tullier, wife; Rosa, infant daughter.

36th—Juan Bautista el Joven; Elena Dowison, wife.

APPENDIX B

Juan Prieto on orders of Martín Navarro equipped each able worker in the seventy-four families of *La Bergere* expedition with farming tools of axes, medium and small hatchets, shovels, hoes, and meat cleavers. The families were: Olivier Terrio, Jean Charles Terrio,

Olivien Aucoing, Charles Aucoing, Marie Josefe LeBlanc, Marquerite Noël, Simon Maserole, Jacques Terriot, Elizabeth Guerin, Joseph Guerin, Pierre Guillot, Marguerite Ebert, Antoine Aucoing, Laura Bourg, Charles Hébert, Claude LeBlanc, Marie Magdeleine Landry, Jean Aucoing, Marie Anastasie Aucoing, Pierre Richard, Tranquile Pitre, Jean Richard, Marie Joséf Richard (widow of Landry), María Gotreau, Jeane Chellon, Ana Hébert, Ursula Brand, Gabriel Moreau, Pierre Landry, Marie La Prince, Pierre Bertrand, Anne Savary, Pierre Gotrau, Jean Baptiste Barrilled, Anne Marie Robechau, Honoré Braud, Prospoer Landry, Jean Pierre Landry, Jean Pierre Bourg, Oliver Le-Blanc, Louis Letollier, Étienne LeBlanc, Jean Baptiste Orele, Jacques Doueson, Isaac Ebert, Natalie Pitre, Cécile Bodrau, Aman Pitre, Ambroise Dugats, Marie Brasseur, Joseph Trahan, Maturin Trahan, Alexois Daigle, Charles Dugast, Pierre Dugats, Anne Orie Dugats, Joseph Bourg, Jean Baptiste Landry, Marie Daigre, Paul Dugats, Simon Dugats, Joseph Dupuy, Prosper Cherver, Magdeleine Dugats, Eustache Daigle, Étienne Dupuy, Fabian Aucoing, Ambroise Pitre, Olivier Trahan, François Frious, Antoine Mollard, Pierre Gotreau, Genevieve Landry, Pierre Aucoing.

(Signed)   Juan Prieto. *

* Prieto to Morales, New Orleans, September 22, 1785, in Cuba, 576, A. G. I.

APPENDIX C

Pedro Aragon y Villegas' list of Acadian
arrivals in New Orleans on *Le Beaumont:* *

1st—Simon D'Aigle; Ana Michel, wife; Eduardo, son, Simon, son; Joseph, son; María Margarita, daughter; Ana Genoveva, daughter; Isabel, daughter; María, daughter.

2nd—Olivier D'Aigle; Victorio, son; Francisco, son; Simon, son; Juan Bautista, son; Onarato, son; María, daughter; Pelagia, daughter; Eulalia, daughter.

3rd—Carlos Henrique; María LeBlanc, wife; María Magdalena, daughter; Rosa Anatasia, daughter; Ursula, daughter; Carlos Robicheau, son of María.

4th—Pedro Richard; Francisco D'Aigle, wife; Anselmo, son; Joseph, son; Augusto, son; María, daughter.

5th—Pedro LaVergne; Pedro, son; María Magdalena, daughter.

6th—Juan Bautista Trahan, son of María Josefa Granchér; Pablo Raymundo, son; María Reyna, daughter; María Margarita, daughter.

* Pedro Aragon y Villegas registration, New Orleans, September 6, 1785, in Cuba, 626 A, A. G. I.

7th—Joseph Traham, son of Ana Granchér; Francisco, son; Mariana, daughter; Julia, daughter.

8th—Joseph Guédry; Magdalena Gaummeau, wife; Joseph, son; María, daughter; Reyna Isabel, infant; Margarita, daughter.

9th—Carlos Commeau; Margarita Josef, wife.

10th—Juan Bautista Ebert; Ana Dorotea, wife; Ana Margarita, infant.

11th—Juan Douaron; Margarita Josefa, daughter.

12th—Pedro Potieu†; Inés Brauzard, wife; Carlos, son; Pedro Lorenzo, son; Francisco, son; Constanza, daughter; Ana, daughter.

13th—Ana Venoi, widow Ebert; Juan Carlos, son.

14th—Juan Bautista Douaron; María Blanca Rainard, wife; Luís Santos, son; Juan Carlos, son; María, daughter; Rosa, daughter; Ursula, daughter.

15th—Francisco D'Aigle; Juana Aulai, wife; Luís, son; Juana, daughter; Adelaida, daughter; Luisa, daughter.

16th—Francisco Arbourg; María Henrique, wife; Francisco, son; Juan Luís, son; Federico, son.

17th—Joseph Traham; Margarita Lavergne, wife; Josef Remigio, son; Antonia, daughter.

18th—Pelagia Douaron, widow La Sende; Juan Eduardo La Sende, son; Emilia, daughter.

19th—Juan Bautista Lagarine; Ana Douaron, wife.

20th—Margarita Douaron, widow Dugats.

21st—Pedro Ebert†; Carlota Potieu, wife; Ana, daughter; Pedro, infant.

22nd—Juan Bautista Ebert†.

23rd—Francisco Alexandro D'Aigle; Rosa Adelaida Bourg, wife; Emilia Adelaida, daughter; Juan Josef, infant.

24th—Rosa Douaron (husband absent).

25th—Juan Guédry; María LeBlanc, wife; Juan, son; Santiago, son; María Josef Belleme, cousin.

26th—Joseph LeBlanc; Santiago, his brother; Francisco, his brother; Magdalena, his sister.

27th—Carlos Guédry; Josef, son; Juan, son; Ana Lorenza, daughter.

28th—Pedro Guédry; Luisa Blandin, wife.

29th—Josef Breaud; María Traham, wife.

30th—Francisco Xavier Baudreaud; Margarita Dugats, wife.

31st—Santiago Moulaison; Maria Douairon, wife; Santiago, son; Rosa, daughter; Sofia, daughter.

† Settled in Atacapas.

32nd—Pedro Guédry; María Josef Hébert, wife; Pedro Josef, son; Juan Pedro, son; Josef Firmin, infant; María Rosa, daughter; Pedro Hébert, his nephew.

33rd—Pablo LeBlanc; Ana Baudreaud, wife; Adelaide, daughter; Rosalia, infant daughter; Rosa Traham, his niece.

34th—Juan Luís D'Aigle, son of Margarita; Angela Dubois (in hospital).

35th—Carlos Granchér; Josef D'Aigle, his nephew.

36th—Juan Bautista D'Aigre; Maria Claudia, wife.

37th—Alein Bourg; María Coummeau, wife; Francisco, son; Genoveva, daughter.

38th—Josef Calliot; Isabel LeBlanc, wife; Santiago, infant son.

39th—Juan Pedro Dugats; Juana Cabou, wife.

40th—Pedro Vincent.

41st—Juan Bautista Douhone.

42nd—Juan Carlos Richard.

43rd—Juan María Granchér.

44th—Pedro Henrique; Margarita Traham, wife; Cecilio Francisco, son.

45th—María Martina, widow Courtin; Santiago, son; Juana Luisa, daughter.

46th—Juan García; Francisca Courtin, wife.

47th—Magdalena LeBlanc, widow Traham; Pablo Traham, son; Simon, son; Alexo, son; María, daughter; Rosalia, daughter.

48th—Josef Costa; Margarita Traham, wife.

49th—Francisco Miguél Betancourt; Victoria la Vergne, wife.

50th—From *Le Bon Papa*: Juan Bautista Guédry; Pedro, son; Francisco, son; Margarita Felicidad, infant; Margarita, orphan girl of 8 years.

(signed)   Pedro Aragon y Villegas
New Orleans, Sept. 6, 1785.

APPENDIX D

Partial list of twenty-three marriages Navarro arranged. The marriages celebrated on November 20, 1785:

Josef Adam, immigrant, with Margarita (19th family, *St. Remy*).

Luís Antonio Charrie, immigrant, with María Haché, (54th family, *St. Remy*).

Santiago Davoir (and family, *La Amistad*) with María Michel (60th family, *St. Remy*).

Augustin Douvan, son of Honorado Douvon and Ana Traham (62nd family, *St. Remy*) with Margarita LeBlanc.*

Fourchet, Guard, alias Lenor, with Francisca Crochet, sister of Augustin Douvon.

Josef Le Jeune, son of Anastasia Gebron, widow Le Jeune (58th family) with Dona María Landry (18th family *St. Remy*).

The marriages celebrated on December 2, 1785:

Luís Pinel (5th family, *St. Remy*) with Blanca Vincent (8th family, *St. Remy*).

Vincente Neveux, immigrant, with Cecilia Hébert (20th family, *St. Remy*).

On December 3, 1785:

Don Luís Joudice, surgeon of *St. Remy,* with Ana Jacques (65th family, *La Amistad*).

Carlos Macle, immigrant, with María Bernard (64th family, *St. Remy*).

On December sixth:

Silvestre Gomez, immigrant, with Carlota Fouquet (65th family, *St. Remy*).

On December twelfth:

Mathurino Aliot, immigrant, with Cecilia Boudreau (35th family, *St. Remy*).

On December fourteenth:

Luís Menard, immigrant, with María Josefa Richard, widow Baset (21st family, *St. Remy*).

Juan Crochet (19th family, *St. Remy*) with María Boudreau (6th family, *La Amistad*).†

* She was the daughter of Carlos LeBlanc and Madalena Gautreau, who died in the hospital of *St. Remy*. Navarro to Morales, New Orleans, December 19, 1785, in Cuba 604B, A. G. I.

† Record is incomplete. In his chart Navarro gives 17 marriages for *La Amistad* expedition and 5 for *St. Remy*.

APPENDIX E

The ninety families of *La Amistad* expedition: Zacarías Boudreaux, Santiago Davoir, Joséf Semer, Luciano Bourgue, Luis Antonio Charrie, Vicente Neveu, Luis Pinel, Juan Carlos Boudreau, Anastasia Sebron, François Landry, Joséf leJeune, Juan François Avarat, Bernard Dugats, Mathurine Alliot, Carlos Pinel, Joséf Boudreau, Juan Carlos Haché, Ursula Hébert, María Moises (widow of Oliver), Juan Bautista le Blanc, Carlos Doucet, Margarita Benoit, Juan Francisco de la Massiere, Colda Baineaud, Juan Bautista Doucet, Juan Bausard, Pelagia Benoit, Estévan Hébert, Luís Dantin, Alexo Breaud, Fabian Guillot, Juan Gautreau, Brigida Part (widow of Boudreau), Joséf Boudreau, Juan Pablo Traham, Benito Caummeau, Eustagio Beltran, Juan Beltrand, Estéban Boudreau, Athanasio Bourg, Ursula Breaud, Juan Tibodeau, Ambrosio Hébert, Marin Boudreau, María Gautreau, Juan Bourgue, Magdalena Blanchard, Ignacio Hammont, María Doucet, Juan Maitrar, Margarita Boudreau, Pedro LeBlanc, Juan Daigle, Francisco Blanchard, Juan Chaison, Francisca Doucet, María Henriqueta Potieux, María Josefa Terriot, Bellony Blanchard, Isabel Douon, Juan Fouget, Joséf Breaud, Chrisostomo Trahan, Mathurino Juan au Coing, Estévan Pelletier, Joséf Adam, Leonor de la Gardé, Juan Bautista Simon, Juan Crochet, and Luís Maurice.*

Second division of twenty families in expedition *La Amistad*. Juan Guzmán, Carlos Giroir, Ana Olivier, Joseph Renard, Pedro Joseph Jacques, Pedro Lorency, Antonio May, Honorado Douvon, María Haché, Luís Menard, Luís Joudice, Carlos Macle, Agustin Douvon, Silvestre Gomez, were equipped on December 15, 1785. Claudio Epifano LeFaibro,† Juan Hainement, Carlos Tardy, Juan Crochet,‡ Francisco Avarat, and Bernardo Dugats were equipped on January 15, 1786.

(Signed) Juan Prieto * *

---

* Prieto to Morales, New Orleans, April 14, 1786, in Cuba 576, A. G. I. Luís Maurice later became associated with the expedition *St. Remy*. The names of three other families are missing.

** *Id*. to Navarro, New Orleans, December 15, 1785, and January 15, 1786, *ibid*.

† Married an Acadian girl, Roaslia Carlota Guzmán and admitted as an Acadian.
———— to Pedro Marigny, New Orleans, New Orleans, January 2, 1786, *ibid*, 608B.

‡ Here he is granted farm tools. He was absent on December 15, 1785.

APPENDIX F

The sixty-two families of *La Villa de Arcangel* expedition: María Richard, Josef Aucoing, Pedro Hébert, Josef Aucoing, Lucie Perpetua Bourgue, Juan Bourgue (father), Juan Bourgue (son), María Terriot, Luís Cloustinet, Juan Longueepree, Alesondro au Coing, Victor Deaforest, Santiago Desforet, Ourdon Tomás Caligán, María Juana Villere, Santiago Forest, Juan Santiago Terriot, Ambrosio Dupuy, Juan Bautista au Coing, María Isabel Desforest, Victor Boudreau, Francisco Pedro le Gorec, Bartholome Henrique, Miguél au Coing, Claudio au Coing, Carlos au Coing, Simon au Coing, Marin Bourgue, Joséf

Hébert, Claudio Gédry, Amano Boudreau, Magdalena au Coing, Juan Bautista au Coing, Juan Pitre, Joséf Ebert, Pedro Enryque, Juan Enryque, Ambrosio Bourgue, Carlos Henryque, Pedro Henryque, Simon Caumeau, Ambrosio Langueepré, Ana Terriot, Josef Ignacio Gaudet, Carlos Henryque, Francisca Guerín (widow of Terriot), Renato Laundry, Victoria Dugats (widow of Henry), Ana Terriot, Carlos Pitre, Pedro Arsement, Joséf Melanson, Carlos Tibodeau, Francisco Xavier Bourgue, Carlos Bourgue, Juan Bautista Terriot, Carlos au Coing, Alexo au Coing, Francisco Hébert, Nicholas Courtua, Santiago Blanchard and Juan Mapre.

(Signed) Juan Prieto. *

Navarro later permitted two extra families to join this expedition, making the total of 62 families. But he does not state which ones they were.

* Prieto to Morales, New Orleans, January 17, 1786, in Cuba, 576, A. G. I.

APPENDIX G

The twenty-seven families of *La Carolina* expedition: Juan de Laune, Cristoval de Laune, Luís Amoureaux, Luís Gaudet, Miguél Doucet, Joséf Doucet, Oliver Boudreau, Ambrosio Hébert, Carlos Blanchard, Basillio Chaison, Nicholas Albert, Ignacio Boudreau, Martín Pitre, Claudio Le Gagneur, Joseph Terriot, Joséf Boudreau, Juan Bautista Doueron, Carlos Gautreau, Pedro Maintay, Joséf Douon, Claudia María LeBlanc, Basilio Richard, María Boudreau, Pedro Montagne Catalan, Estévan Francisco Angilbert, Guido Gueriven and Renato Armeau.

(Signed) Juan Prieto. *

* Prieto to Morales, New Orleans, January 17, 1786, in Cuba, 576, A. G. I.

BIBLIOGRAPHY

Manuscripts

Archives Départmentales de la Vienne, Poitiers.

Le Marquis de Pérusse des Cars et projet de la colonie du Poitou. Dépôt 22, liasses 32, 33, 40, 89, 98, and 129. Cs3, 245s (1772?), Dependencies on Poitou.

Archives du Ministère des Affaires Étrangères, Paris.

Correspondance politique Angleterre.—Mémoire Acadienne au Nivernois, December 2, 1762, CDXL, ff. 208-20; Lettre September 2, 1762, CDXLVII, f. 13; Copie d'une lettre sur les Acadiens remité de M. le duc de Nivernois, December 2, 1762, CDXLVIII, ff. 216-24; Négociationes pour la paix, *ibid.*, f. 213, *et seq.*; Lettre au Nivernois, December 11, 1762, *ibid.*, ff. 68, 267-355; Mémoire sur les Acadiens, 1763, CDXLIX, ff. 24, 150-51, 334-53; Nivernois au Praslin, March 14, 1763, CDL, ff. 4, 83-87; Mémoire Acadienne au Nivernois, l'humble requête de habitans, London, July 7, 1763, *ibid.*, ff. 415-46; Lettre des Acadiens, Halifax, Agust 13, 1763, CDLI, ff. 57-76, 123-25, 206-208, 322, 438-39; Choiseul au Guerchy, Versailles, November 22, 1763, CDLII, ff. 203-205; Guerchy au Choiseul, December 6, 1763, *ibid.*, f. 238.

Correspondance politique Espagne.—DLI, f. 26; DLV, f. 20; Acadiens à Louisiane, 1783, DCX, ff. 6-58; Acadiens à Aranda, 1783, DCXI, f. 34; "A son Excélence, Monseigneur Le Comte De Vergennes," Nantes, April 4, 1784, DCXII, ff. 287-89, 334, 367; Dépêches, 1784, DCXIII, ff. 185, 334; Émigration, le solde, 1785, DCXVI, f. 269, *et seq.*; Lettres, 1785, DCXX, ff. 57-104.

Mémoires et Documents Angleterre.—Instructions à M. de la Rochette pour le duc de Nivernois, April 18, 1763, XLVII, ff. 9-10; Choiseul au Nivernois, Supplement XIII, 1763, *ibid.*, ff. 11-15; Mémoire; Familles Acadiennes, 1777, *ibid.*, ff. 18-28; Mémoire, Transport d'Acadiens, 1763-85, *ibid*.

Archives du Ministère des Colonies, Paris.

Colonies. C^{14}, XXVIII; Canada: Serie G^1 458, Réfugiés, 1765, I, ff. 27-39, 138-39; II, f. 122; CXXII, ff. 3, 5, 27-29, 58, 88; Acadiens, 1762-73, CDLXXXII, CDLXXXIII, and CDLXXXIV; Acadiens, 1774-1790, CDLVIII, CDLIX.

Archives Morbihan, Vannes.

Canada français, Le Loutre correspondance, I, 1888; Registres des Acadiens de Belle-Ile-en-mer, II, 1889; Registres des Acadiens de Belle-Ile-en-mer, III, 1-60.

208   *ACADIAN ODYSSEY*

Archives Nationales (Palais Soubise), Paris.

"Amérique du Nord. Réglement des limites," in Acadie, IV, C¹¹E (1751);
ibid., V, January 23, 1753. Colonies: Serie B—— Orders du Roi, dés-
pêches, minutes du Conseil de la Marine, CX, ff. 11-313; CXV, ff. 56,
121, 127, 155, 177, 333: CXVI, ff. 12-15, 64-70: CXVII, ff. 40, 41, 83, 89,
116-17, 159, 196, 206, 229-340, 360-67, 389-91, 405, 426-30, 454, 471-97;
CXIX, Cayenne, f.6; CXX, ff. 16-17, 47, 86, 110, 113-16, 153, 195, 225,
270-75, 323, 343-58; CXXI, ff. 1-18; CXXII, ff. 23, 181-82, 278, 397;
CXXV, ff. 195-99; CXXXI, ff. 326-30: CXXXIV, ff. 154-60; CXLIII, ff.
127-215, 349, 648, 672. Colonies: Serie C¹¹D, Acadie (1707-11), VII;
Mémoire du duc Nivernois, February, 1763, *ibid.,* ff. 235-99;
Mémoire remis au duc de Nivernois, *ibid.,* f. 241; Mémoire du duc de
Vergennes, *ibid.,* f. 320 *et seq.;* Projet du Poitou, 1713-88, Art. 2 (Obser-
vationes), *ibid.,* ff. 296-300; Acadie, 1713-88, *ibid.,* ff. 270-77: Acadiens,
1774-76, *ibid.,* ff. 300-303; Corsica, *ibid.,* f. 306; Belle-Isle-en mer, *ibid.,* ff.
307-13; Acadie, Réfugiés, Mémoire sur les Acadiens en France, Pensions
aux Acadiens, IX, ff. 252-320; Mémoire sur l'Acadie, 1693-1749, X; Serie
C¹³A, Foucault à Dubuq, February 28, 1765, CLV, f. 108; Serie C¹³A,
Mémoire des habitans et négociants de la Louisiane sur l'événement du
Octobre, October 29, 1768, XLVIII, ff. 245-55; Serie G¹, Réfugiés, CXXII,
ff. 3-5, 27-29, 50-88. Finances: Help to Acadians, 1773-1788, and Marquis
de Pérusse des Cars projet, subsidy, solde, to Louisiana, liasse F¹⁵ 3.495;
Help to Acadians, liasses F¹⁵ 3.492, 3.493; Government help and registration
of Acadians, 1792-93, liasse F¹⁵ 3.494; Côtes du Nord, F¹⁵ 3.331B, F¹⁵ 3.352A;
La Manche F¹⁵ 3.356A; Statistics on Acadians, F¹, F⁴, F¹⁵, Guerre: A¹,
Histoire d'Acadie, vol. 3341; A¹, Acadie, 1749-54, vol. 3393; A¹, Acadie.
Correspondance de abbé Le Loutre; C¹¹E, "Memorial presented by His
Majesty's Commissioners to the Commissioners of His Most Christian
Majesty in answer to their Memorial of the 4th of October, 1751, con-
cerning Nova Scotia or Acadie," V, ff. 1-267; Serie C¹¹E, Correspondance
Génerále, Memoires, Letters, Orders, General Manuscript History of
Acadia, 1604-1755, IV, V, VI.

Archivo General de Indias, Seville.

(A legajo often contains from 100 to 3,000 manuscripts of letters, royal
orders, ministerial dispatches, colonial reports from governors, comman-
dants, and subjects.) Legajos, Cuba, 3, 85, 86, 109, 114, 119, 149A, 197,
187A, 187B, 188A, 188B, 189A, 520A, especially Libro Maestro de la
Contaduría Principal, 573A, 573B, 576, 593, 594, 597, 602B, 604A, 604B,
606, 608A, 608B, 626A, 626B, 633, 705, 1375, 2351, 2355, 2357, 2358,
2360, 2361, 2362, 2363.

Archivo Historico-Nacional, Madrid.

"Discusiones sommaria sopra gli antichi limiti dell' Acadia . . . . . . "

Impre. 3n Basilea por Samuel Tourneisan, italiano y françés, 1755, in Estado-Legajo 5.002; Envió de acadianos residentes en Francia a la Louisiana por cuenta de España, 1783-86, in Estado-Legajo 3885 (13); Documentary history of the transactions of Peyroux de la Coudrenière, Oliver Terrio, Ignacio Heredia, Manuel d'Asprès, José de Gálvez, Count de Floridablanca, Charles Gravier, Count de Vergennes with Count de Aranda, in Estado-Legajo 3885 (13), cartas 1-84. (Carta 53 was missing).

Archivo Segreto Vaticano, Vatican City.

Collegione Nunziatura di Fiandra, Bruxelles, November 22, 1763, Leg. 135.

Biblioteca de Palacio Antigua Real, Madrid.

Noticia de los acaecimientos de la Louisiana en el año de 1769, in Miscelanea, tomo XIII.

Bibliothèque de Bordeaux, Bordeaux.

Recueil de pièces relatif aux Acadiens, Lemoine, Ms. 1480.

Bibliothèque Nationale, Manuscript Department, Paris.

Joly de Fleury, "Mémoire sur les Acadiens," submitted to Louis XVI, immediately after his coronation, in Commerce et Colonies, vol. 1722, ff. 179-204.

Origines Françaises, August 23, 1749, vol. 9281; "Notes sur l'Acadie et Isle Royale," *ibid.*, vol. 9282, ff. 1-134.

British Museum, Manuscript Department, London.

Papers relating to Nova Scotia, 1720-1791, in Dr. Andrew Brown's Collection: Early History of Acadia, Add. 19049; Early Acadia, 1710-57, Add. 19069 and Add. 19070; Acadians most loyal in 1793, Add. 19071; English fears of Acadians, removal, Add. 19072, No. 32, 31; Acadia, 1749-90, causes of the war, twenty-six different papers on Acadian removal, Add. 19073; Meteorological observations in Nova Scotia, Add. 19074; General notes on Acadians, Add. 19075; Early history, 1492-1691, Add. 19076; and Relation d'Acadie un corsaire hollandoise de Carrasso, Adds. 19303 and 19393.

Printed Sources

Akins, Thomas B. (ed.). *Selections from the Public Documents of the Province of Nova Scotia* (Halifax, 1869).

Calendar of State Papers, Colonial Series (London, 1860———), *America and the West Indies,* I (1574-1660), V (1661-68), VII (1669-74), IX–XL (1675-1733).

Canada Yearbook, 1941 (Ottawa, 1941).

Annual Report on Canadian Archives (Ottawa, 1873), II (1905), ed. Placide Gaudet.

Census of Canada, 1870-71 (Ottawa, 1873-78), 5 vols.

Charlevoix, Pierre François Xavier de. *History and General Description of New France,* 6 vols., tr. J. G. Shea (New York, 1900).

Collection de Manuscrits contenants lettres, mémoires et autres documents historiques relatifs à la Nouvelle France, 4 vols. (Quebec, 1883-85), I, 115-24.

Denys, Nicolas. *The Description and Natural History of the Coasts of North America* (Acadia), tr. and ed. William F. Ganong (Toronto, 1908).

French, B. F. (ed.) *Historical Collections of Louisiana, embracing many rare and valuable documents relating to the natural, civil and political history of that state,* 5 vols. (New York, 1846-53).

Gagnon, C. O. (ed.). *Lettre de M. L'abbé Le Guerne missionnaire de l'Acadie* (Quebec, 1889).

Grant, William L. (ed.). *Acts of the Privy Council of England,* Colonial Series, 1613-1783, 6 vols. (London, 1908-12).

———. *Voyages of Champlain, 1604-1618* (New York, 1907).

———. *Hakluytus posthumus; or Purchas his pilgrimes, containing a history of the world in sea voyages and land travels,* 20 vols. (New York, 1905).

Hutchinson, Thomas. *History of the Colony and Province of Massachusetts Bay from 1749 to 1774,* ed. John Hutchinson, 3 vols. (Cambridge, 1936).

Lescarbot, Marc. *Nova Francia, A Description of Acadia, 1606,* tr. P. Erondelle, 1609 (London, 1928).

———. *Histoire de la Nouvelle France,* 5 vols. (2d ed., Paris, 1612).

Thwaites, Reuben G. (ed.). *Jesuit Relations and Allied Documents,* 73 vols. (Cleveland, 1896-1901). See vols. I to IV especially.

Winthrop, John. *The History of New England from 1630 to 1649,* ed. James Savage, 2 vols. (Boston, 1825-26).

Monographs

Addison, Joseph. *Charles the Third of Spain* (Oxford, 1900).

Brebner, John Bartlet. *New England's Outpost,* in Columbia University *Studies in History, Economics, and Public Law,* No. 293 (New York, 1927).

Cantillion, Phillippe de. *Essai sur la nature du commerce en général* (Paris, 1754).

Casgrain, l'abbé Henri Raymond. *Un Pélerinage au Pays d'Évangeline* (3d. ed., Paris, 1889).

Couillard Després, Azarie. *Observationes sur l'histoire de l'Acadie française* (Montreal, 1919).

————. *En marge de la tragédie d'un peuple de M. Émile Lauvrière; ou Erreurs sur l'histoire de l'Acadie refuteés* (Bruges, 1925).

Daubigny, Eugène Théodore. *Choiseul et La France d'outremer après le traité de Paris* (Paris, 1892).

Dionne, Narcisse E. *Le parler populaire des Canadiens français, ou Lexique des canadianismes, acadianismes* (Quebec, 1909).

Ditchy, Jay K. *Les Acadiens Louisianais et leur parler* (Paris, 1932).

Doughty, Arthur George. *The Acadian Exiles,* Vol. X, in George M. Wrong and H. H. Langton (eds.), *Chronicles of Canada* (Toronto, 1916).

Dubois, Émile. *Chez nos frères les Acadiens; notes d'histoire et impressions de voyage* (Montreal, 1920).

Fontaine, L. U. *Cent trent-cinq ans après, ou La renaissance canadienne* (Montreal, 1890).

Gautheron, René. *Le Patrimonie Acadien. Nouvelle Écosse* (Rennes, 1932).

Geddes, James. *Study of an Acadian-French Dialect Spoken on the North Shore of the Baie-des-Chaleurs* (Halle, 1908).

Jego, J. Baptiste. *Le drame du peuple Acadien; Reconstitution historique en neuf tableaux et une pose plastique de la dispersion des Acadiens, d'asprès "La tragédie d'un peuple" Émile Lauvrière* (Paris, 1932).

Lalanne, Charles Claude. *Histoire de Châtelleraud et du Châtelleraudais* (Châtellerault, 1859).

Lanco, Joseph M. (ed.). *Les Acadiens à Belle-Ile-en-mer* (Josselyn, 1924).

Lauvrière, Émile. *Deux traîtres d'Acadie et leur victime; les Latour père et fils Charles d'Aulnay* (Paris, 1932).

————. *La tragédie d'un peuple, histoire du peuple Acadien de ses origines à nos jours,* 2 vols. (Paris, 1922).

Le Gallen, Léandre. *Belle-Isle histoire politique, religieuse et militaire* (Vannes, 1906).

Le May, Leon P. *Histoire de Belle-Isle* (Vannes, 1880).

Longfellow, Henry W. *Evangeline* (Boston, 1896).

Martin, Ernest. *Les exilés Acadiens en France aux XVIIIe siècle et leur éstablissement en Poitou* (Paris, 1936).

Michael, Wolfgang. "Great Britain (1759-63)," in *Cambridge Modern History,* VI (New York, 1909).

Mirabeau, Victor de Riquetti, Marquis de. *L'Ami des hommes, ou Traité de la population* (Rouxel edition, Paris, 1883).

Morse, W. I. *Acadiensia nova, 1598-1779, new and unpublished documents and other data relating to Acadia* (London, 1935).

————. *Gravestones of Acadie, and other essays on local history, geneology and parish records of Annapolis county, Nova Scotia* (London, 1929).

————. *The Land of New Adventure* (the Georgian era in Nova Scotia) (London, 1932).

Papuchon, Alexis. "La Colonie Acadienne du Poitou," in *Bulletins de La Société des Antiquaires de L'Ouest* (2ᵉ trimestre, Poitiers, 1908).

Rameau de Saint-Père, Edmé. *Une colonie féodale en Amérique (L'Acadie, 1604-1881)*, 2 vols. (Paris, 1887-1889).

Richard, Édouard. *Acadia; missing links of a lost chapter in American history, by an Acadian*, 2 vols. (New York, 1895).

Rigaud, R. P. *Vie de La Bonne Soeur Elizabeth* (Paris, 1867).

Roberts, Charles Douglas. "Echoes from Old Acadia," in *Canadian Leaves,* ed. G. M. Fairchild (New York, 1887), 145-73.

Smith, Philip Henry. *Acadia. A Lost Chapter in American History* (Pawling, N. Y., 1884).

Tull, Jethro. *The horse-hoeing husbandry; or, An essay on the principles of tillage and vegetation wherein is taught a method of introducing a sort of vineyard culture into the corn fields in order to increase their product and diminish the common expense* (London, 1733).

Ville, Léon. *En Acadie, Martyre d'un Peuple* (Paris, 1927).

Voorhies, Felix. *Acadian Reminiscences, with the true story of Evangeline* (Boston, 1907).

Webster, John Clarence. *Acadia at the End of the Seventeenth Century; letters, journals and memoires of Joseph Robineau de Villebon, commandant of Acadia, 1690-1700 and other contemporary documents* (St. John, N. B., 1934).

Williams, Catherine, Read. *The Neutral French; or The Exiles of Nova Scotia* (Providence, 1841).

General Histories

Arthur, Timothy Shay. *The History of Georgia, from its earliest settlement to the present time* (Philadelphia, 1852).

Bancroft, George. *History of the United States from the discovery of the continent,* 10 vols. (Boston, 1859-75).

Barde, Alexandre. *Histoire des comites de vigilance aux Attakapas* (Saint-Jean-Baptiste, La., 1861).

Beer, George Louis. *The Old Colonial System, 1660-1754* (New York, 1912).

Belknap, Jeremy. *The History of New Hampshire, Comprehending the events of one complete Century from the discovery of the River Pascataqua,* 3 vols. (Boston, 1791-92).

Bolton, Herbert E., and Thomas M. Marshall. *The Colonization of North America, 1492-1783* (New York, 1936).

Calnek, William Arthur. *History of the County Annapolis, including old Port Royal and Acadia, with memoires of its representatives in the provincial parliament, and biographical and genealogical sketches of its early English settlers and their families,* ed. A. W. Savary (Toronto, 1897).

Chambers, Henry E. *Mississippi Valley Beginnings; an outline of the early history of the earlier West* (New York, 1922).

Couillard Després, Azarie. *Histoire des seigneurs de la Rivière du Sud et de leurs alliés canadiens et acadiens* (Paris, 1912).

Danvila y Collado Manuel. *Reinado de Carlos III,* 6 vols. (Madrid, 1893-96).

Eaton, Arthur Wentworth H. *The History of Kings County, Nova Scotia, heart of the Acadian land, giving a sketch of the French and their expulsion; and a history of the New England planters, who came in their stead, with many genealogies,* 1604-1910 (Salem, Mass., 1910).

Fiske, John. *New France and New England* (Boston, 1902).

Gayarré, Charles. *History of Louisiana,* 4 vols. (New York, 1854-66).

Grant, William Lawson. *History of Canada* (London, 1919).

Haliburton, Thomas C. *An Historical and Statistical Account of Nova Scotia,* 2 vols. (Halifax, 1829).

Hannay, James. *The History of Acadia from its first discovery to its surrender to England, by the treaty of Paris* (St. John, N. B., 1879).

Hanotaux, Gabriel, and Alfred Martineau. *Histoire des colonies françaises et de l'expansion de la France dans le monde,* 6 vols. (Paris, 1929).

Herbin, John Frederic. *The History of Grand Pré, the home of Longfellow's "Evangeline," by the only descendant of the exiled people now living in the Grand-Pré of the Acadians* (4th ed., St. John, N. B., 1911).

Hicks, John D. *The Federal Union, A History of the United States to 1865* (Boston, 1937).

Hildreth, Richard. *History of the United States of America, from the discovery of the continent to the organization of government under the federal constitution,* 3 vols. (New York, 1849).

Houck, Louis. *A History of Missouri from the Earliest Explorations, and settlements until the admission of the state into the union,* 3 vols. (Chicago, 1908).

Kirke, Henry. *The First English Conquest of Canada with some account of the earliest settlements in Nova Scotia and Newfoundland* (London, 1871).

Lauvrière, Émile. *Histoire de la Louisiane française,* 1673-1939 (University, La., 1940).

214   *ACADIAN ODYSSEY*

MacGregor, John. *British America* (London, 1932).

Murdoch, Beamish. *A History of Nova Scotia or Acadie,* 3 vols. (Halifax, 1865-67).

Nettels, Curtis P. *The Roots of American Civilization; a history of American colonial life* (New York, 1938).

Ogg, Frederic Austin. *The Opening of the Mississippi; a struggle for supremacy in the American interior* (New York, 1904).

Parkman, Francis. *Half Century of Conflict,* 2 vols., Pt. VI, in *France and England in North America* (Boston, 1891-1903).

————. *Montcalm and Wolf,* Pt. VII, in *France and England in North America* (Boston, 1910).

————. *The Old Regime in Canada* (Boston, 1902).

————. *Pioneers of France in the New World,* Pt. I, in *France and England in North America* (Boston, 1891-1903).

Prudhomme, Louis Marie. *Voyage à la Guiane et à Cayenne fait en 1789 et années suivantes; contenant une description géographique de ces contrées, l'histoire de leur découverte; les possessions establissemens des Français, des Hollandais, des Espagnols et des Portugais* (Paris, 1798).

Rameau de Saint-Père, Edmé. *La France aux colonies; études sur le developpment de la race française hors de l'Europe* (Paris, 1859).

Raymond, Wilham O. *The River St. John, its physical features, legends and history, from 1604 to 1784* (St. John, N. B., 1910).

Seignobos, Charles. *A History of the French People,* tr. Catherine Alison Phillips (London, 1933).

Stevens, William Bacon. *A History of Georgia from its first discovery by Europeans to the adoption of the present constitution,* 2 vols. (New York, 1847).

Thwaites, Reuben G. *France in America 1497-1763,* vol. VII, in *The American Nation Series* (New York, 1905).

Vergennes, Charles G. *Mémoire, Historique et Politique sur La Louisiane, par M. de Vergennes, ministre de Louis XVI, accompagné d'un précis de la vie ce ministre, et suivi d'autres mémoires sur l'Indostan, Saint-Domingue, la Corse et la Guyane* (Paris, 1802).

Williamson, William D. *The History of the State of Maine,* 2 vols. (Hallowell, 1839).

Winsor, Justin (ed.). *Narrative and Critical History of America,* 8 vols. (Boston, 1884-89), especially vols. IV and V.

Wrong, G. M. *The Conquest of New France; a chronicle of the colonial wars,* X, in Allen Johnson (ed.), *The Chronicles of America Series,* 56 vols. (New Haven, 1920-51).

Zimmerman, Alfred. *Die Kolonialpolitik Frankreichs* (Berlin, 1870).

————. *Die Europäischen Kolonien* 15 vols. (Berlin, 1896-1903), IV, 220-27.

Periodicals

"The Acadians in Pennsylvania," in *American Catholic Historical Research,* VII (April, 1911), 108-11.

Acadiensis, a quarterly devoted to the interests of Canada (St. John, N. B.) (1901——), vols. I to VIII.

De Bow's Review (May, 1847), 411.

Dow, George Francis. "The French Acadians in Topsfield and Their Life in Exile," in *Topsfield Historical Society Collection,* XIV (1909), 137-147.

————. "The French Acadians in Essex County and Their Life in Exile," in *Essex Institute Historical Collections,* XLV (October, 1909), 293-307.

Gaudet, Placide. "Un Épisode de l'expulsion des Acadiens," in *Bulletin des Recherches Historiques* (Paris, February, 1908).

Grandmaison, Lèonce de. "L'histoire pathétique du peuple Acadien," in *Etudes,* CLXXV (April 20, May 5, 1923), 129-53, 276-93.

Griffin, Sara Swan. "The Acadian Exiles," in *Lowell Historical Society, Contributions* II, No. I, 89-107.

Huot, Antonio. "Les Acadiens de la Louisiane," in *Revue Canadienne,* LVII (July, 1909), 32-47.

Lart, C. E. "Notes on the Fate of the Acadians," in *Canadian Historical Review,* V (March, 1924), 108-17.

Lauvrière, Émile. "L'Acadie et l'Amérique latine," in *Revue Amérique Latine,* VII (March-April, 1924), 193-202, 316-27.

————. "Le peuple Acadien au XVIIᵉ siècle," in *Revue Historique Colonies Française,* XIIᵉ, Ann. 3ᵉ trimestre (1924), 429-44.

"Mémoire sur les Acadiens presenté a nos Siegneurs Clergé en France, assemblés á Paris en Juillet 1775," in *Revue de l'Aunis* (1867).

New York Mercury (November 30, 1762).

Nova Scotia Historical Society Collections, 9 vols. (Halifax, 1879), especially vols. I to VI on Acadia and Acadians.

Patterson, George. "Honorable Samuel Vetch, First English Governor of Nova Scotia," in *Nova Scotia Historical Society Collections,* IV (1885), 22 ff.

Poirier, Pascal. "Des Acadiens desportés à Boston en 1775," in *Proceedings and Transactions of the Royal Society of Canada,* 1908, 3d ser., II (1909), 132.

"Proclamation aux Acadiens de M. Wilmot gouverneur de la Nouvelle-Écosse," in *Revue Historique Colonies Françaises,* XVI (November 28), 703-704.

"Proposed Capture of Nova Scotia by the Americans; treaty with the Indians; Attitude and suffering of the Acadians," (containing the report of Colonel John Allan), in *American Catholic Historical Research,* VII (October, 1911), 375-80.

Raymond, William O. "Nova Scotia under English Rule," in *Proceedings and Transactions of the Royal Society of Canada,* 1910, 3d ser., IV (1911), 57.

Reed, William B. "The Acadian Exiles or French Neutrals in Pennsylvania," in *Historical Society of Pennsylvania Memoires,* VI (1858), 283-316.

Robinson, Berton E. "Grand Pré of the Acadians," in *Canadian Geographical Journal,* XI (August, 1935), 77-84.

Rogers, Norman McLead. "Acadian Exiles in France," in *Dalhousie Review,* V (April, 1925), 11-21.

Shepherd, William R. "The Cession of Louisiana to Spain," in *Political Science Quarterly,* XIX (1904), 439-58.

Sollers, Basil. "Party of Acadians who sailed from the Potomac, bound for the Mississippi," in *Maryland Historical Magazine,* IV (September, 1909), 279-81.

Willard, Abijah. "An Unwritten Chapter of Evangeline," in *Magazine of History,* IX (January, 1909), 10-12.

Wilmot, Montague, "Proclamation aux acadiens de M. Wilmot, gouverneur de la Nouvelle-Écosse," in *Revue Historique Colonies Françaises,* XVI (November, 1928), 703-704.

Winslow, John. "John Winslow's Journal," in *Nova Scotia Historical Society Collections,* III (1879), 71-196, N. S. A.

INDEX

Acadia, 1, 46, 51, 64; name of, and its corruption, 3; any of several Mimac words, 4; first successful colonization of, 4; civil war in, 5; first settlers of, 5; government in, 6; subject to four treaties, 7, 8; population in 1697, in 1713, 8; in 1714, in 1755, 16; ancient boundaries, 9, 14; attempted returns to, 20; new, established, 161

Acadians, dispersal of, ix; character of, 5; language of, 6; agricultural ability, 6, 88, 118; social customs of, 6; religious character of, 6; philosophy of, 7; accused of Indian atrocities, 9; education of, 11; as neutrals, 12; loyalty to king of France, 12, 13, 25, 26; in league with French, 14; fear of English, 15; refugees for, 18; estimate of deportees, 18; attitude of American colonies toward, 19; emigrate to Santo Domingo, 19; perish in mid-Atlantic, 19; unwanted in Acadia, 20; enslaved, 21; scattered along Atlantic coast, 23; appeal to Nivernois, 24; overwhelmed with joy, 28; chaplain's overtures to, 29; dissension among, 29; send delegates to Nivernois, 30, 32; distrust La Rochette, 31; at Falmouth, 32; refuse return to France, 33–35; population in 1763, 35; fear French tropical colonies, 36; camp mortalities of, 41; census of, in Anglo-American colonies, 45–47; petition liberation, 46–49; population along Nova Scotian coast, 52; native capacities and limitations of, 55; willing to return to New Brunswick, 64; classes of, in 1773, 70; abandon Poitou, 78; internal rift of, in 1777, 82–87, 134; lose unity of purpose, 87; pitiful flight of, in 1778, 88; aim in 1783, 92; resist absorption into French population, 93; impolitic conduct of, 98, 99; petition Vergennes, 100; in Paimboeuf and

Nantes, 102; potential wealth, 106; noble, 107; D'Asprès pays 2,000, 118; fear removal to Louisiana, 122; discouraged, 124; average cost of removal to New Orleans, 156; transfer loyalty to Louisiana, 161; contributions to Louisiana, 97, 162

Adolphus, Gustavus, 59

Agricultural schools, in colonies, 95–96

Alexander, Sir William, settles Scots in Acadia, 4

Ambition, Le, 43

Amboise, x, 60

American colonies, attitude of, toward Acadians, 19; encroachment of, on Louisiana, 118; Aranda's prophecy concerning, 126

American Revolution, 18, 83; help from France to, 92; prevents Acadian immigration, 93

Amherst, General Jeffrey, 16; armistice terms to French, 27

Andalusia, 66

Annapolis, 47

Anne, Queen, 8

Aragon y Villegas, Pedro, 137, 148–49

Aranda, Count de (see Bolea), x, 90, 130; removes two families, 91; pressures Charles III, 97; legalizes Spain's agreement with Peyroux, 101; reports 1,508 Acadians for Louisiana, 108; responsible for their removal, 109; sends transportation bids to Madrid, 113; reveals royal cedula of October 22, 1783, 97, 113; urges early departure of Acadians, 121; submits five questions to Charles III, 125; fears collapse of Acadian colonization in Louisiana, 126; receives royal approbation for colonization, 127; effects Acadian removal, 128; notifies Navarro to welcome Acadians, 131; fails to obtain desired quota, 154; final account to Spanish court, 154

217

Date Due